Economic Policy Coordination in the Euro Area

T0313016

The European debt crisis has given new impetus to the debate on economic policy coordination. In economic literature, the need for coordination has long been denied based on the view that fiscal, wage and monetary policy actors should work independently. However, the high and persistent degree of macroeconomic disparity within the EU and the absence of an optimum currency area has led to new calls for examining policy coordination.

This book adopts an institutional perspective, exploring the incentives for policymakers that result from coordination mechanisms in the fields of fiscal, monetary and wage policy. Based on the concept of externalities, the work examines cross-border spillovers (e.g. induced by fiscal policy) and cross-policy spillovers (e.g. between fiscal and monetary policies), illuminating how they have empirically changed over time and how they have been addressed by policymakers. Steinbach introduces a useful classification scheme that distinguishes between vertical and horizontal coordination as well as between cross-border and cross-policy coordination. The author discusses farther-reaching forms of fiscal coordination (e.g. debt limits, insolvency proceedings, Eurobonds) with special attention to how principals of state organization affect their viability. Federal states and *Bundesstaaten* differ in the incentives they offer for debt accumulation – and thus in their suitability for fiscal coordination.

Steinbach finds that the originally strict separation between policy areas has undergone significant change during the debt crisis. Indeed, recent efforts to coordinate policy are no longer limited to one policy area, but now extend to several areas. Steinbach argues that further fiscal policy coordination can be effectively deployed to address policy externalities, but that the coordination mechanisms used must match the form of state organization in the first place. Regarding wage policies, there are significant barriers to coordination. Notwithstanding some empirical successes in the implementation of a productivity-oriented wage policy, the high heterogeneity of national wage-setting institutions is likely to prevent any wage coordination.

Armin Steinbach is an economist and lawyer at the German Ministry of Economics in Berlin, Germany. He is the author of books on economic policy and has published in academic journals such as the *Journal of International Economic Law*, *Columbia Journal of European Law* and *American Review of International Arbitration*. He held visiting scholar positions at Harvard and Oxford University and received a doctorate in law from the University of Munich and a doctorate in economics from the University of Erfurt in Germany.

Routledge studies in the European economy

Economic Policy Coordination in the Euro Area

Armin Steinbach

Routledge
Taylor & Francis Group

LONDON AND NEW YORK

First published in paperback 2024

First published 2014
by Routledge
4 Park Square, Milton Park, Abingdon, Oxon OX14 4RN

and by Routledge
605 Third Avenue, New York, NY 10158

Routledge is an imprint of the Taylor & Francis Group, an informa business

British Library Cataloguing in Publication Data
A catalogue record for this book is available from the British Library

Library of Congress Cataloging in Publication Data
Steinbach, Armin.
Economic policy coordination in the Euro area / Armin Steinbach.
  pages cm
  Includes bibliographical references.
  1. European Union countries–Economic policy. 2. Eurozone. I. Title.
  HC240.S676 2014
  339.5094–dc23   2013045366

ISBN: 978-1-138-02397-0 (hbk)
ISBN: 978-1-03-292784-8 (pbk)
ISBN: 978-1-315-77615-6 (ebk)

DOI: 10.4324/9781315776156

Typeset in Times New Roman
by Wearset Ltd, Boldon, Tyne and Wear

Contents

Figures

Tables

1 Introduction

Discussion about the necessity of economic policy coordination and the appropriate governance structure has accompanied the EU integration process for some time. The current coordination system is asymmetric: monetary policy is set centrally by the ECB, while economic policy, especially fiscal policy and wage policy, is determined on the national level.

Today's coordination system has long been controversial. The Werner Report and the MacDougall Report stressed that a monetary union requires centralized decisions for national budgets as well as an enlarged Community budget.[1] The Werner Report concluded by calling for the creation of a central bank and a European economic government. But the goal of aligning budgetary policy to Community targets was abandoned when the monetarist view gained prominence in the EU. From its perspective, the privileged position of the central bank, together with rule-based fiscal policy, made additional coordination and transfer of sovereignty to the European level unnecessary. Instead, policymakers decided to base monetary union on a "thin" model that required little transfer of institutional sovereignty. In the run-up to Maastricht, the main task of budgetary policy switched from stabilizing aggregate demand to supporting the inflation targets of monetary policy. To this end, the Delors Report provided for the establishment of an effective cap for budgetary deficits.[2] It called for binding and contractual fiscal rules but nevertheless advocated the "soft" coordination of national policies at the EU level. European-wide mechanisms of economic governance were not a feature of its recommendations. For many years, policymakers forwent comprehensive economic policy coordination because they assumed that economic growth in the EU could be achieved through a centralized stability-oriented monetary policy and some more or less binding fiscal rules.

The coordination debate has grown more heated over the course of the European sovereign-debt crisis. The macroeconomic divergences between eurozone states cast doubt on the views expressed by many economists predicting that a monetary union would synchronize economies across the EU. There has been much political disagreement about what do to in response. Some politicians have demanded that states that lose competitiveness and pile up debt be forced from the Union. Others have called for greater integration at the EU level to mend its "birth defect" – the absence of political and monetary union – and standardize fiscal policies. As the sovereign-debt crisis continues, a number of European legislative decisions have been introduced. Most measures have sought to compel a sharper form of fiscal discipline at the national level, including legislation to strengthen fiscal rules (e.g. Sixpack, Twopack, Euro Plus Pact, European Redemption Pact). These proposals have also encompassed an additional means of coordination beyond fiscal policy: the monitoring of macroeconomic imbalances through a range of parameters. All in all, this new legislation represents a qualitative advancement in the area of EU economic policy coordination.

Given the developments of recent years, this book tries to answer the question of whether more economic policy coordination is necessary and which additional forms of coordination in the field of fiscal, monetary and wage policies are possible and useful, with a view to avoiding future crises.

1.1 Basic criticisms of economic policy coordination

Any study of economic policy coordination and governance issues must begin by addressing misgivings expressed by economists concerning the need for coordination. Critics of coordination follow two lines of attack.

The first basic criticism relates to the preconditions that are supposed to indicate the need for coordination: it is commonly argued that a prerequisite for coordination is the existence of identifiable variables that disrupt the long-term equilibrium of target economic variables. This premise – a key component of the underlying theoretical model – limits the applicability of economic policy coordination from the start. Why? In a model that expects rational outcomes, monetary disturbances in wage and price flexibility exert a real influence in the short term only when they are permanent and unexpected; disturbances that are expected or publicized do not. Hence, as long as nominal variables (e.g. price levels) do not factor in the objective function, the predictions of game theory remain irrelevant in the short term.[3] In the long term, a rational model offers no incentives whatsoever for discretionary monetary policy. The same is true of fiscal policy, given sufficient flexibility for prices and wages. The critics argue instead for greater flexibility in the labour and goods markets, which promises to decrease economic interdependence, thus eliminating the need for coordination.[4] I consider this point in detail below. Though I will not take issue with the philosophical assumptions of the Keynesian and monetarist views, I cannot avoid addressing the basic conflict between these views when it comes to discussing economic policy coordination. I will also consider current empirical evidence of the persistence of macroeconomic heterogeneity and, on that basis, investigate existing forms of coordination and proposed forms of coordination with regard to the incentives they provide for policymakers.

The second precondition that is supposed to indicate the need for coordination is the absence of an automatic correction mechanism once a disruption occurs (such as an asymmetric shock). An ideal monetary union ought to provide such a correction mechanism by adjusting prices, wages, migration or fiscal transfers based on optimal currency area theory. The critics of economic policy coordination argue that efforts should be directed not at strengthening coordination, but at reducing obstacles in the way of adjustment (through, say, higher wage flexibility or easier migration).

If the first line of attack against economic policy coordination sees no need for coordination based on the theoretical model, the second line of attack emphasizes the practical problems of coordination. It contends that we can be certain neither about the state of the economy on which coordinated activity is based nor about how or whether other states will act. Critics point out that the existing literature on international macroeconomic policy coordination unrealistically assumes that policymakers all operate on the same model, preferring the Nash bargaining solution to the Nash non-cooperative solution in most cases. The problem with this assumption is that policymakers differ in the models they use. In sum, there are three obstacles to successful international coordination: (1) uncertainty as to the position of the economy, (2) uncertainty as to the correct objective and (3) uncertainty as to the correct model linking policy actions to their effects in the economy.[5]

These concerns about the uncertainty involved in coordination cannot be dismissed, nor should they be. Research has indicated that coordination among policymakers who differ about models is likely to reduce national prosperity, not raise it.[6] I will argue, however, that uncertainty about the homogeneity of coordinating states with regard to models can be reduced, if not eliminated, with "hard" coordination that excludes discretionary measures. The same applies to uncertainty about the position of the economy. Indeed, I will claim that persistent macroeconomic heterogeneities make coordination necessary in the first place.

1.2 State of the research

The stabilization potential of fiscal policy within the EMU has been the subject of many studies, including Bofinger and Mayer, Enderlein, van Aarle and Garretsen, van Aarle *et al.* and Hagen and Mundschenk.[7] Often, such studies use "stabilization games" to examine the interaction between centralized monetary policy and national fiscal policy.[8]

A frequent approach for investigating coordination options uses an economic model to determine dependencies and externalities between policies. In many cases, however, the interdependencies identified depend on the choice of economic model. Dullien developed a model in which monetary policy can influence aggregate demand in a world without real balances by influencing interest rates via changes in short-term interest rates.[9] On the basis of this model, Dullien finds that the central bank and wage bargainers must work in concert to guarantee stable prices and expanding output. In other words, a policy mix for optimal employment and inflation levels combines stability-oriented wage demands with an expansionary monetary policy.[10] The core assumption of studies in support of coordination is that monetary policy can have (permanent or temporary) effects on output and employment even in a world in which all economic actors behave completely rationally.

One rationale for international policy coordination can be found in game theory.[11] The techniques of game theory provide useful tools for analysing the strategic aspects of policy coordination.[12] Researchers identify the benefits of coordination usually by comparing non-cooperative and cooperative strategies. The so-called Cournot–Nash equilibrium serves as the non-cooperative reference point, also known as the disagreement point. The Cournot equilibrium is a special case of the Nash equilibrium. The same applies to the Bertrand equilibrium.[13] Players seek to provide best responses to maximize their outcome for a given objective by varying their strategies based on the decisions of other players. The Cournot–Nash equilibrium lies at the intersection of the reaction curves but is typically located outside the contract curve, signalling Pareto inefficiency. When players maximize a collective utility function – in other words, when they cooperate – each increases his or her payoff. The position of the equilibrium point on the contract curve depends on the bargaining power of the players. The Stackelberg equilibrium, in which "followers" know what the "leaders" are doing, lies between the non-cooperative Cournot–Nash equilibrium and the cooperation solution. The Stackelberg equilibrium seems particularly suited for the analysis of ECB activity and national fiscal policies, as the EU consists of a leader (the wage bargaining partners) and followers (ECB, fiscal policymakers).[14] The reason why cooperative solutions are Pareto efficient is intuitive: externalities and trade-offs between policies (e.g. monetary and fiscal policies) are internalized through cooperation.

Game theory can be extended to many dynamic situations in real life, especially given the fact that the same game is played every year. In sequential bargaining and repetitive games, the best strategy is shaped over time with a number of refinements, including subgame perfection, open loops and closed loops. This suggests that cooperative solutions are more likely because the lack of cooperation in repetitive situations may be punished with "infinite periods".

Investigations that rely on game theory usually start with the underlying economic model. For instance, Pusch uses a market constellation model to investigate the interaction of agents and game theory.[15] Like most other investigators, Pusch assumes a working coordination mechanism. He believes that unions will always act strategically and that wage policy coordination will always be possible (though, empirically, this does not hold true for every case). Furthermore, all three agents in his study (central bank, unions, governments) employ an individual utility calculus whose interactions open up many possibilities for game theory. Dullien uses game theory to identify why an optimal policy mix between monetary policy and wage policy fails to materialize.[16] Based on his analysis, he proposes three reasons: (1) coordination problems, (2) a lack of cooperation between European wage bargainers and the central bank and (3) risk-averse central bankers.[17]

But game theory has an Achilles' heel when used as a tool for assessing coordination: its predictions very much depend on the underlying economic model. A game theory model can in principle accommodate uncertainties associated with agent behaviour, but it will have problems taking into consideration uncertainty or ignorance about which economic model to use, as this part of the equation deals with agent payouts. In this respect, the critics of coordination are right to stress the problems caused by uncertainty, especially where game theory is concerned.

1.3 This study's approach

The purpose of this study is to examine the need for economic policy coordination within the eurozone and describe the form it might take. In contrast to recent research, this study steers clear of a key criticism of economic policy coordination – namely, uncertainty about the underlying economic model. Previous studies all make basic assumptions about the functional relationships between monetary policies, fiscal policies and wage policies, thus leaving them open to attack. By contrast, I analyse existing and potential economic policy coordination and the incentives they generate from the perspective of institutional economics. The advantage of this approach is that the underlying economic model no longer needs to be identified. Furthermore, it allows monetarist and Keynesian approaches to coordination to be compared and assessed with regard to their institutional structures.

The study begins in Chapter 2 with an empirical review of macroeconomic heterogeneity within the eurozone so as to determine the need for economic policy coordination in the first place. I then examine the criteria used to establish an optimal currency area. My aim is to understand why, even after the creation of the eurozone, there remain macroeconomic asymmetries – asymmetries that call for the kind of stabilization offered by coordinated economic policy.

In Chapter 3 I propose a coordination classification scheme that distinguishes between vertical and horizontal coordination, as shown in Table 1.1. I then break down horizontal coordination into *cross-border* coordination (e.g. fiscal policy within the Stability and Growth Pact (SGP)) and *cross-policy* coordination (e.g. fiscal policies and wage policies). This distinction (which previous studies do not use) is necessary for a clear understanding of the historical evolution of coordination within the eurozone and of the economic implications for each form of cooperation. I use the term "vertical coordination" to distinguish between different forms of coordination with regard to their bindingness. Here, I make a basic distinction between soft, hard and centralized coordination.

Table 1.1 Classification of coordination methods

		Horizontal coordination	
		Cross-border coordination	*Cross-policy coordination (fiscal, monetary, wages)*
Vertical coordination	Soft coordination Hard coordination Centralized coordination		

Source: author's description.

Next, I discuss the rationale for economic policy coordination by way of external effects, as the existence of economic heterogeneity in the eurozone is not per se sufficient to explain the necessity of coordination. Rather, externalities, public goods, club goods and interdependence between policy areas provide the real rationale for coordination.[18] I also consider Keynesian and monetarist perspectives on coordination and present empirical findings on the externalities of national economic policy. In doing so, I employ the distinction between cross-border and cross-policy coordination. The external effects in cross-border coordination consist of spillovers – the effects of measures (fiscal policy, say) on other countries. Coordination is usually necessary if positive spillovers, negative spillovers or effects on community goods (e.g. euros, price level) result from the actions of individual states. With cross-policy coordination (fiscal policy, monetary policy, wage policy), the external effects arise from interdependencies between different policy areas. In theory, the existence of interdependencies between policy areas depends on whether the underlying economic model is Keynesian or neoclassical.

In Chapter 4, I classify the coordination mechanism used in the eurozone up to the outbreak of the sovereign-debt crisis. This temporal caesura is necessary to illustrate the development and expansion of EU coordination. Up to the sovereign-debt crisis, the strongest form of coordination was centralized monetary policy. The SGP – which coordinates the fiscal policies of EU states – is a type of hard coordination. The Broad Economic Policy Guidelines, the Macroeconomic Dialogue and the Luxemburg Process all employ a version of soft coordination. It turns out that prior to the sovereign-debt crisis, coordination was unable to sufficiently internalize the externalities, given the strong asymmetries between EU institutions and actors. This is because an autonomous central bank bears the sole responsibility for monetary policy, while more or less "hard" procedures are in place for other policy areas.

In Section 5.1, I investigate the options for farther-reaching economic coordination of fiscal, wage and monetary policy. In the area of cross-border coordination for fiscal policy, I present recent reforms and assess them with regard to the externalities identified in the previous section, especially with regard to whether the SGP succeeds in internalizing the externalities. In addition, I discuss farther-reaching fiscal coordination (debt limits, insolvency proceedings, Eurobonds) in view of the different principles of state organization in which they may be implemented. Federal states and union states differ in the incentives they offer for debt accumulation – and thus in their suitability for fiscal coordination.

In addition to my analysis of fiscal coordination, I argue in Section 5.2 that the strict separation in accordance with the monetarist "assignment approach" during the debt crisis has undergone significant changes. The newly established macroeconomic monitoring system represents hard, cross-policy coordination accompanied by soft, cross-policy coordination (the Europe 2020 strategy or the European semester, say). In attaching effective conditionality to a European Financial Stability Facility/European Stability Mechanism (EFSF/ESM) programme, the EU has also moved to hard, cross-policy coordination, entailing the comprehensive reform of fiscal, wage and structural policy in member states. Ultimately, the ECB's purchase of government bonds expands monetary policy into the realm of fiscal policy.

In Section 5.3, I investigate the possibility of coordinated wage policies that are productivity-orientated and seek steady growth in macroeconomic inflation and unit labour costs. Specifically, I analyse the institutional framework in the EU member states with regard to horizontal, cross-border wage coordination. In doing so, I investigate the extent to which the existing wage negotiation systems of EU member states permit a common wage policy. To this end, I outline the degree of coordination offered by wage negotiation systems in the EU. It turns out that in all EU member states, wage negotiations take place on many levels. For each country, I select sector-specific and company-specific components. I classify coordination forms by their centrality, their organization and their tariff fixation.

In addition to wage policy coordination within EU member states, I regard existing cross-border wage coordination between unions. Empirical investigation has shown that the implementation of a productivity-oriented wage policy in national wage agreements can work. Yet it has also shown that the national wage-setting systems vary greatly. An EU-wide wage policy thus seems unlikely and not desirable given institutional barriers and disincentives. To create the conditions for a common European wage policy, the national wage-setting systems must be standardized. But the standardization of wage policy institutions and employment policy strategy is, I argue, unrealistic for several fundamental reasons.

In Section 5.4, I turn to the coordination of monetary and fiscal policies. The usefulness of such coordination greatly depends on the underlying macroeconomic model. The ECB (along with other proponents of neoclassical economics) had difficulty accepting a coordinated monetary policy whose goal is growth. In its view, monetary policy can at most trigger short-term growth effects and accelerated inflation, but in the long run the effects of monetary supply and monetary policy remain neutral. From a Keynesian perspective, by contrast, the ECB can perform an important function for coordinated economic policy. This is why Keynesians propose that the mission of the ECB be expanded to include price stability, economic growth and employment as equal-ranking objectives, as is the case in the United States. Ultimately, the ECB accepts a stronger mixture of monetary policy and fiscal policy in practice than it does in theory. The ECB's purchase of government bonds until mid-2012 had a fiscal-policy-like influence, because it improved the refinancing conditions in the countries affected. In the summer of 2012, the ECB began to explicitly coordinate bond purchases and the European Stability Mechanism's (ESM) conditional credit line extension. This linked the monetary measures of the ECB with a macroeconomic adjustment programme designed to fundamentally change the economic policy structure in the receiving states. The result is a tight coordination of monetary policy with other economic policy areas – and a rejection of the traditional assignment approach.

Notes

1 The Werner Report (1970), MacDougall Report (1977).
2 Delors Report (1989).
3 See Vaubel (1983, 17), Buiter (1985, 42) and Maennig (1992, 169ff.).
4 Feldstein (1988, 3), Issing (2001a), Vaubel (1983, 13).
5 Frankel and Rockett (1988).
6 Frankel (1989).
7 Bofinger and Mayer (2003), Enderlein (2004), van Aarle and Garretsen (2000), van Aarle *et al.* (2004) and Hagen and Mundschenk (2002).
8 Dixit and Lambertini (2001), Uhlig (2002).
9 Dullien (2004).
10 Dullien (2004, 9).
11 Hamada and Kawai (1997, 87ff.).
12 Mooslechner and Schürz (1999, 174).
13 Pindyck and Rubinfeld (2009, 614).
14 Pusch (2009, 100ff.).
15 Pusch (2009).
16 Dullien (2004).
17 Dullien (2004, 9).
18 Le Cacheux (2007, 40).

2 Asymmetric shocks and heterogeneity following the creation of the EMU

This chapter begins with a claim: the need for economic policy coordination in a monetary union depends primarily on three factors. These are: (1) the severity of asymmetric shocks – that is, supply or demand shocks that only affect some regions of a currency union; (2) the relevance of endogenous shocks, i.e. the effects that result from a combination of centralized monetary policy and diversified national economies; and (3) the degree of structural heterogeneity in output, inflation and current account balances between national economies. Generally, economic heterogeneity in a monetary union is not a problem per se as it may reflect acceptable or welcomed diversity, such as the "catching-up" of less advanced economies, leading in the long run to overall convergence. But there are forms of "negative" divergence that hamper growth in the EMU and do not serve long-run convergence. In the absence of appropriate policy responses or adjustment mechanisms, negative divergence can contribute to the macroeconomic underperformance of the eurozone and may also lower the effectiveness of the common monetary policy, as this policy might set false incentives for certain member states.[1]

Drawing on the intense economic debate about what constitutes an optimum currency area (OCA),[2] I make three arguments: (1) that the EU does not represent an OCA; (2) that asymmetric shocks affect the euro countries differently due to their heterogeneity; (3) that no adjustment mechanisms can dampen these effects. In this way, we must ask whether the creation of the monetary union has brought about greater uniformity in business cycles across member states.

Before the EMU came into effect, many economists assumed that a common business cycle would be possible for eurozone countries.[3] Nevertheless, many studies had identified business cycle divergence between member countries. Particularly in the case of numerous smaller economies, no robust findings of economic convergence and synchronization with the eurozone average could be observed. Furthermore, these analyses were inconclusive about whether this heterogeneity resulted from structural differences or from differences in monetary and fiscal policy responses to macroeconomic shocks.

2.1 Theoretical studies on business cycle convergence in the EMU

The studies carried out since the formation of the EMU come to different conclusions about business cycle convergence. In many theoretical studies, it is argued that business cycle convergence can be achieved through the harmonization of economic policy and increased real economic integration. Economists have argued that the centralization of monetary policy can eliminate national monetary policy both as a stabilizer and trigger of asymmetric shocks. The same applies to the fiscal policy restricted by the SGP. It has been posited that in terms of real economic effects, the harmonization of business cycles will occur as intra-industry trade intensifies.[4] According to a core argument, the dominance of intra-industry trade will increase the symmetry of demand-side shocks, leading to greater international correlation of business cycles.[5] Frankel and Rose presented empirical evidence for the existence of a strong positive link between bilateral trade intensity and the international convergence of business cycles.[6] Furthermore, some years after the launch of the EMU, the main EU institutions argued that the strong synchronization of business cycles between eurozone members should contribute to reducing the likelihood of asymmetric shocks in the currency union.[7]

Another theoretical argument for convergence and the decline of general economic fluctuations has been the expectation of an increase in price and wage flexibility within the monetary union. When monetary policy is centralized and fiscal policy restricted, an increase in price adjustment in contrast to quantity adjustment is expected.[8] According to this logic, prior to the introduction of the EMU firms and policymakers could rely on the stabilizing intervention of monetary and fiscal policy and thus externalize the effects of price and wage stickiness. As a result, prior to the EMU price and wage dynamics were in place that were unable to respond flexibly to exogenous shocks. Accordingly, it was believed that the restriction of economic policy autonomy by the monetary union and the SGP would increase the ability of the private sector to respond to shocks more flexibly in the future, decreasing the need for stabilizing interventions on the member-state level.[9]

By contrast, some economists projected that business cycles would diverge as industrial concentration and sector specialization in the eurozone increased.[10] Krugman argued that the process of economic integration (mainly, the expansion of interregional trade as a result of the EMU) would lead to greater local/regional specialization and concentration of production,[11] which might cause some euro area regions to become more vulnerable to idiosyncratic (sectoral/industry-specific) shocks and, in turn, lead to an increased likelihood of various regionally specific crises and recessions within the euro area.[12] However, in the first few years of the EMU, there was little evidence for increased specialization.[13]

2.2 Empirical studies of economic convergence in the EMU

Generally, the economic state of euro countries is determined by responses to shock and monetary transmission, by supranational monetary policy, by economic policy on the country level and by the flexibility of goods and factor markets. This study does not undertake a detailed analysis of these aspects and their interactions. Rather, I limit myself to selected empirical findings on the importance of asymmetric shocks and monetary policy transmission differences (endogenous shocks) in the eurozone. Both factors play an important role in determining the need for market-based adjustment mechanisms and national stabilization policy. Also crucial is whether the creation of a monetary union provides greater uniformity to business cycles and transmission in the member states. I then sketch alternative market-based mechanisms for absorbing economic shocks.

I begin by considering the level of structural heterogeneity in output and inflation. This is important for multiple reasons. For one, it tells us whether uniform interest rate policy by the ECB is the best response to the underlying macroeconomic data or whether it could result in distorting effects when national economies are heterogeneous. Moreover, it can give us an idea about whether OCA criteria are satisfied, helping us determine whether there's need for coordination in the first place.

2.2.1 Heterogeneity with regard to capacity utilization

Country-specific differences in capacity utilization indicate the severity of asymmetric shocks within the eurozone. Figure 2.1 shows the country-specific differences in capacity utilization since the beginning of the 1980s, expressed in terms

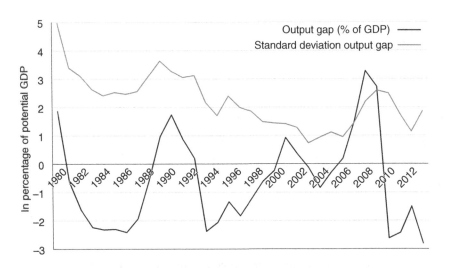

Figure 2.1 Output gaps (source: IMF, World Economic Outlook Database).

of output gaps. The output gap measures the difference between actual output and its estimated potential.[14]

The variation in capacity utilization levels is expressed in Figure 2.1 as the standard deviation of the output gap. The average output gap (in per cent of GDP) characterizes the average potential deviation or deviation trend.[15] While the standard deviation offers a measure for dispersion in potential utilization by the member states, the average output gap quantifies the average amount of deviation from the potential. Fluctuations in average output gaps underscore the existence of business cycle divergence.

The figure points to business cycle convergence in the second half of the 1990s and in the years immediately following the creation of the EMU.[16] In this period, the standard deviation shows declining divergence in potential utilization in the eurozone, with a slightly reduced volatility relative to the 1980s and 1990s. Accordingly, the economic conditions for a general monetary policy were more favourable from the mid-1990s to 2005 than at the beginning of the 1990s. Yet we should note that economic divergence at the beginning of the 1990s was strongly tied to German unity and its monetary and fiscal policy consequences. Accordingly, homogenization in the second half of the 1990s grew out of special circumstances. For the period since 2005, economic fluctuations have increased considerably, and additional convergence of business cycles is not in the offing. During the financial crisis, the standard deviation declined between 2008 and 2010, which indicates that all countries were affected by the financial crisis equally. Since 2011, the standard deviation in the eurozone has been increasing, an indication that EU member states exited the crisis in very different ways.

Figure 2.2 illustrates the range of country-specific output gaps in the eurozone. At the end of the 1990s and after the start of the EMU, the spectrum

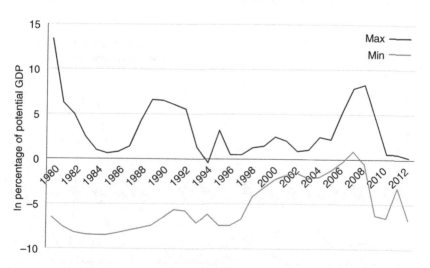

Figure 2.2 Divergence of output gaps (source: IMF, World Economic Outlook Database).

declined slightly. Since 2004 divergences have increased considerably. During the 2008–2009 financial crisis, the distribution declined briefly but has since increased again.

In sum, the utilization of capacities in the eurozone does not provide empirical support for theoretical forecasts made before the monetary union that projected a convergence in capacity utilization. Consequently, the finding of increasing business cycle convergence since the creation of the eurozone must be ruled out. A significant decline has not been witnessed for average output gaps or for standard deviations. On the contrary, the divergence in output gaps in the eurozone has actually increased. Divergence with regard to potential utilization illustrates the persistence of country-specific differences – and a lack of economic convergence.

2.2.2 Heterogeneous inflation levels

Figures 2.3 and 2.4 present inflation differentials in the eurozone. They point to a strong convergence in price level growth in the 1980s and 1990s.[17] The reduced divergence results from a decline in the average inflation rate. The convergence in inflationary expectations before the monetary union facilitated homogenous inflation rates in the 1990s. Another factor was the self-restraint of national central banks in the European Monetary System (EMS). In the first two stages of the EMU, divergence in inflation rates – expressed by the standard deviation – was reduced. By the third stage, convergence in inflation rates came to a standstill. Since then, divergence has remained constant. Since 2006, a significant rise in volatility has been observed in the standard deviation. More recently, the

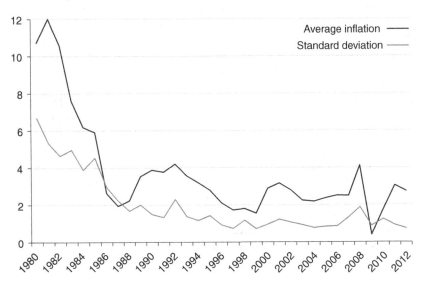

Figure 2.3 Inflation in per cent (source: author's calculations, based on IMF, World Economic Outlook Database).

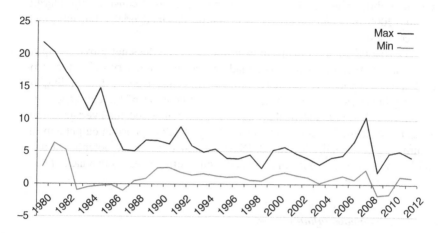

Figure 2.4 Dispersion of inflation rates (source: author's calculations, based on IMF, World Economic Outlook Database).

financial crisis brought about heterogeneous inflation rate growth, with increasing divergence between nations. Indeed, the inflation differential when the ECB increased the prime interest rate in April 2011 was at a record high. It ranged from 0.9 per cent (Ireland) to 2.2 per cent (Germany) to 5.5 per cent (Estonia), with a spread of 4.6 per cent.[18] By comparison, in 1997, the base year for the euro convergence test, the difference was 0.7 per cent. This means that divergence in inflation in April 2011 was almost seven times as high as it was at the monetary union's formation. Even in previous years when the ECB increased the prime rate, the difference in national inflation rates did not exceed 2.8 per cent.[19] This finding is confirmed by Engel and Rogers,[20] who found no evidence of price convergence following the introduction of the euro, neither in general nor for a specific convergence movement. Similar results are reported by Lutz,[21] who investigates four alternative datasets of disaggregated prices.

Are there sound explanations for persistent inflation differentials within the eurozone? One reason supporting the conventional negative assessment of inflation differentials within the eurozone is the possibility that they might be associated with a loss of competitiveness in countries with higher inflation rates. Comparatively high inflation might be attributable to an asymmetric increase in productivity in the respective economy, and thus represent a (Balassa–Samuelson type) equilibrium phenomenon.[22] According to the estimations of Gischer and Weiss,[23] for instance, a portion of the inflation differential in the eurozone is attributable to Balassa–Samuelson effects. Honohan and Lane,[24] by contrast, find for the period 1999–2001 that the nominal depreciation of the euro against the US dollar affected national inflation rates within the eurozone heterogeneously, raising inflation especially in those countries which trade heavily with non-EMU partners. Arnold and Verhoef,[25] however, demonstrate that their results no longer hold true if lagged inflation is added as a regressor, or as soon as the outlier

Ireland is eliminated from the panel. Other empirical studies argue against the occurrence of Balassa–Samuelson effects.[26] Indeed, the Balassa–Samuelson effect cannot explain the observed persistent differences in inflation, because euro countries with high productivity growth usually show below-average inflation rates, not above-average inflation rates (as predicted by the effect).[27]

The differences in potential utilization that result from asymmetric demand and supply shocks, together with country-specific differences in economic structure and in output and inflation, play an important role in inflationary differences.[28]

An important source of divergence in inflation rates is changes to nominal labour unit costs. The euro crisis has shown that the loss of competitiveness experienced by several eurozone members was induced by high collective wage agreements, leading to higher inflation rates than most central and northern EMU countries.[29]

Figure 2.5 shows how relative unit labour costs since the beginning of the European monetary union have diverged. As we can see, the costs in countries such as Portugal, Spain, Greece and Ireland have increased rapidly since the introduction of the euro, while the relative labour unit costs in Germany and Austria decreased markedly. Figure 2.6 shows the significant effect this had on the development of inflation rates within the eurozone.

Figure 2.6 shows that inflation correlates heavily with nominal labour cost growth, which shows strong divergent trends among member states. Countries with low unit labour cost growth in past years, such as Germany and Austria, are also among the countries with low inflation. In contrast, Ireland, Greece, Spain and Portugal have seen high unit labour cost growth and high country-specific inflation. The dashed regression line indicates a strong correlation between unit labour cost growth and inflation.[30] This is supported by estimations from Tatierska, who showed that in eight of the 11 euro area countries there is a plausible

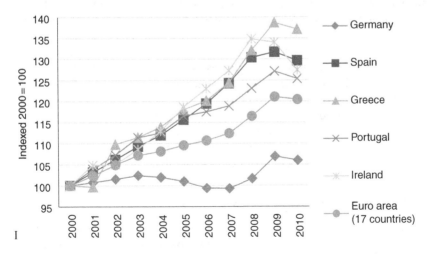

Figure 2.5 Relative unit labour costs since 2000; year 2000=100 (source: Ameco).

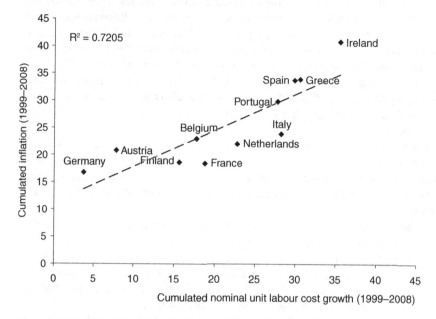

Figure 2.6 Inflation and growth of unit labour costs in Europe, 1999–2008 (source: European Commission, Ameco; graph from Zemanek *et al.*, 2009).

relationship between unit labour costs and price level dynamics. The average time needed to adjust prices in line with movements in unit labour costs is estimated to be around eight months.[31]

Thus, persistent inflation differentials in the eurozone are also indicative of a continuous divergence in economic competitiveness. The steadily rising divergence implies that there is neither wage competition nor wage standardization within the eurozone. Apparently, relative wages have not been adjusted to diverging competitiveness and have failed to correct rising imbalances.[32] Altissimo *et al.* argue that structural rigidities and in particular downward rigid prices and wages in the eurozone have prevented an adjustment of real exchange rates.[33] In this context, the European Commission shows that country-specific unit labour costs respond differently to positive and negative output gaps.[34] In Portugal, Italy, Greece and France losses in competitiveness during the downturn have been greater than in Germany and Austria. Generally, this pattern is attributed to different degrees of nominal wage rigidity.

2.2.3 Heterogeneous account balances

Another indicator of macroeconomic divergence is current account imbalances. Imbalances within the eurozone increased massively from the creation of the monetary union in 1999 to the beginning of the economic crisis. From 1998 until directly before the crisis in 2007, average divergence in current account imbalances doubled. In 1998 the average account imbalance – whether in the form of surpluses or deficits – was just under 3 per cent of GDP; in 2007 it was more than 6 per cent (see Figure 2.7). The increase seems even greater given that currency rates were relatively stable in the two years before the creation of the monetary union. A comparison of the imbalances directly before the crisis of 2008–2009 with those in the early 1990s is telling. Back then, the average imbalance was just under 2 per cent of GDP, a mere one-third of its 2007 level.[35] Curiously, the external balance of the monetary union changed minimally during this period, going from a slight surplus to a small deficit. This indicates that growing current account imbalances in euro countries were primarily a problem *within* the monetary zone.

If we examine imbalances by country (Figure 2.8), we notice extreme deficit levels in three countries in particular: Spain, Greece and Portugal. By the time the financial crisis hit, these countries had current account deficits of around 10 per cent of GDP or more. In each country, the account balance worsened considerably in relation to the year before the monetary union was created. Greece's deficit increased by more than 10 percentage points. Notably, Portugal's deficit worsened in the initial years of the monetary union, while Spain and Greece's grew more slowly, picking up speed only after 2005.

In diametric contrast, the account balances of other countries improved dramatically over this period, in particular those of Germany, Austria and the Netherlands. From 1998 to 2007, the current account balance of Germany improved by 8.5 percentage points. In Austria and the Netherlands, the balance improved by roughly 5 percentage points. Aside from Germany, the Netherlands and Luxembourg displayed significant current account surpluses immediately before the crisis, equalling 8.7 per cent of GDP and 9.7 per cent of GDP, respectively.[36]

Most economists blame the growing imbalance levels since 1999 on changes to unit labour prices. They argue that countries whose labour unit costs increased

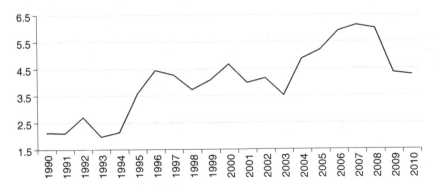

Figure 2.7 Average current account balance as a percentage of GDP (source: IMF, 2012).

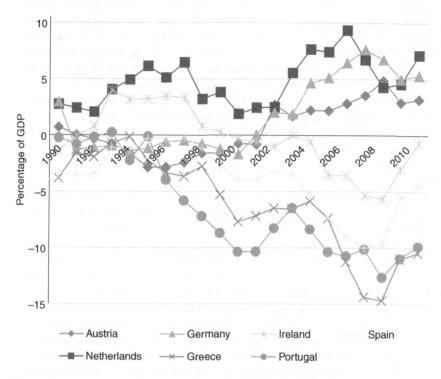

Figure 2.8 Current account imbalance (percentage of GDP) (source: IMF, 2012).

at a higher than average rate lost market share to countries with lower labour unit costs – on domestic as well as export markets. This displacement of market share manifests in above-average import growth and below-average export growth, leading to ever greater divergence account balances.

Figure 2.9 shows that from 1999 to 2007, changes to labour unit costs correlated highly with changes in account balances within the eurozone. Countries that lost significant amounts of price competitiveness (measured by the relative increase in labour unit costs) saw their account balances generally worsen. By contrast, countries that were able to lower prices saw their account balances markedly improve. Cost divergences appear, therefore, to be a key factor behind strong increases in account balance deficits and surpluses.[37]

2.2.4 Monetary policy transmission differences can amplify heterogeneity

Heterogeneity among economic structures within the eurozone can be intensified by monetary policy transmission. The harmonization of transmission reduces the risk of shock caused by monetary policy and the risk of greater asymmetric shock caused by transmission differences. If monetary policy has different

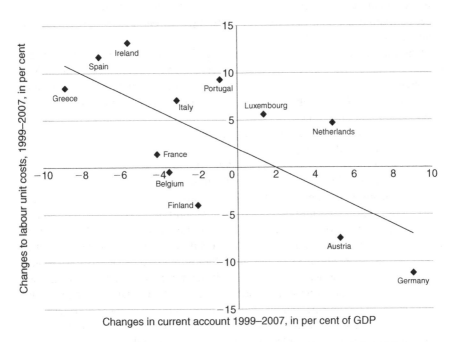

Figure 2.9 Changes to labour unit costs and account balances, 1999–2007 (source: Dullien, 2010, 23).

effects within the eurozone, there is the danger that asymmetric shocks may result, even when the initial conditions are the same. For small economies at the periphery of the eurozone, where the risk of asymmetric shock is greater and the real effect of fluctuating euro currency rates is stronger,[38] this can mean rising volatility and a growing need for alternative mechanisms for absorbing shock.

The possible differences in monetary policy's real economic effects can be discussed by examining transmission mechanisms.[39] The central issue is the influence of monetary policy on demands for consumer goods, capital goods and net exports. The idea that monetary policy might have heterogeneous effects has motivated a number of empirical studies investigating the role of transmission differences in the eurozone, though their findings lie outside the scope of this study.[40] Instead, I want to consider the likelihood that one country's business cycle will deviate from the EMU average. In such a case, the monetary policy of the ECB may cease to have a stabilizing effect; indeed, it may even serve to destabilize.

The position of each EMU country relative to the eurozone average plays an important role in measuring heterogeneous economic development. Since the ECB bases its interest rates exclusively on average data, the pressure on states with greater than average business-cycle divergence is stronger than on states with business cycles that correlate with the average, so that monetary policy for individual countries is occasionally too restrictive or too lax. This kind of maladjustment occurs when the two central factors influencing monetary policy – i.e. the output gap and inflation rate – strongly deviate in one eurozone state from the eurozone average.[41]

Real interest rates that are very low or negative bring about positive business cycles. Negative real interest rates may increase consumption levels and raise real investment, accelerating growth above the production potential and causing an inflationary effect. In the EMU rising inflation has an almost paradoxical effect: as inflation rates increase, real interest rates decrease. This cycle cannot correct itself purely via monetary mechanisms; quite the contrary: monetary policy can increase divergence.

This effect of monetary policy is at odds with the classical approach of many researchers who, before the EMU was created, assumed that cyclical differences in the eurozone could be offset by the real currency exchange rates.[42] These studies predicted that countries with high inflation rates would lose their competitiveness in the medium term, would see declining export demand, and would have to import more and more goods. As a result, the domestic economy would cool down in the medium term and the inflation rate would decline. An exact opposite scenario was expected to occur in countries with lower growth and inflation. These projections were rooted in the belief that national price levels converge in the domestic market when the mobility of goods and services remains high, resulting in a uniform real interest rates. But economists who advocated this perspective failed to consider whether and to what extent this adjustment process actually works for large and small economies. As it turns out, the process *does* work for small and open economies, which face high competition levels from abroad due to trade interdependencies. By contrast, even if large and open national economies have trade interdependencies, they also have large domestic markets.[43] Consequently, adjustments to real exchange rates in large economies take incomparably longer than in small economies.

2.2.5 Interim findings

My initial claim was that the need for economic political coordination in a monetary union depends primarily on the severity of asymmetric shocks, the relevance of the impact of uniform monetary policies and on the degree of structural heterogeneity in output, inflation and current account balances. Above, I showed that the EMU has yet to lead to lower macroeconomic heterogeneity; indeed, the convergence process appears in some places to have come to a halt.[44] Moreover, countries are being pressured to harmonize their economies because of the ECB's decision to base its interest rate policy on average values. The possibility that the ECB interest rate policy will generate endogenous shocks cannot be excluded, even if the starting situation is the same in each country. This can result in volatile economic development and a growing need for alternative shock absorption mechanisms. In sum, my empirical findings provide good reason to analyse the stabilizing potential of coordinated economic policy.

2.3 Possible mechanisms to adjust for heterogeneous development within the eurozone

The more politically and economically homogenous countries are, the less prosperity they lose when entering a monetary union. When no homogeneity is present, imbalances can arise, as individual regions must deal with suboptimal real interest rates. The resulting business cycle divergence can generally be offset by ensuring sufficient factor flexibility in individual member countries, yet what these adjustment factors are, and whether they apply to the EMU, remains uncertain. From an economic perspective, a monetary union with a single monetary policy can be successful only if structural divergence within the union can be overcome via adjustment mechanisms. Strictly speaking, the presence of an adjustment mechanism suffices to meet the criterion of an OCA.

The attempt to identify criteria for OCAs makes sense only in monetary areas that experience asymmetric shocks. For this reason, while economic heterogeneity is not a suitable criterion for investigating OCAs, the test for economic homogeneity is crucial when investigating monetary policy integration. As I have shown above, the euro countries show little economic and structural similarity.[45] Accordingly, it is necessary for eurozone member states to have at their disposal adjustment instruments to neutralize asymmetric shocks. However, in a monetary union, instruments such as monetary and exchange rate policies are no longer available for individual countries. Therefore, OCA theory states that the following adjustment mechanisms can potentially be used to handle asymmetric shocks: labour mobility, price and wage flexibility and fiscal policy. Yet which of these adjustment mechanisms could be effectively used to manage asymmetric shocks within the eurozone?

2.3.1 Labour mobility

Empirical studies have shown that labour mobility is not a key adjustment mechanism in the EU or the eurozone.[46] In some countries, particularly the United States, evidence indicates that labour mobility has served as an adjustment factor.[47] When asymmetric shocks occur, labour drifts from more weakly developed economies into more strongly developed regions. For the European monetary area, however, such movement can all but be excluded, as spatial mobility is weak at both the international and interregional levels.[48]

As illustrated by Table 2.1, in the EU-27 only 0.18 per cent of the working-age population changed residence to another EU country. Geographic mobility of labour thus appears much lower in the EU. However, there are major reasons for differences between the United States and EU. These are mostly related to socio-economic and cultural phenomena including language and labour legislation, but also that, in the EU, free movement is a rather recent phenomenon compared to the long history of migration in the United States. It may therefore be more appropriate to compare internal mobility in the United States to the mobility of working-age residents not between, but within EU countries. Comparing

Table 2.1 Comparison between the EU and the US, 2008

	US (%)	EU-27 (%)
Share of working-age residents who moved from a different region/state within the same country	2.80	1.03
Share of working-age residents who moved from an EU country/ US state	2.80	0.18

Source: Gakova and Dijkstra (2010).

the share of working-age residents who moved to another region of the same country – 1.03 per cent in the EU versus 2.8 per cent in the United States – somewhat reduces the gap in mobility between the two.[49]

The European Commission has also been sceptical about whether labour mobility can absorb shocks in the eurozone. Though it concedes that regional mobility in already existing federations could abet adjustment when regional shocks occurs, it rejects the possibility of something similar for the EU as a whole on account of cultural and linguistic differences, although high-income groups in certain border regions may represent an exception. Strong labour mobility also contains certain risks. Should labour – especially highly qualified labour – drift from economically weak regions to economically strong regions because of low wages, peripheral regions would likely stagnate further, while centres would reap even greater benefits. The increase in economic and social divergence could make integration considerably more difficult.[50]

2.3.2 Price and wage flexibility

Extensive economic debate has been conducted with regard to price and wage flexibility. In most Western European countries, real and nominal wages have limited flexibility because of labour market regulation.[51] Markets for goods also show substantial price rigidity.[52] Yet the findings of Dullien and Fritsche do not support the conjecture that the absence of floating exchange rates and the loss of monetary policy independence accelerate the deregulation of goods and labour markets.[53] Accordingly, flexibility and market-based shock absorption are not endogenous values for currency rate regimes.[54]

These findings have been confirmed by more recent studies, including those carried out by the ECB. Heinz and Rusinova use a Phillips curve panel framework to estimate the degree of real wage flexibility in 19 EU countries.[55] Specifically, they examine how real wages vary depending on the cyclical position of an economy, labour market institutions and the level of inflation. Their results show that real wage flexibility appears to be somewhat higher in Central and Eastern European countries than in the euro area, both with respect to the response to unemployment and productivity. This difference may be related to differences in labour market institutions and, in particular, wage bargaining institutions. There is agreement that more flexible labour, goods and capital markets are necessary for accelerating and improving market-based shock absorption within the monetary union.[56]

A number of studies have examined the impact of labour market institutions, focusing in particular on the impact of institutions on wage dynamics. Much of the empirical literature concentrates on the centralization of wage bargaining, but it is generally inconclusive about its effect on economic outcomes.[57] Some authors find supportive evidence for the Calmfors–Driffill hypothesis, which postulates a hump-shaped relationship between the level of coordination in wage negotiations and the degree of real wage moderation. According to this hypothesis, centralized bargaining produces moderate results because it internalizes the negative effects of excessive wage growth on the entire economy.[58] Alesina and Perotti divide countries into three broad institutional groups, based on the level of wage bargaining, and find support for the hump-shaped relationship between this indicator and wages.[59] Nunziata also finds that wage bargaining institutions play a major role in influencing wage dynamics;[60] however, he suggests that wage growth moderates with higher levels of coordination. Nunziata finds no significant effect in countries where coordination levels remained stable, and argues that increasing coordination in the 1990s was particularly relevant for moderating labour costs in Ireland, France and Italy.

Considering both the level of wage bargaining and type of coordination, Kittel finds that countries with uncoordinated labour markets tend to respond less flexibly to shocks than those that rely on some kind of coordination.[61] In addition to the level of coordination, another impacting factor identified in the literature is union density and coverage, and a negative relationship has been established between union density and flexibility.[62]

2.3.3 Fiscal transfer

An alternative to adjustment by means of currency exchange rates is adjustment by means of fiscal transfer. The use of this approach can be found in the best-known cases of integrated monetary areas outside Europe: the United States and Canada.[63] In both countries, factor mobility plays a role as an adjustment instrument, while regional economic phenomena trigger tax equalization payments to reduce structural divergence.[64]

In theory, equalization plans can be designed in such a way that high-production EMU states with strong economies pay unilateral financial transfers to economically weaker countries. To date, however, public transfers between member states on a larger scale have not been politically feasible. On the one hand, they would strongly strain budgets in donor countries given the already precarious fiscal situation. On the other hand, a comprehensive financial equalization mechanism like the regional ones practised within individual countries will be hard to implement as long as the EU has yet to develop a real community identity. Of course, the community might carry out transfer payments itself, yet the problem with this approach is the fact that public finances in the union are decentralized. The EU budget amounts to 2.1 per cent of all government expenditure of the EMU member states, whereas in the United States more than 65 per cent of the total government expenses reflect those of the central government. The ever reoccurring debate about how much individual EU countries should pay makes clear that a significant ramping up of community finances is out of the question, at least in the medium term.

2.3.4 Fiscal policy stabilization

The last option involves resorting to nationally controlled fiscal and wage policies. First, a word about fiscal policy: On the national level, fiscal policy remains the only political instrument that provides a stabilizing effect for asymmetric shocks in the short term when monetary policy is centralized.[65] Hence, the value of fiscal policy as a stabilization option increases even when structural and economic heterogeneity in the eurozone remains almost constant. When asymmetric shocks occur and differences arise in monetary policy transmission, the stabilization function of fiscal policy tends to gain in importance.

The stabilizing potential of fiscal policy within the EMU has been the object of many studies. Analysis of the stabilizing potential of fiscal policy in the EMU can be found in the work of Beetsma and Jensen, Bofinger and Mayer, van Aarle and Garretsen, van Aarle *et al.* and Hagen and Mundschenk, among others.[66] Most of these researchers use "stabilization games" to examine the interaction between centralized monetary policy and national fiscal policy.[67]

Economies affected by asymmetric shocks may deploy expansive fiscal policy to equalize export losses. But they should do so only when the losses result from the reduction of foreign demand or from the effect of changed preference structures. If above-average cost increases or below-average productivity in the export sector is the cause, then the domestic policy cannot be deployed as a long-term corrective. Under these conditions, what's needed are wage price drops. However, the SGP has wrapped a tight corset around the budget policies of EMU states. The reference values governing new debt and gross debt ratios leave little leeway for the kind of expansive fiscal policy that can fight economic disequilibrium. Why the strict regulation? Inflated debts negatively influence interest and price levels in the eurozone. The liability of EMU countries for the government debts of fellow member states is generally barred on account of the no-bailout clause. This is why a strict stability course for all member states is absolutely necessary, regardless of whether a crisis mechanism like the one established during the government debt crisis exists.

Fiscal policy, despite its potentially important role as a stabilization instrument, faces a number of practical challenges. First, the delayed identification of shocks and the long decision-making process in tax and spending policy reduce the effectiveness of fiscal measures. Both of these factors are traditionally referred to together as the "outside lag." Second, the spillover of fiscal policy on neighbouring states via the net export channel dampens fiscal policy multipliers as well as the efficiency of unilateral stabilization in open economies. Third, targeted policy relies on the availability of useable real-time data. For instance, strategies geared towards output gaps encounter problems when it comes to data and forecast quality, since output gaps vary based on projected output, a purely theoretical concept whose quantification is highly uncertain. Targeted economic policy, to take another example, depends on the accuracy of projections about the effects of exogenous shocks.[68]

These three considerations – together with the comprehensive research that supports them and the weaknesses of unilateral fiscal policy I discuss above – explain why I am uninterested in further exploring the stabilizing potential of national fiscal policy. Rather, my main objective is to investigate the extent to which policy coordination can help reduce heterogeneity in economic development.

2.3.5 Interim findings

New economic adjustment instruments within the EMU are needed first and foremost because of lack of homogeneity between member states. The eurozone is a monetary union, but at the same time it is not an OCA. The eurozone does not fulfil some important OCA criteria, especially those related to labour mobility as well as price and wage flexibility. As a monetary union, the euro area is potentially exposed to asymmetric shocks. The inappropriateness of a single interest rate in an environment of macroeconomic heterogeneity exacerbates the lack of convergence. New economic adjustment instruments are also needed because currently the only feasible measures are wage and fiscal policies, which are limited in their applicability. Adjustments through wage policy have limited flexibility due to labour market regulation and centralized wage negotiations, while adjustments through fiscal policy are tightly restricted by European regulation. Finally, as I argued in the last section, national fiscal policies are problematic as a stabilizing measure. In the next chapter, therefore, I turn to coordinated economic policy and take a closer look at its stabilizing potential.

Notes

1 Priewe (2007b).
2 For the classic OCA theories, see Mundell (1961), Mundell (1973), Kenen (1969) and McKinnon (1963).
3 See Vogel (2007, 27), Frenkel and Nickel (2002), Agresti and Mojon (2001) and Rothschild (2003).
4 See Belke and Baumgärtner (2002) and Belke and Heine (2001).
5 Frankel and Rose (1998) based their analysis on data from 21 industrialized countries collected between 1959 and 1993.
6 Frankel and Rose (1998)
7 See Szelag (2008, 17), European Commission (2004) and Issing (2005).
8 See Kreiner (2002) and Michaelis and Pflüger (2002).
9 See Burda (2001).
10 See Midelfart-Knarvik *et al.* (2002) and Frenkel and Nickel (2002).
11 Krugman (1993).
12 See Szelag (2008, 17) and Krugman (1993).
13 See Buscher and Grabisch (2009).

14 Output gaps for advanced economies are calculated as actual GDP minus potential GDP as a percentage of potential GDP. Estimates of output gaps are subject to a significant margin of uncertainty. For a discussion of approaches to calculating potential output, see De Masi (1997).
15 No data are available for Luxembourg. For the rest of the eurozone, data collection begins with a country's entry into the European monetary system.
16 See Belke and Gros (1998) and Belke and Kösters (2000).
17 Rogers (2001), Hill (2004) and Faber and Stokman (2005).
18 Based on data from March 2011 taken from Eurostat (2011).
19 Steinbach (2011).
20 Engel and Rogers (2004).
21 Lutz (2004).
22 See Michaelis and Pflüger (2002).
23 Gischer and Weiss (2006).
24 Honohan and Lane (2003).
25 Arnold and Verhoef (2004).
26 See Beck *et al.* (2009), Zemanek *et al.* (2009), Alesina *et al.* (2001) and Michaelis and Pflüger (2002).
27 Lommatzsch and Tober (2006).
28 Angeloni and Ehrmann (2007).
29 All in all, competitiveness worsened. Above-average inflation rates lowered real interest rates in the southern countries – increasing foreign capital revenue, improving the economy and raising wages, but ultimately reducing price competitiveness. See Krämer (2010, 382).
30 See Zemanek *et al.* (2009).
31 See Tatierská (2010).
32 See Zemanek *et al.* (2009).
33 See Altissimo *et al.* (2006).
34 See European Commission (2006).
35 See Dullien (2010).
36 See Dullien (2010).
37 See Dullien (2010, 23).
38 The more open a member country is to the rest of the world, the more nominal currency rate fluctuations affect production and price levels. Hence, small yet open economies at the periphery of the eurozone, such as Finland, Ireland and the Netherlands, tend to be more vulnerable to currency rate fluctuations than other eurozone countries. See Clements *et al.* (2001) and Honohan and Lane (2003).
39 See Mishkin (1995).
40 For a comprehensive analysis of existing studies, see Vogel (2007, 39ff.).
41 See Enderlein (2004).
42 See Frankel and Rose (1998).
43 See Maclennan *et al.* (1998).
44 See Bofinger and Mayer (2005).
45 See Bayoumi and Eichengreen (1993).
46 See Decressin and Fatás (1995), Obstfeld and Peri (1998), OECD (1999) and Eichengreen (1993).
47 See OECD (1999, 119ff.), Busch (1994, 92f.) and Dohse *et al.* (1998, 112f.).
48 See Dohse *et al.* (1998, 113).
49 See Gakova and Dijkstra (2010).
50 European Commission (1990).
51 Deroose *et al.* (2004).
52 Altissimo (2006), Burda (2001) and Obstfeld and Peri (1998).
53 Vogel (2007, 44) and Dullien and Fritsche (2008).
54 Dullien and Fritsche (2008).

55 Deroose *et al.* (2004); Obstfeld and Peri (1998); Heise *et al.* (1994, 74).
56 Heinz and Rusinova (2011).
57 Du Caju *et al.* (2008).
58 Calmfors (1993).
59 Clar *et al.* (2007).
60 Alesina and Perotti (1997).
61 Nunziata (2005).
62 Kittel (2001).
63 See Bayoumi and Masson (1995).
64 See Sala-i-Martin and Sachs (1992) and Fatas (1998).
65 For a broad analysis, see Enderlein (2004).
66 See Dixit and Lambertini (2001), Uhlig (2002) and Vogel (2007, 19).
67 Beetsma and Jensen (2004), Bofinger and Mayer (2003), van Aarle and Garretsen (2000), van Aarle *et al.* (2004) and Hagen and Mundschenk (2002).
68 Vogel (2007, 46).

3 Prerequisites for coordination and options for its design

In the previous chapter we concluded that even after the introduction of the EMU, economic heterogeneity remains that justifies the need to examine the potential for coordination within the eurozone.

Against this backdrop, the study proceeds as follows: the first step is to classify the various forms of coordination that are possible in order to establish a clear understanding of the term. In a second step, I discuss the need for coordination based on interdependencies and externalities. This discussion is necessary because the continued existence of economic heterogeneity in the eurozone is not sufficient in itself to justify the need for coordination. Spillovers, the existence of public goods and club goods, and interdependence between policy areas all provide a rationale for coordination. The study will discuss the various theoretical views of Keynesians and monetarists on the need for coordination, as well as the empirical evidence for the generation of externalities by national economic policy.

3.1 Definition and forms of coordination: vertical and horizontal coordination

A study of economic policy coordination requires clearly defined classification of the different forms of coordination. In the economics and political science literature, the term coordination is used for different forms of coordination.

I deem it appropriate to differentiate between vertical and horizontal coordination. *Vertical coordination* is used as a means of defining various coordination mechanisms in terms of the degree to which they are obligatory or binding.[1] In this regard, policy coordination can take the form of soft coordination, hard coordination or centralized coordination.[2] For example, it may be said that monetary policy in the eurozone is a form of centralized coordination, while the SGP may be classified as hard coordination. Ultimately, however, these terms reflect the degree to which fulfilment of goals, policies and rules are obligatory. The various forms of vertical coordination are discussed in detail in Section 3.4.

In addition to the criterion of vertical coordination, which reflects the degree of obligation associated with coordination mechanisms, I view the classification of *horizontal forms of coordination* as necessary. The existing economics and political science literature rarely makes a clear distinction as to whether it is referring to coordination between individual members of the EU or the eurozone in a specific policy area (e.g. for fiscal policy, the SGP), or whether the coordination being referred to represents aligning different policy areas with one another (for example, coordination between fiscal and monetary policy). Both forms of coordination are discussed, yet not kept distinct terminologically.[3] The lack of a clear distinction is problematic. Differentiating between these forms of economic policy coordination is necessary to enable a clear assessment of different forms of coordination within the EU. Only then can we clearly understand the development of coordination within the eurozone and clarify the various economic and political implications of each form of cooperation. Accordingly, a distinction should be made between types of *cross-border coordination* between members of the eurozone. This coordination may be limited to certain aspects of economic policy, such as fiscal coordination within the framework of the SGP or the centralization of monetary policy at the ECB. This form of horizontal coordination is referred to in the following as the *cross-border coordination* that takes place within a specific policy area.

The second distinct form of horizontal cooperation is the coordination of various areas of economic policy. Here, we are concerned with the degree to which interdependencies between monetary, fiscal and wage policies make it necessary to ensure that these areas are not viewed as independent, but rather coordinated (e.g. so that wage and monetary policies are unified). This form of coordination is referred to in the following as *cross-policy coordination*.

In this way, the parameter of "horizontal coordination" allows us to distinguish between cross-border and cross-policy coordination. Likewise, within the context of horizontal coordination, the two forms of coordination (cross-border and cross-policy) are not mutually exclusive. It is conceivable that coordination is cross-border, but only relates to a single policy area (as in the above-mentioned case of monetary policy). It is also possible that coordination is cross-border but also embraces various policy areas, such as the area of macroeconomic dialogue, in which negotiating parties, central banks and finance ministers are brought together.[4] This entails a combination of cross-border and cross-policy coordination.

Based on the foregoing analysis, Table 3.1 illustrates the range of classifications for the various forms of coordination used for this study. The classification

Table 3.1 Classification of coordination methods

		Horizontal coordination	
		Cross-border coordination	*Cross-policy coordination (fiscal, monetary, wages)*
Vertical coordination	Soft coordination Hard coordination Centralized coordination		

Source: author's description.

scheme allows, on the one hand, a clear categorization of one of the two horizontal forms of coordination. The study will also show that overlaps taking place within the box in the table are also possible. In such a case, we are dealing with a form of coordination that is both cross-policy and cross-border in nature.

3.2 Requirements for the need for coordination

In a world with no interdependencies, the question of coordinating economic policy within the eurozone would not arise. Yet in light of spillovers, the existence of public and club goods, as well as interdependence between policy areas, a clear rationale for policy coordination exists. In terms of the nature of externalities and interdependencies, a distinction should be made between the two forms of horizontal coordination, i.e. cross-border and cross-policy coordination.

3.2.1 Requirements for the need for cross-border coordination

The forms of coordination described previously are united in that they are based on the idea of external effects and communal goods. Economic theory holds that a need for intergovernmental coordination arises when national policy has implications (of a positive and negative nature) on other national economies or community goods. If an expansive national fiscal policy has implications for other countries (for example, because of a high level of debt caused by a devaluation of the common currency), it makes sense to establish coordinated fiscal rules. Thus, there is usually a need for cross-border coordination when positive or negative externalities and effects arising from the activities of individual states impact other countries and communal goods.[5] For the purposes of this study, a concept of externality is used that is not based on market failure. This means that both conventional external effects and monetary external effects are cited for the purpose of establishing the need for coordination.

•   The effect of an activity on a third party that is not considered in the associated economic decision is deemed to be an externality or external effect. In economic terms, externalities are a reason for market failure, and they may make government intervention necessary. However, this does not apply to monetary externalities, which include the effects of decisions on income distribution between people and institutions over which impacted third parties have no control, but which are governed by a price system. Monetary external effects represent the normal functioning of a price system. They are therefore of an indirect nature, and are a consequence of market relationships. Essentially, they are nothing more than a display of changed scarcity relationships. They control the allocation of resources and are therefore desirable from an efficiency perspective. Monetary external effects are not a form of market failure.

- However, monetary effects are relevant to the question of the need for coordination. For example, if expansive fiscal action leads to an external effect for another EU member (e.g. a higher interest rate; an increasing probability of bailout; or cross-border trade effects), there is possibly a monetary effect, because these changes are represented by changed price relationships (higher bond yields; higher price levels). While these external effects are played out in the market, they nevertheless represent fiscal policy decisions in one country having an adverse impact on the options for decision-making in another country. This is the reason why the SGP was set up: namely, to reduce the scale of negative external (monetary) effects.

- A common good or collective good is a good that is freely accessible to all potential buyers. Common goods may be provided by the state or by private suppliers. Public goods belong to the category of common goods. In terms of consumption, they are marked by the qualities of non-excludability and non-rivalry. Unlike externalities which take place between states and therefore influence national goods, collective goods are economic variables that apply equally to all member states. Examples of collective goods include the exchange rate, price levels the interest rates in the currency area, the internal market and the balance of payments.

To illustrate the difference between externalities and collective goods, we shall consider the fiscal action of a single state that spills over to the commodity and financial markets of other countries. However, if the objective of price stability is affected by this action, the collective good of price stability is also changed for all countries. In relation to collective goods, there is the problem of freeriding, which is used as a justification for the stability pact. If a member state uses excessive debt to drive up interest rates on the common capital market, it can externalize the costs of debt.

Thus, coordination also responds to the collective action problem of providing collective goods shared by the members of a monetary union.[6] The existence of collective goods in the EMU, such as a common price level and low financing costs, creates new channels of externalities among the member states. Policies that affect policy-relevant eurozone aggregates have economic implications for the other member states because the ECB will react to them and the reaction will be felt by all member states. For example, with regard to fiscal stability, the collective action is to ensure consistency between national policies and the EMU's objective of monetary credibility, i.e. to prevent member states from freeriding on the fiscal prudence of their fellow EMU members and to encourage policies that improve collective goods. The problem is that an EMU member that runs excessive deficits will not face a higher real exchange rate vis-à-vis the rest of the currency zone, while all members may share the burden of a higher interest rate and a loss of international competitiveness. Member states can thus externalize the costs of excessive deficits, which diminishes the incentive for fiscal restraint from the perspective of a country. This invites freeriding.[7] Expansive national fiscal policies, especially of the larger member states, can endanger the collective good of monetary credibility and affect related variables such as the average inflation rate, the exchange rate and the stability of financial markets and the banking sector. National policies that affect the average inflation rate or the exchange rate can have an impact on the ECB's interest rate decisions or ECOFIN's judgement on exchange rates. Excessive deficits also endanger the credibility of the ECB. If an EMU member defaults on its public debt, this can lead to capital losses among its creditors, including the commercial banking system. A banking crisis that spreads in the EMU would put the ECB under pressure to buy up the bonds of the government in distress, even if this were to destabilize prices in the eurozone.[8] If markets expect that the ECB will succumb to this pressure its credibility would be endangered.

Thus, the EMU increases the degree of economic interdependence between eurozone member states. Sharing a common currency and a single monetary policy means that there is a higher probability that economic policies and developments in one member state will spillover into the rest of the euro area. Coordination of economic policy instruments across the member states of a monetary union is justified when this spillover is significant.[9]

3.2.2 Requirements for the need for cross-policy coordination

A distinction can be drawn between cross-border externalities and cross-policy interdependencies. There is a need for policy coordination if we acknowledge interdependencies between individual policy areas. Assuming, for example, that monetary decisions have fiscal consequences, the need to coordinate these policy areas seems obvious.

Accordingly, the need to coordinate various policy areas arises only if we start from the proposition that there are interdependencies between various policy areas. This insight is not generally accepted in economic theory. The need for long-term coordination arises only if one accepts that the problem of effective demand plays a short-term and a long-term role in a monetary economy and that various economic actors (government, the central bank and collective bargaining parties) use their tools to exert a joint influence on the sub-aggregates of aggregate demand.[10] Only under these conditions is it necessary to coordinate the use of resources by aligning the activities of economic policy actors for the purpose of achieving common goals (e.g. high employment, low inflation, growth, equitable income distribution). To this end, it is viewed as particularly necessary to take interdependencies in the use of resources into account. By contrast, if we start on the basis that the market system has the ability to regulate itself and is stable – and accept the validity of Say's Law – a clear division of roles (so-called "assignment") in economic policy is sufficient to achieve these economic goals. The assignment approach asserts that interdependencies between policy areas do not exist or can be adequately accommodated through informed strategic action.

3.2.2.1 The Keynesian view on the need for policy coordination

The Keynesian view rejects the validity of Say's Law and the classical dichotomy between the monetary and the real sphere, since they do not apply either in the short or the long term. The private sector is unstable and is therefore in need of a policy to stabilize effective demand over the short and long term. To this end, coordinated monetary, fiscal and wages policies are needed that are geared towards the medium to long term. According to this view, in the short term, the central bank's interest rate policy influences effective demand, and in particular private investment, via delayed effects on the capital market interest rate, and in the long term it affects functional income distribution.[11] Monetary policy therefore has considerable real effects in the short and long term.[12] Its short-term effects are asymmetrical, however: by raising interest rates the central bank can put a stop to any boom, but cutting interest rates when businesses have depressed profit expectations cannot end a recession. To end a recession, the support of fiscal and/or wage policy is required.

The Keynesian view further asserts that the nominal wage policy agreed to by the parties to collective agreements has an indirect influence on employment.[13] It influences the nominal unit labour costs for a given level of labour productivity and the price level for a given mark-up applied by businesses when setting prices. Changes to distribution are only possible if permitted by the factors that influence the mark-up, such as the intensity of competition on commodity markets or the long-term prevailing interest rate. The level of employment is a product of effective demand on the commodity market, the development of which is essentially determined by private investment, which is in turn dependent on the relationship between the expected profit rates and the interest rate.

Fiscal policy can stabilize the business cycle in the short term by accepting cyclical deficits and surpluses, and in the long term it can increase effective demand and potential growth by means of a policy of investment-oriented lending. Moreover, the distribution of available income can be modified by means of tax and social policy, and this can in turn influence consumer demand, which is the largest demand aggregate. Government competition policy influences the level of competition on the commodity market and also therefore mark-ups and functional income distribution.

On account of the interdependencies of the instruments used by the economic actors and the fact that the target variables are in each case influenced by different instruments, the Keynesian approach prohibits a strict assignment of actors and instruments to just one single economic policy goal.[14] As a result, coordination of the means employed is indispensable. This coordination may be achieved implicitly by individual actors taking account of the interdependencies, or it may be achieved explicitly in the framework of institutionalized *ex ante* coordination. What is vital, however, is that the actors are aware of the interdependence of their activities and that there is agreement on the likely effects of the instruments used. As such, coordination requires a minimum level of consensus with regard to the analysis of economic circumstances, the diagnosis and forecasting of the economic situation and the economic objectives to be achieved.[15]

3.2.2.2 Monetary neoclassical assignment: the irrelevance of coordination

However, if we start from the assumption that the market system has the ability to regulate itself and is stable – and that Say's Law is valid – a clear division of roles (so-called "assignment") in economic policy is sufficient to achieve overall economic goals.[16] The assignment approach claims that there are no interdependencies between policy areas or that they can be adequately taken into account through informed strategic action. In this sense, both the neoclassical and monetary variants of macroeconomic theory advocate clear assignment in economic policy.[17] If we assume that there is a stable real exchange economy (in which Say's Law and the "classical dichotomy" between a monetary and real sphere apply, with inflation as a "monetary phenomenon"), then monetary policy has sole responsibility for bringing about price level stability.[18] If, in the monetary model, monetary policy can also influence (through adaptive expectations) output and employment levels at least in the short term, then real short-term influence is also excluded in the neoclassical model (with rational expectations in terms of this model). With suitable institutional arrangements, monetary policy can achieve the aim of price level stability in the long term (and in the short term in the neoclassical model) without real economic costs in the form of high unemployment and lower growth. The only responsibility for (real) wage policy is to provide market clearance in the labour market by securing the agreement of a real wage rate for full employment or a compatible real wage structure with full employment. The level of employment in an economy is therefore only determined on the labour market. The state is responsible for an incentive-based regulatory framework and for correcting market failures. There is no responsibility for growth and employment. Such a clear assignment makes coordination of economic policy unnecessary. The influence and responsibility of economic actors are clearly regulated. There are no interdependencies in the use of resources.

This view has clear consequences for the institutionalization of economic policy. It implies politically and economically independent central banks that are required only to bring about price level stability – central banks that, in this way, prevent the political exploitation of the time inconsistency of monetary policy and, by extension, the development of inflationary expectations. It implies the greatest possible restriction of fiscal policy in order to avoid outgoing disturbances in the market process, particularly the crowding out of private investment. It also implies flexible labour markets in which balanced real wage rates that are compatible with full employment can take effect without restrictions.

The ECB follows this neoclassical monetary approach, which accepts the neutrality of monetary policy in the long term and unsettling effects of fluctuating and high inflation.[19] According to this economic perspective, the central bank's primary objective is to maintain price level stability and a low inflation rate.[20] The ECB asserts that it can best serve economic policy by ensuring consistency in price level policy. There is therefore no trade-off between inflationary and growth targets. The first takes precedence and achieves the latter as a natural consequence. In terms of the division of responsibilities, this means clear assignment, i.e. a clear separation between monetary, wage and fiscal policy. Active coordination, by which the ECB establishes agreements between policy areas and ensures a common approach, is something that the ECB rejects as counterproductive. The ECB sees coordinated policy as impractical due to massive implementation problems.[21] First, it considers a suitably coordinated response to shocks to be difficult, because the impact of shocks and policy reactions can only be fully elucidated on the basis of a generally agreed upon economic model. In this regard, however, agreement is absent. Second, the ECB notes that coordination blurs responsibilities, resulting in weaker mechanisms for goal fulfilment. Third, there are difficulties in regard to enforcement because there are no tools for monitoring and implementing coordinated actions. Given these factors, the ECB deems that another approach is more suitable. With the correct institutional structure and a clear division of tasks, there is no need for ad-hoc coordination.

According to the prevailing view, the independence of the central bank has paramount importance, because only the central bank can take disciplinary action on the political decisions of the other economic actors. Further coordination on budgetary policy is deemed unnecessary and existing coordination is viewed as harmful, as it defuses competition between regions and prevents necessary structural reforms and job-creating wage stratification.[22]

Accordingly, the best outcome in a monetary union is achieved when each actor performs its designated role. A successful economic policy depends on a clear division of responsibilities (i.e. assignment), in which the central bank is responsible for the price level only, the government is responsible for structural reforms, budgetary consolidation and reliable framework conditions, and trade unions are responsible for employment growth.[23] Mixing up actors' responsibilities is viewed as leading to undesirable results.

3.2.3 Interim findings

Based on the discussion thus far, we arrive at the following insight: a justified need for cross-border coordination depends on the identification of externalities between national economic policies. Externalities can either directly affect macroeconomic indicators of other economies or influence collective club goods, the exchange rate of the common currency, currency-area price levels and the interest rate. It is therefore necessary to clarify whether there is empirical evidence for such spillovers.

As regards the question of cross-policy coordination, no clear statement about the prerequisites for coordination can be made on the basis of economic theory. This is because theoretical disputes also have implications for whether there is a need for cross-policy coordination. If one affirms the Keynesian perspective and the existence of interdependencies between various policy areas, then one must also acknowledge the need for such cross-policy coordination. However, if one follows the classical monetary perspective, each policy area should be considered separately. This study therefore focuses on the empirical question of whether there are in fact such interdependencies.

3.3 The existence of externalities as a basis for the need for coordination

3.3.1 Cross-border externalities as a by-product of economic policy

To start, I shall investigate the existence of cross-border spillovers for the first form of horizontal coordination – that is, cross-border coordination. Cross-border spillovers are externalities that result from the national economic policies of other states or from the euro as a collective good. In the following, both fiscal and wage policy spillovers come under consideration. However, monetary policy cross-border spillovers can be viewed as non-existent due to the common monetary regime within the eurozone.

3.3.1.1 Cross-border fiscal policy spillovers

Changes in the fiscal policy of a nation in a monetary union affects not just the economy in various other countries, but also the key aggregates on a European level depending on the size of the country taking the action and the size of the change itself. For example, an expansive fiscal policy in one country leads to a change in key macroeconomic variables in another country. The country impacted by this externality may see the change either as desirable or as counterproductive, depending on the country's economic policy objectives. Evidence of external effects generated by national fiscal policy in a monetary union can be shown on the basis of the traditional analytical framework of the Mundell–Fleming model.[24] The transmission of external effects primarily occurs via trade and capital market effects.

In terms of trade flows, we can generally expect the transmission effect to increase with the foundation of a monetary union, as a monetary union should lead to an intensification of trade (with increased transparency in good prices, competition is encouraged and trade intensity can increase). However, this effect may be small in the eurozone, since the European single market meant that trade barriers had largely been removed even before the monetary union came into being. The effect of a fiscal change on interest rate levels in another country is also strengthened as part of the integration of financial markets in a monetary union. If the markets are less segmented, the interest-driven effects of an expansionary fiscal policy on foreign countries increase.[25] However, both effects (trade and interest effects) act in different ways, so that it is not clear a priori whether this strengthens the arguments for coordinating economic policy. It is therefore uncertain whether fiscal policy in a monetary union is a "locomotive policy" or a "beggar-thy-neighbour-policy". Accordingly, the Mundell–Fleming model therefore offers no compelling argument for or against fiscal policy coordination.[26] The need for fiscal policy coordination in a monetary union is directly linked to the sizes and signs of the spillovers and externalities resulting from national fiscal policies.[27] Determining the sizes and signs of fiscal spillovers is crucial, since they ultimately determine whether coordination should lead to a more expansionary or a more restrictive fiscal stance in the member states. For example, if governments perceive negative spillovers in a static game, they would consider a non-cooperative ("beggar-thy-neighbour") policy in response to bad economic shocks as too expansionary and would agree on a more restrictive stance in all countries. By contrast, if governments perceive positive spillovers, coordination should eliminate the freeriding behaviour of individual countries and promote more expansionary policy in response to bad economic shocks. In a dynamic setting the situation is more complicated as the size, signs and persistence of the spillovers may change significantly over time.[28]

What are the results of econometric studies on the existence of fiscal spillovers? There are studies on spillovers outside of the eurozone and studies examining spillovers within the eurozone. Outside of the eurozone, a number of studies use vector autoregressive (VAR) models to analyse macroeconomic spillover.[29] Ahmed *et al.* study macroeconomic spillovers between the United States and the rest of the OECD using a two-country SVAR (structural vector autoregressive) model.[30] Canova and Dellas analyse bilateral trade interdependence and common disturbances in a group of ten industrial countries.[31] Kim undertakes a comparative study of the G-7 countries, modelling them as interdependent in fluctuations in world commodity prices and exchange rates.[32] Kim and Roubini identify the effects of US monetary policy on the non-US G-7 nations.[33] They find that two offsetting effects are at work: (1) an exchange rate depreciation is expansionary via the trade channel; and (2) a rise in the Federal Funds rate (and, in response, a domestic interest rate increase) decreases interest-sensitive spending worldwide, with a subsequent fall in US output decreasing demand for the exports of other countries.[34]

More relevant for the purpose of this analysis are fiscal spillovers occurring within the eurozone since the inception of the EMU. In this regard, Beetsma and Giuliodori use an SVAR model to study the cross-border spillover of fiscal shocks via the trade channel.[35] Fiscal expansion in Germany, France and Italy is shown to increase their imports from other European countries significantly. This finding supports the argument in favour of coordinating fiscal policies in the eurozone. Furthermore, Caporale and Girardi examine the dynamic effects of fiscal imbalances in a given EMU member state on the borrowing costs of other countries in the eurozone.[36] The estimation of a multivariate, multi-country time series model (specifically a Global VAR, or GVAR) for the EMU period suggests that euro-denominated government yields are strongly linked with each other. The results show that the percentage of variability in the long-term interest rates of EMU countries explained by domestic factors is modest relative to that accounted for by foreign (that is, EMU aggregate) shocks. From a more general perspective, the evidence of close linkages between EMU economies suggests that fiscal developments in a given country are likely to reverberate throughout the eurozone. The authors conclude that greater coordination among EMU member states aimed at tackling worsened issuance conditions and liquidity evaporation in the secondary markets for euro-denominated government bonds should be pursued, especially in the present period of financial turmoil.[37]

3.3.1.2 Cross-border wage policy spillovers

In terms of wage policy, there are no binding agreements in the EU or the euro-zone that impose specific regulations for wage growth. The absence of uncoordinated wage growth combined with a single currency brings about the potential for external effects between the members of the eurozone. As shown above, different wage growth rates within the eurozone affect prices in the various national economies. Yet price levels are crucial to price competitiveness. Wage growth in one country can therefore affect the relative competitiveness of other countries, and a change in comparative cost benefits may, for example, have an effect on the macroeconomic variables in another country. Permanently low wage agreements may increase relative competitiveness such that the competitiveness of other member states becomes significantly weaker. In particular, the sovereign debt crisis in the eurozone shows that wage growth that is continually higher than productivity growth and inflation can weaken competitiveness so profoundly that current account deficits and unsustainable debt positions arise. High public debt levels have led in turn to significant increases in interest rates on bond markets, with negative effects for the stability of the euro as a collective good.[38]

Prior to the establishment of the EMU, countries with above-average or below-average inflation rates were able to maintain their competitiveness by devaluing or revaluing their currency. This meant that in Germany, for example, where the inflation rate was below the EU average for many years, it was possible to use revaluation to offset worsening terms of trade. This method of adjustment is now foreclosed, and this has two consequences. First, inflation differentials across countries, originating from nation-specific shocks, cumulate into changes in external competitiveness, which give rise to international trade spillovers. Goods from countries with high inflation lose price competitiveness and will export less, leading to current account deficits. Inversely, countries with relatively low inflation rates are able to improve their price competitiveness. Second, a low or high inflation rate leads to high or low real interest rates because the single currency means that different wage growth levels can lead to diverging inflation rates. This has consequences for real interest rate levels in member states, which in turn has ramifications for each country's aggregate demand.[39] High real interest rates lead to a slowdown in economic development because of a lower willingness to invest. Conversely, low real interest rates stimulate growth. A combination of nationally differentiated wage-induced inflation differentials and a uniform monetary policy creates real economic effects which cannot be compensated for with interest rate policies at the national level. This is because a uniform interest rate prevents the process of adjustment using revaluation and devaluation.

Figure 2.6 illustrated the high correlation between wage agreements and inflation. If inflation rates differ due to divergent wage growth, the monetary transmission channel of the ECB interest rate will have differing effects on each national economy. As the ECB interest rate is based on the average of the euro countries, wage-induced inflation differentials will lead to externalities for national economies that do not match this average. The bottom line is that wage-induced effects on national inflation rates mean that the suitability of a given monetary policy is being continually undermined. Clearly, the more inflation rates diverge, the greater the asymmetric impact of the interest rate on each individual economy.

The transmission of negative demand stimuli on foreign countries is another source of external effects arising from wage policy. Wage restraint can temporarily lead to a reduction in nominal aggregate demand if employment does not respond flexibly to wage changes and if business investments are not sufficiently stimulated despite improvements in profit expectations. Due to lower domestic demand compared to the baseline scenario, imports also increase more slowly, such that this effect dampens aggregate demand abroad.[40]

Little attention has been devoted in the empirical literature to international spillovers resulting from labour market policies. However, some isolated works have sought to identify spillovers generated by labour market policies, including wage setting. Spange, for example, shows that wage rigidities are transmitted between countries through international trade. He analyses the effects of real wage rigidities in a stochastic two-country general equilibrium model, demonstrating that real wage rigidities in one country make consumption more volatile in both countries. Moreover, he finds that expected consumption is affected by rigidities.[41]

Braun and Spielmann find that labour market policies can have spillover effects, supporting the view that there are benefits to international policy coordination.[42] They study the effects of wage subsidies in an international duopoly model with unionized labour markets and discuss the costs and benefits of policy coordination. They find that wage subsidies paid in one country have external effects – both for the domestic country but also for the trading partner. Given these spillover effects, they identify a need for coordinating labour market policies internationally. They note, however, that the harmonization of labour market policies seems feasible only for countries with sufficiently similar labour market institutions.[43]

Dao uses a dynamic open economy model to analyse the effects of national wage bargaining on a domestic economy and on a foreign trading partner.[44] The model is calibrated to Germany and the rest of the eurozone. Labour markets are unionized and wages are bargained collectively to better account for European institutional features. He finds that compared to a competitive labour market setting, unionization dampens the positive domestic response and triggers positive spillover to the foreign economy through the real wage rigidity induced by rent-seeking unions. When the model is enriched with nominal rigidity and a common monetary policy for both countries, the dampening and positive spill-over effects are further reinforced in the short run.[45]

In sum, both theoretical as well as empirical analysis suggest that there are potential international spillovers resulting from national wage policy, yet the magnitude and signs of these spillovers are not clear, as they vary from case to case. Nevertheless, in view of the identified spillovers, a need for international coordination is generally advocated in the literature.

3.3.2 Cross-policy externalities as a basis for the need for coordination

In addition to cross-border spillovers, the existence of cross-policy spillovers may result in a rationale for horizontal coordination. In this regard, however, the term *interdependence* expresses more precisely the interactions between policy areas (monetary, fiscal and wage policies) than does the term *externality*. Indeed, the issue here is to what extent mutual dependencies between policy areas make a case for coordination.

3.3.2.1 Interdependencies between monetary and fiscal policy

Interdependencies between fiscal and monetary policies are assumed to exist in the economic literature. However, there is much disagreement as to whether this results in a need for coordination, and, if so, what instruments are required.

At present, the SGP only provides for the cross-border coordination of fiscal policy. Its objective is to address the cross-border externalities of national fiscal policy described above. However, spillovers from fiscal policy can also impact monetary indicators.[46] In particular, a fiscal expansion or contraction in one or more eurozone countries may affect both short- and long-term interest rates, an effect that is transmitted to other countries via the eurozone's common monetary policy and/or integrated capital markets. Numerous studies use a VAR model to estimate the spillovers from fiscal policy on monetary policy (and vice versa) in the eurozone. Monetary and fiscal policy interactions have been examined both from a theoretical and empirical perspective. In theoretical analyses, the empha-sis has been on strategic elements.[47] Empirical analysis has focused on the related question of the complementarity and substitutability of monetary and fiscal policy.[48] In the first case, a restrictive monetary policy is accompanied by a restrictive fiscal policy and vice versa. In the second case, a restrictive monetary policy is accompanied by an expansionary fiscal policy response and vice versa.

Studies using a VAR model to estimate spillovers between fiscal and monetary policies show that fiscal and monetary policy should not be treated individually and conducted separately from each other. Muscatelli *et al.* use a VAR of the output gap, inflation, the short-term interest rate and a fiscal-stance measurement to analyse the interactions between monetary and fiscal policies in the G-7.[49] They find that monetary and fiscal policies are increasingly being used as strategic complements and that the responsiveness of fiscal policy to the business cycle has decreased since the 1980s. Van Aarle *et al.* estimate the short- and medium-term effects of monetary and fiscal policy innovation, and estimate demand and supply shocks on this basis.[50] Their model allows them to trace the effects of structural supply and demand shocks and macroeconomic policy innovation on real output, prices, interest rates and fiscal balances. They find that large differences in country adjustments are induced by monetary and fiscal policy innovation. They also identify considerable cross-country differences in the interdependencies between macroeconomic policy instruments. Jacobs *et al.* focus on the importance of fiscal policy rules for the conduct of monetary policy in the eurozone.[51] They conclude that monetary and fiscal policy should not be conducted in isolation.[52]

Other studies have sought to compute the welfare effects of coordinating fiscal and monetary policies. These studies often yield welfare effects amounting to 0.5–1.5 per cent of GDP.[53] Breuss and Weber examine the case for coordinating European monetary policy with national fiscal policies, considering fiscal and monetary spillovers.[54] They come to the conclusion that complete coordination and harmonization of monetary and fiscal policies can produce welfare effects amounting to 0.56 per cent of GDP. However, to achieve this policy coordination, the provisions of the SGP would have to be violated, and not all countries would be better off, which would mean a violation of the Pareto criterion. If the constraints of the SGP remain in place or if fiscal policies alone are coordinated – a scenario which can certainly be described as very realistic given the ECB's independence and its explicit refusal to participate in coordination – the benefits of coordination disappear almost entirely.

Neck and Haber simulate the effects of a productivity shock and a fall in demand in five scenarios.[55] The study comes to the conclusion that in the case of productivity shocks, scenario 1 (no active economic policy) proves to be the optimal scenario, followed by the cooperative solution. The best response to demand shocks is a cooperative fiscal policy. Under these assumptions, cooperation is therefore often the best strategy.

Weyerstrass *et al.* also demonstrate the benefits of monetary and fiscal policy coordination in different coordination scenarios using the MSGM world macro model.[56] Similarly, Buti *et al.* find evidence to suggest that an inconsistent policy mix simply cannot be avoided (in the face of demand shocks) when monetary and fiscal authorities assign different weights to real and monetary objectives.[57] Faced with a demand shock, a monetary authority that is preoccupied with price stability and reluctant to alter interest rates will favour a high level of fiscal stabilization and (contingent on that fact) a low degree of monetary stabilization. On the other hand, a fiscal authority that gives little or no weight to price stability and more importance to output stabilization will pursue a high degree of monetary stabilization in the wake of a demand shock. With each authority expecting in these circumstances the other to do more, the result is a failure in coordination and an inconsistent set of monetary and fiscal policies.[58]

On the other hand, there are contributions that argue against the need for coordinating fiscal and monetary policies. Alesina *et al.*, Alesina, Scheide and Issing contest that coordination is not necessary,[59] asserting that although a case can be made on theoretical grounds for a "policy mix" approach in which fiscal and monetary policy are determined jointly, any possible benefits are heavily outweighed by the political-economic shortcomings.[60] The essence of the case made by Alesina *et al.* is that if the respective authorities "keep their houses in order", all will be well. In terms of who does what, it falls to monetary policy (and thus the ECB) to deal with symmetric shocks and adjustments, while fiscal policy has the primary responsibility for asymmetric shocks, and is the purview of national finance ministries.[61] While the opponents of explicit coordination generally approve of coordination that takes the form of an informal exchange of views and information,[62] they argue that any further coordination is associated with the danger that clarity regarding specific functions, mandates and responsibilities of each policy area will be lost. Ultimately, opponents of explicit coordination argue that it would reduce the transparency of the economic policy framework for the general public and prevent political decision-makers from being individually accountable. It is stated that as an alternative, implicit coordination could be achieved *ex post* if national governments and economic actors made a credible commitment to a uniform monetary policy for maintaining price stability when deciding on their own actions.[63] The opponents of coordination of fiscal and monetary policy consider a clear definition of the objectives, instruments and competences to be adequate and superior because of the information, implementation and incentive problems of explicit coordination.[64] It is striking, however, that these studies do not question whether a potential for coordination might theoretically result from interdependencies.

The bottom line is that theoretical and empirical studies confirm that fiscal and monetary policies are interdependent (as I will show below). The question of the need for coordination is less clear. Nevertheless, the majority of theoretical and empirical studies confirm a potential need for coordination due to interdependencies between fiscal and monetary policies. If a need for coordination is rejected in past studies, then this rejection is not based on the finding of a lack of interdependence between fiscal and monetary policies. Instead, the opponents of coordination cite the problems of transparency and incentive as well as political and economic obstacles to its realization. Moreover, the opponents of explicit coordination highlight the difficulty of identifying shocks for carrying out coordinated policies to manage the economic situation. On this point, opponents also argue that, ultimately, one must agree on the specific macroeconomic model that will be used to quantify how the economic situation will change as a result of a shock.[65]

3.3.2.2 *Interdependencies between wage and monetary policy*

It has already been shown that various economic schools of thought dispute the macroeconomic effects of wage and monetary policy. This is separate from the question of whether wage and monetary policies affect one another, and whether monetary policy may lead to externalities for wage policy, or vice versa.

The most obvious interdependence between monetary and wage policies lies in the externality that wage bargaining behaviour may exert on monetary policy-makers. As wages increase above productivity growth and lead to inflationary pressure, the central bank may find itself forced to conduct a restrictive monetary policy in order to preserve the currency's value. This restrictive monetary policy has negative consequences for the whole economy. Thus one sector's wage increase might lead, via the central bank's reaction, to a contraction of aggregate demand.[66] Following this argument, the magnitude of the resulting externality depends on how the central bank reacts to wage increases. At the same time, the degree to which wage bargainers take this reaction into account depends upon the bargaining structure, since the central bank's reaction gets internalized to a varying degree depending upon the size and fragmentation of unions.

The existence and degree of monetary externalities thus largely depends on the wage bargaining structure, i.e. the effects of decentralized and centralized wage bargaining.[67] Much of the macroeconomic literature about wage bargaining in the EMU starts by considering the interaction between wage bargaining and monetary policy. Early contributions found that the more centralized unions are, the more they take this externality into consideration. In a highly coordinated wage bargaining structure, a single centralized union would take the possible externality effect into account when bargaining for wage increases, because their influence would grant assurance of a corresponding reaction from monetary policymakers. By contrast, a single-sector union would care only about its own wage increases and thus have the power to inflict macroeconomic harm. Very small wage bargainers are only price-takers, and do not have the bargaining power to push for wages high enough to cause unemployment.[68] Consequently, not only very centralized, but also very decentralized unions can be expected to minimize monetary externalities, while unions between these two extremes would generate externalities. This point has been elaborated by Hall and Franzese.[69] They argue that when a central bank starts to conduct a disinflationary monetary policy, the real costs in terms of output loss and unemployment might depend on the coordination of the wage setting process. Smaller wage setters might: (1) be unable to judge the consequences of their wage demands on monetary policy; (2) judge their own influence on the aggregate price level to be negligible; or (3) be afraid that other wage bargainers will push for higher wages in their respective sectors, thus putting pressure on macroeconomic price levels and on monetary policy. As a result, smaller wage setters might be less inclined to change their behaviour when the central bank signals a change in its policy stance.

By contrast, according to Hall and Franzese, in a highly coordinated wage bargaining process the credible signal of the central bank to disinflate may be enough to induce employers and unions to settle for lower wage increases.[70] Consequently, the central bank would not need as restrictive a monetary policy as in the uncoordinated case. It follows that the more coordinated the wage bargaining, the lower the likelihood of disinflation. Based on a cross-country econometric analysis for 1955–1990, Hall and Franzese find strong empirical support for their claim that the combination of an independent central bank and a highly coordinated wage bargaining process yields the best results in terms of inflation and unemployment.[71]

With regard to the optimal relationship between monetary policymakers and the wage bargaining structure, many studies conducted prior to the introduction of the EMU attempted to forecast its effects.[72] Soskice and Iversen formalized the interaction between wage growth,[73] international competitiveness and unemployment under the specific conditions of monetary union in a model that assumed a non-accommodating monetary policy. According to their model, it was feared that higher wage claims – especially in Germany (and to a lesser extent also in other countries) – might lead to a monetary reaction that would drive up eurozone unemployment. These authors analysed a scenario in which German wage bargainers gained a strong influence in determining European wage and inflation dynamics. This line of argumentation, which assumes an interaction between wage setting and monetary policy, is especially relevant when examining the role of the German union IG Metall, which is the major player in wage negotiations in Germany, although its influence in recent years has waned. Prior to monetary union, IG Metall's wage leadership and the credible threat of the Bundesbank to respond to inflationary wage agreements with a restrictive monetary policy led in Germany to an implicit coordination of monetary and wage policies. In the eurozone, however, this type of interaction between economic players does not exist.[74] The decentralization of wage policy means that the ECB lacks a "tango partner" when it comes to wage policy, and there is the problem of freeriding behaviour on the part of unions. Clearly, if one's own contribution to overall inflation is low and a targeted response on the part of the ECB is not possible, then there is less willingness for wage restraint.[75]

A further spillover that may result from the relationship between monetary policy and wage bargaining is the time-inconsistency problems that occur when nominal wage and price contracts of some duration must be fixed before the trajectory of monetary policy is known with certainty. In such contexts, which are common in the industrialized world, wage and price contractors will agree on nominal wages and prices higher than the real levels they seek in order to allow for the possibility that future inflation will lower their real wages and returns. As a consequence, wage and price agreements will be more inflationary than they might otherwise be. This is a powerful theory in economics. As a consequence, there is a common acknowledgement across the diverging economic schools that coordination should at least consist of informal information exchanges between monetary and wage policymakers, in order to increase transparency and information and reduce time-inconsistencies.[76] By contrast, there are contributions in the literature finding that additional transparency in monetary policy would not lead to moderate wage policies. Grüner *et al.* find that higher monetary policy uncertainty has a negative effect on wage inflation in the continental European economies and in Japan. If labour unions cannot be certain how their wage setting behaviour will influence the behaviour of the central bank, they tend to be less aggressive and more cautious in formulating wage demands.[77]

Institutional political economists interested in the political-economic management of inflation and unemployment have examined the interaction between monetary policy and wage bargaining.[78] One strand of the institutionalist approach derives from the modern neoclassical economics of monetary policy and stresses the importance of the monetary authority's anti-inflationary conservatism and credible autonomy from the current government. The central claim is that credibly autonomous and conservative central banks achieve nominal (e.g. inflation) benefits at no real (e.g. employment) costs on average.[79] Another strand is based on the study of interest intermediation in democracies and stresses institutions in labour and goods markets. Its central claim is that coordinated wage/price bargaining fosters restrained agreements by internalizing certain externalities inherent to the bargains, thereby providing real and perhaps also nominal benefits. Each argument emphasizes a single institution in the macropolitical economy: central bank independence from political authority or wage/price bargaining coordination across the economy.

However, there is no unanimous answer on whether a conservative – i.e. highly inflation averse – central bank should be preferred over a liberal – i.e. employment-focused – central bank. The standard view was formulated by Rogoff,[80] who states that a conservative central bank increases welfare for the economy when labour markets are decentralized. However, focusing on the characteristics of the central bank, Skott, Sorensen, Grüner and Hefeker, Guzzo and Velasco and Cukierman and Lippi have studied the impact of monetary policy and labour market institutions on macroeconomic outcomes.[81] These authors partly contradict the standard finding of Rogoff – namely, that with highly centralized wage setting structures, liberal central bankers might discipline inflation-averse labour unions because unions fear an inflationary response by the liberal central bank. However, this finding is based on the assumption that unions are inflation averse.[82]

3.3.3 Interim findings

We thus find that the effort to determine the need for coordination should distinguish between cross-border externalities and cross-policy interdependencies.

In the first case – that is, cross-border externalities – coordination of national economic policy is required if the actions taken by individual states lead to positive or negative spillovers, impacting the macroeconomic indicators of other euro economies or community goods. Numerous theoretical as well as empirical studies have demonstrated that international spillovers result from national fiscal and wage policies. However, no definitive answer can be given as to whether these externalities are negative or positive.

In the second case – that is, cross-policy interdependencies between monetary, fiscal and wage policy – opinions differ on the need for coordination. There is a sharp dividing line between monetarist and Keynesian perspectives. In any event, empirical studies have revealed spillover effects between different policy areas. Thus, there is evidence for interdependencies between monetary and fiscal policy as well as between monetary and wage policy.

3.4 Vertical forms of coordination

The previous section examined the need for horizontal coordination – i.e. cross-border and cross-policy forms of coordination. Based on the classification set forth in this study, the next step is to examine vertical forms of coordination in order to categorize existing and potential forms of coordination.

One can distinguish between different degrees of vertical coordination. As mentioned, policy coordination can take the form of soft coordination, hard coordination or institutionalized cooperation.[83] The key differentiator between these various forms of coordination is the extent to which the agreed upon goals, policies and rules are binding. Accordingly, vertical coordination can be understood in terms of the *depth* of coordination, whereas the horizontal forms of coordination discussed above may be seen as the *breadth* of coordination.

While it is sensible to distinguish between three forms of vertical coordination (soft, hard and centralized), the forms of possible coordination – and, by extension, degree to which coordination is binding – are wide-ranging. This may hamper clear classification.[84] Moreover, unlike the three-form scheme presented here, the literature often distinguishes between discretionary and rule-based coordination.[85] However, the literature does not draw a clear distinction between discretionary and rule-based approaches. Discretionary coordination need not take place solely on extraordinary occasions. Furthermore, rule-based approaches usually permit some freedom of action.[86] In terms of compliance with the targets defined through coordination efforts, it should be emphasized that the decisive criterion is the degree to which coordination is binding, because this largely determines whether an agreement made by individual member states will actually be observed.

3.4.1 Soft coordination

The aim of soft forms of coordination is to bring about convergence and the alignment of national policies or political outcomes. In terms of means, soft coordination may rely on indicators and benchmarks for identifying best practices, the drafting of guidelines, the exchange of information through dialogue, peer pressure and peer review arrangements, or multilateral monitoring through bodies that can impose soft sanctions (naming, shaming and blaming).[87]

Agreements reached through soft coordination are somewhat non-binding in nature. Accordingly, sanctions are not imposed when rules and policies are not complied with. This offers nations a wide range of manoeuvre both in terms of time and the scope of coordination.[88]

With regard to timing, soft coordination may run on a fixed schedule (i.e. weekly, monthly, annually) or it may begin only with the arrival of a specific event that was defined in advance. A third option is ad-hoc coordination, i.e. when states come to recognize a need for international agreement.[89] A "loose form", similar to the G-8 meetings,[90] and an "institutionalized form" are both conceivable.[91]

In terms of the scope of coordination, soft coordination offers a wide range of manoeuvre. The degree of coordination[92] can range from simple information sharing[93] and the coordination of interim targets to the complete harmonization of all goals and fiscal instruments. If coordination is restricted to information sharing, policymakers may exchange information about policy targets and priorities, but they will make their decisions independently. In this connection, the exchange of information on macroeconomic issues may improve the strategic action of autonomous actors. This is because the actors keep each other informed of their intentions. Reactions thus become more predictable – conflicts are easier to anticipate and recognize, and thus become less costly. If, for example, the ECB and the parties to wage agreements keep each other informed of wage demands and possible interest rate reactions, both sides can improve expectations, avoiding future overreactions.[94] In the case of pure information sharing, actors draw on improved knowledge regarding the actions and reactions of the other parties, yet only collaborate to address externalities to the extent that their autonomy is preserved.

Soft coordination takes the form of guidelines, channels of communication and collaborative frameworks, and seeks to achieve a balance between policy credibility, political stability and policy flexibility. Generally, collaborative exchange takes place on a multi-annual basis. Soft coordination places great emphasis on policy learning and consensus building.[95] Mechanisms such as peer review and benchmarking are used to promote a unified approach. This form of coordination is distinguished by the fact that it focuses on the collaborative improvement of policy, rather than on implementing sanctions or constraints. Particularly on the supply side, soft coordination may also provide incentives to governments to stick to agreed approaches in order to reduce the spillover effects of divergent policies.

Against this backdrop, there are four reasons for member states to support soft coordination:[96]

1. It is easier to reach compromises and reduces *ex ante* negotiation costs: actors with diverging interests and expectations can reach agreements more easily. The lack of sanctions and limited binding obligations make soft coordination easier. These features, in particular, are what account for its appeal and have led to the rapid expansion of soft coordination in the EU.

2. Reduced loss of sovereignty: the transfer of sovereignty is limited because actors maintain a higher degree of control. In the EU, soft methods of coordination facilitate access to policy areas that were previously the exclusive responsibility of member states. The price of this lies in the largely non-binding nature of the requirements.

3   Easier management of uncertainty in terms of future costs: actors do not run the risk of agreeing to arrangements that impose future costs they could have otherwise avoided.
4   Soft forms of coordination can have an "alibi" function: if coordination is required for specific economic reasons, but an obligatory form of coordination is rejected, then agreeing to soft coordination can be furnished as evidence of political action, without having to engage in any binding or onerous agreement. An example of this function is the non-binding and vague announcements made by euro members regarding the establishment of a European economic government under the Euro Plus Pact (see Section 5.2.4).

3.4.2 Hard coordination

Hard coordination, by contrast, can be said to exist if the coordination outcomes of participating states are binding and non-compliance or a lack of compliance is subject to negative sanctions. Sanctions are associated with rule-based coordination. The establishment of rules or control mechanisms means *ex ante* coordination. The introduction of control mechanisms requires the clarification and definition of objectives, which are used as the basis for setting targets. It is clear that rule-based coordination is more challenging than soft coordination, as it requires the will and skill of players to interact and to make and agree on binding arrangements. Hard coordination may take the form of a one-time exchange whereby trade-offs are made or may involve the setting of norms (e.g. hammering out agreements on certain standards).[97] Within the scope of wage and monetary policy coordination, for example, a one-time exchange might involve swapping some amount of wage growth for an interest rate cut. By contrast, one can speak of coordinated standards when parties agree to long-term rules that guide action. For example, one might introduce a rule according to which wage growth must be aligned with productivity growth and interest rates are managed such that inflation below a minimum threshold is avoided. Regular exchange is a good foundation for the development of norms, because a norm can be developed by explaining and institutionalizing previous exchanges. Although exchange transactions are still possible when norms are in place (whereby one thing is exchanged for another at essentially the same time, and, accordingly, there is only a minor risk of one party failing to fulfil its obligations), the establishment of norms necessitates further safeguards to prevent non-compliance and freeriding.[98]

Regarding the internalization of external effects, there are differences between the various forms of coordination. In the case of pure information sharing through soft coordination, externalities resulting from the actions of other actors can only be internalized in so far as the autonomous strategic action of each actor is preserved.[99] However, if binding exchange agreements can be established, coordination can take place through exchange deals that take into account and counterbalance the externalities of each actor's behaviour. While the pure exchange of information is only useful for encouraging transparency and the recognition of externalities, the establishment of norms offers – ideally – a means for the complete internalization of externalities, because rules can be identified and established taking external effects systematically into account. Through binding exchange deals with rule-based action, we can expect less uncertainty and a stabilization of expectations. Binding arrangements help to avoid the difficulties that are associated with a discretionary coordination process.[100]

Rule-based coordination also increases credibility between the coordinating entities and vis-à-vis third parties. A rule-based coordination system increases the credibility of action for fiscal policy and for the ECB. By improving the predictability of future economic policy action, it results in the improved allocation of resources.[101] Binding agreements also help to reduce the influence of lobby groups. While rules cannot make the political system resistant to the influence of group interests, they can curtail the demands of particular interest groups and contain rent seeking. Rule-based coordination also reduces negotiation costs, which accrue quickly under discretionary coordination processes.[102]

In contrast to soft coordination, hard coordination has four key characteristics:[103]

1   Increased commitment to adhere to agreements: by imposing a high degree of obligation, hard coordination increases the costs of non-compliance. The budgetary policy rules of the SGP, for example, pursue this objective.
2   Reduced *ex post* transaction costs: once hard coordination comes into force, the costs of agreement are reduced, as the targets that have been decided upon no longer have to be renegotiated. The monitoring of actors is simplified if implementation offers little room for interpretation.
3   Reduced uncertainty with regard to the behaviour of other actors: after all actors have agreed to a set of binding rules, the risk of individual participants deviating from the rules is significantly reduced.
4   Hard coordination is long term: while soft coordination can be discontinued at any time, hard coordination is usually permanent or long term and may provide no exit option. For example, European law does not provide for an exit from the SGP or the euro, because the obligations imposed by the SGP are intended as permanent.

We should not ignore the drawbacks when considering the benefits of hard coordination versus soft coordination. There may be considerable difficulties in the implementation of rule-based systems. First, the setting of rules in economic policy necessitates a common understanding and interpretation of underlying economic mechanisms. However, there is often no consensus among economists on a given issue. We have already discussed the conflict between the neoclassical and Keynesian doctrines regarding the meaningfulness of coordination. If "inadequate rules" are agreed upon due to political calculations or because of a lack of knowledge of economic relationships, the rules may inadvertently trigger effects that damage the well-being of national economies. Second, the introduction of a binding rule system may require the passage of laws and possibly institutional changes. The more heterogeneous the existing institutional structures and mechanisms in the countries involved, the more difficult this becomes. This is because common rules that are equally applicable to all member states must be compatible with institutional conditions. Furthermore, the adjustment of institutional conditions – i.e. the removal and redesign of institutional structures – invariably calls forth resistance from those who are affected (e.g. bureaucrats, interest groups and politicians). The effort to resist such changes by those affected are positively correlated with expected losses. The implementation of rules may therefore be fraught with implementation and acceptance problems, as such rules raise issues of national sovereignty, and institutional arrangements – once introduced – tend to become deeply entrenched.

3.4.3 Centralized coordination

Centralized coordination should be regarded as a special form of coordination. With centralized coordination, national decision-making powers are transferred to a centralized and supranational body. This involves the permanent transfer of sovereign powers to transnational decision-makers. Decisions are either made collectively by member states or by an institution that acts on behalf of these states. The main arguments in favour of centralized coordination are: (1) the reduction of the costs to reach consensus and make decisions;[104] (2) the elimination of the destabilizing effects of national decisions; and (3) the management of externalities produced by decisions in individual nations.

However, centralized coordination poses problems, particularly of a bureaucratic nature. This method of coordination augments the difficulties that already exist on the national level with interest groups and the independence of executive functions. Administrative inefficiencies increase.[105] Moreover, if the supranational executive is unable to call upon a legislative body that has adequate decision-making powers, there may be a breakdown in parliamentary control and the mechanisms of democracy.

In all other respects, the same difficulties experienced with hard forms of coordination apply. The creation of a central decision-making body requires a consensus on the function and substance of the decision-making for which the body will be responsible. In this regard, significant problems may arise concerning appropriate decision-making standards, as such standards may be contested in academic circles or disputed due to political or economic interests. Furthermore, the establishment of new, centralized institutions is associated with a loss of national sovereignty, which may cause resistance on the national level and face acceptance problems.

3.5 Interim findings

The preceding chapter began by drawing a distinction between vertical and horizontal coordination. Such a distinction is appropriate for two reasons. First, it provides an improved framework for analysing the different reasons why coordination is needed. This, in turn, makes it possible to examine forms of coordination currently discussed and that are conceivable for the future. Second, this distinction aids in the effort to trace the history of coordination in the EU before and during the euro crisis.

According to the proposed categorization scheme, on the horizontal axis we can make a distinction between cross-border and cross-policy coordination. By extension, determining the need for coordination should be based on whether there are cross-border externalities or cross-policy interdependencies. With a view to cross-border coordination, externalities arise either directly because of the effects of national trade on the macroeconomic indicators of other economies or because of communal goods, such as the exchange rate of the euro, price levels and interest rates. Externalities are substantiated here both theoretically and empirically. In the case of cross-policy interdependencies between monetary, fiscal and wage policies, opinions diverge sharply on the need for coordination based on the monetary and Keynesian perspectives. Nevertheless, empirical studies have revealed spillover effects between different policy areas. There is clear evidence for interdependencies between monetary and fiscal policies and between monetary and wage policies.

On the vertical axis, the degree to which an agreement is binding is used as a characteristic for defining the various mechanisms of coordination. This chapter elucidated general characteristics and motives for coordination of varying "depth".

This systematic classification delivers the foundation for the next chapter. The categorization scheme posited here provides a framework for assessing the forms of coordination implemented within the EU and their evolution before and during the euro crisis. It also provides a useful toolbox for examining current and future forms of coordination.

On a theoretical basis, it was shown that policy arrangements should not ignore the mutual interdependence between the policy fields. Fiscal policies have an impact on the strategic behaviour of the central bank and wage setters. In turn, fiscal policy decisions and their effects in the economy may depend on distortions resulting from wage-setting behaviour. Moreover, the outcome of coordination depends on the conservativeness of the central bank. A conservative central bank has beneficial effects under fiscal leadership vis-à-vis the central bank. Fiscal coordination improves outcomes in the case of a conservative central banker, whereas it leads to worse outcomes with a populist one.

Notes

1 For a different concept of horizontal and vertical coordination see Ribhegge (2011, 207ff.).
2 Begg (2003) distinguishes between hard and soft coordination. See also Currie *et al.* (1989, 24); Bayer (1999, 271).
3 Italianer (2001, 93ff.); Maennig (1992, 108).
4 See Section 4.1.2.
5 Koppitz (2010).

6 See for the following Schwarzer (2007, 20).
7 Schwarzer (2007, 20); Begg *et al.* (2003, 67); Aizenman (1994); Allsopp and Vines (1996); Beetsma and Bovenberg (1999).
8 Eichengreen and Wyplosz (1998, 71f.).
9 Schwarzer (2007, 20).
10 Hein (2002a, 359ff.).
11 See for the following Hein and Truger (2004, 22f.).
12 Sesselmeier (2002).
13 Hein and Truger (2004, 22).
14 Hein and Truger (2004, 23).
15 Priewe (2002).
16 Gottschalk (2002).
17 Issing (2002), Jerger and Landmann (2006, 267), Snowdon *et al.* (1994, 137ff.).
18 See for the following Bartsch *et al.* (2001, 1).
19 Niechoj (2004); Hein (2002b, 252).
20 Issing (2001a).
21 ECB (2003, 48).
22 Schatz (2001, 571f.).
23 Hein (2002b, 251f.).
24 Fleming (1962) and Mundell (1963, 1964). Comprehensive formal analytical studies include Feuerstein (1992), Papadoupoulou (1992) and Boss *et al.* (2004, 71).
25 Levin (1983, 341).
26 Fabeck (1995, 19).
27 See for the following Bartolomeo *et al.* (2005, 2).
28 Bartolomeo *et al.* (2005, 2).
29 See for the following Weyerstrass *et al.* (2006, 9).
30 Ahmed *et al.* (1993).
31 Canova and Dellas (1993).
32 Kim (1999).
33 Kim and Roubini (2000).
34 Weyerstrass *et al.* (2006).
35 Beetsma and Giuliodori (2004).
36 Caporale and Girardi (2011).
37 Weyerstrass *et al.* (2006).
38 Boss *et al.* (2004, 71f.).
39 Angeloni and Ehrmann (2007).
40 Boss *et al.* (2004, 72).
41 Spange (2003).
42 Braun and Spielmann (2010).
43 Braun and Spielmann (2010).
44 Dao (2008).
45 Dao (2008).
46 See for the following Weyerstrass *et al.* (2006, 9).
47 For an overview see Buti *et al.* (2001).
48 Mélitz (2000).
49 Muscatelli *et al.* (2002).
50 Van Aarle *et al.* (2003).
51 Jacobs *et al.* (2007).
52 Weyerstrass *et al.* (2006).
53 Mooslechner and Schürz (1999, 181); Breuss and Weber (2001, 144).
54 Breuss and Weber (2001).
55 Neck and Haber (1999). Fixed instruments, two scenarios with regulatory binding and discretionary economic policy, and EMU scenarios – one with non-cooperative fiscal policies and one with cooperative fiscal policies.

56 Weyerstrass *et al.* (2006).
57 Buti *et al.* (2001).
58 Leith and Wren-Lewis (2000).
59 Alesina *et al.* (2001), Alesina (2003), Scheide (2004) and Issing (2002).
60 Begg *et al.* (2003, 67).
61 Buti and Giudice (2002).
62 Issing (2002, 312).
63 Issing (2002, 312).
64 Vogel (2007, 19).
65 See Section 1.1.1.
66 Dullien (2004, 14).
67 Boss *et al.* (2004), Soskice (1990), Calmfors and Driffill (1988), Sisson and Marginson (2002), Traxler and Kittel (2000), Traxler *et al.* (2001), Flanagan (1999).
68 Calmfors and Driffill (1988), Dullien (2004, 12).
69 Hall and Franzese (1998).
70 Hall and Franzese (1998)
71 Hall and Franzese (1998), Dullien (2004, 15).
72 See for the following Glassner and Pusch (2010, 15), Guzzo and Valesco (1999), Cukierman and Lippi (1999), Jerger (2002), Altissimo (2006), Heise (2002), De Grauwe (2006), Deroose *et al.* (2004), Buscher and Gabrisch (2009), Dullien and Fritsche (2008).
73 Soskice and Iversen (2001).
74 Hall and Franzese (1998), Iversen (1998).
75 Hancké and Soskice (2003).
76 Issing (2002, 312), Boss *et al.* (2004, 38).
77 Grüner *et al.* (2005, 5).
78 See for the following Franzese (2001), Mooslechner and Schürz (1999).
79 Rogoff (1985).
80 Rogoff (1985).
81 Skott (1997), Sorensen (1991), Grüner and Hefeker (1999), Guzzo and Velasco (1999) and Cukierman and Lippi (1999, 2001).
82 Grüner *et al.* (2005, 9).
83 Currie *et al.* (1989, 24) and Begg *et al.* (2003) distinguish only between hard and soft coordination.
84 Italianer (2001, 93), Maennig (1992, 108).
85 Maennig (1992, 218), Fabeck (1995, 113).
86 Cooper (1985, 370), Frenkel (1987, 208).
87 Begg *et al.* (2003, 69), Wagener *et al.* (2006, 487), Weidenfeld and Wessels (2006).
88 See for the following Fabeck (1995, 113ff.).
89 On different forms of ad-hoc coordination, see Grober (1988, 112).
90 The relative absence of a specific and tangible form of coordination and the lack of results related to it are typical of this form of discretionary coordination.
91 This is not to be confused with centralized coordination. In its institutionalized form in terms of soft coordination, it remains non-binding and it only provides an external framework for international coordination.
92 See Scheide and Sinn (1987, 3) for a comparison of different degrees of coordination.
93 Currie *et al.* (1989, 24), Horne and Masson (1987, 29), Steinherr (1985, 286).
94 Boss *et al.* (2004, 51).
95 Begg *et al.* (2003, 69).
96 Schäfer (2005, 194).
97 Niechoj (2004), Marin (1990), Czada (1997).
98 Coleman (1995, 344ff.).
99 Niechoj (2004).

100 Frenkel *et al.* (1988, 160).
101 Frenkel *et al.* (1988, 160); Currie *et al.* (1989, 37).
102 Frenkel *et al.* (1988, 160); Maennig (1992, 219).
103 Schäfer (2005, 194).
104 Welfens (1990, 7).
105 Fabeck (1995, 116).

4 Coordination in the EU before the government-debt crisis

Economic policy coordination in the EU is based on a complex set of rules and procedures. They lay down various forms of coercion for disciplining member states as a means of counteracting the incentives for non-cooperative behaviour and freeriding. According to the Treaty of Lisbon, the member states are to conduct their economic policies with a view to contributing to the achievement of the objectives of the European Community. Accordingly, they are to regard their economic policies as a matter of common concern and coordinate them within the Council.[1] As far as monetary policy within the eurozone is concerned, defining and implementing the monetary policy of the Community is one of the basic tasks to be carried out by the ECB. The defined primary objective of this policy is to maintain price stability.[2] In other words, monetary policy in the eurozone is centralized and institutionalized at the supranational level. The ECB can decide and implement monetary policy autonomously as a centralized form of coordination. Yet simultaneously, economic policies – including budgetary and structural policies – are decentralized, i.e. formulated and implemented at the national level. In light of the inescapable interdependencies between monetary and economic policy, various means of coordinating these policy domains between member states and the EU as a whole have arisen. These means of coordination can be categorized on the basis of the above analysis as either horizontal or vertical in nature.

In this chapter I identify the forms of coordination within the EU before the outbreak of the government-debt crisis, and examine whether they were well suited for dealing with the externalities and interdependencies discussed above. I begin in the next section by considering farther-reaching forms of coordination and their recent reforms. By distinguishing between coordination before the government-debt crisis and coordination after, I seek to highlight how coordination approaches have changed in the EU over time.

4.1 Soft coordination in the EU

As we saw in the last chapter, soft coordination policy uses joint policy objectives, reporting and surveillance mechanisms, member state recommendations and peer pressure ("naming and shaming") for its disciplining measures. With this form of coordination, policy decisions in the EU regarding labour markets, wage prices and institutional structures are general in scope and call mainly for "naming and shaming" measures when countries fail to adhere to regulations. Soft coordination aims to create convergence by means of best practice (comparison of individual state measures) and peer pressure (influence from other countries).

The 2000 Lisbon Summit endorsed the use of soft coordination in existing coordination activities and promoted its use in fields outside economic policy. The heads of state noted the ability of soft coordination to help in sensitive areas, i.e. where there is little consensus about which measures to take and how to distribute burden. This ability is why soft coordination is now known in the EU as an "open method".[3] The "openness" refers to the considerable latitude of its guidelines: instead of providing binding regulation it offers national actors opportunities for exchange without increasing state accountability. An endogenous process with many actors, soft coordination defines the spectrum of potential practices. At the same time, however, though its guidelines are not legally binding, they do contain an implied moral injunction. The Broad Economic Policy Guidelines of the Member States and of the Community (BEPGs) and the Macroeconomic Dialogue belong in this category of coordination.

4.1.1 Broad Economic Policy Guidelines, integrated guidelines and national reforms

The BEPGs make up the heart of the EU economic coordination cycle pursuant to Article 120 of the Treaty on the Functioning of the European Union (TFEU). The guidelines, introduced by the Maastricht Treaty, are designed to steer the implementation of financial and economic policy. The relaunch of the Lisbon Strategy in 2005 assembled the BEPGs and Employment Guidelines (Art. 148 of the TFEU) under the Integrated Guidelines for Growth and Jobs for a three-year period. The idea was to improve the fit between economic and employment policy in the medium term.[4] The new procedures stipulated that member states must submit a new national reform programme every three years and a progress report every year that describes measures for implementing guidelines.

The introduction of the BEPGs is the first time the European Commission has pursued a concept of sound macroeconomic policy based primarily on arguments from neoclassical and monetarist economic theories. The guidelines aim at the consolidation of state finances through balanced budgets, at price stability and at moderate wage increases (i.e. no higher than productivity growth plus inflation). The BEPGs also propose structural reforms to foster growth in the goods and labour markets. According to the BEPGs, the main task of the ECB is to ensure price stability. Fiscal policy is supposed to implement the balanced budget targets stipulated in the SGP, while wage policy has the task of facilitating a high employment rate (through stability-oriented wage agreements) and increasing the rate of return on investments. Last, structural policy must ensure market flexibility, including that of the labour market.

The BEPGs coordination of monetary policy, wage policy and fiscal policy is designed to keep wages moderate, avoid public deficits and carry out structural reforms.[5] Coordination in this sense means having state actors obligate themselves to carry out the basic objectives that have been defined, which involves a clear allocation of responsibilities to macropolitical actors. Here, coordination is not viewed as a mutual reliance between actors because the effects of their actions are interdependent, thus making individual objectives unobtainable without coordination. Instead, responsibilities are clearly assigned to individual policy actors.

Accordingly, for the EU coordination consists in an alignment of economic policy, not in a coordination of measures between countries. The BEPGs do *not* stipulate that member states undertake coordinated budget adjustments (e.g. that consider the budget balancing efforts of other states). The SGP sets budget deficit targets only for fiscal policy in individual countries. The targets are suited neither for the monetary union nor for international coordination; their real purpose is the prevention of unsound fiscal policy.[6] Likewise, the BEPGs recommend that wage policy foster employment for all EU countries, without requiring coordination between them. As with fiscal policy, wage policy does not address the possible spillovers and negative side-effects of policy measures highlighted by advocates of international economic coordination. Rather, it focuses on pursuing objectives by maintaining a steady course. An important exception is the area of tax policy. Here, the BEPGs advocate stronger coordination (harmonization) of value-added tax, of corporate tax and of tax on interest earned from savings.

Even if generally unknown by the general public, the BEPGs build the backbone of the EMU: on the one hand, they contain recommendations for *all* economically relevant policy areas; on the other, all other coordination must deliver results in line with BEPG recommendations. In balance, the guidelines, together with the national reform programmes that came after their introduction, seek to implement a soft version of coordination on an international level. Instead of carrying out cross-policy coordination, they follow the neoclassical assignment approach, assigning each policy area its own tasks independent of its interactions with other fields.

4.1.2 The macroeconomic dialogue

At the 1999 Cologne Summit, the European Council initiated another soft form of coordination: the Macroeconomic Dialogue (MED). The MED brings together the social partners and representatives of the ECB, the Commission and ECOFIN twice a year for a confidential exchange of opinions on how to improve macroeconomic performance and support non-inflationary growth and employment. The participants are responsible for coordinating monetary, wage and fiscal policy among themselves. The MED is a forum for different viewpoints; it does not issue reports or guidelines. The meetings are supposed to build trust and limit misconceptions among key actors so as to avoid extreme situations – particularly output losses – by improving mutual understanding of policy tasks and intentions. Fiscal authorities receive supplementary information on monetary and wage developments that they did not previously have at their disposal.

The MED imposes no restriction on the actors in their fields of responsibility, a feature that the ECB in particular eagerly points out. According to the ECB's interpretation of the primary laws governing its autonomy, "Clear boundaries define the cooperation between community organs, community institutions, and the ECB."[7] For economic policy cooperation, "The views exchanged between the ECB and other economic policy decision-makers remain non-binding."[8] The ECB expressly forbids the *ex ante* coordination of monetary policy with other policy areas.

The MED is the first form of eurozone coordination to take a cross-policy approach. Its ultimate goal is to find an optimal form of coordination governing the interactions between wage policy, fiscal policy and monetary policy. In its vertical hierarchy, it follows the principle of soft coordination, favouring a pure exchange of viewpoints between the participants over binding rules.

In practice, the work of the MED faces several obstacles.[9] For one, already existing rules in some policy areas leave little leeway for comprise – the ECB must continue to meet price stability targets. The hands of finance ministers continue to be partly tied by the SGP. Furthermore, the MED's emphasis on participant autonomy makes it hard to pursue effective coordination.

The ECB emphasized repeatedly while the MED was being debated that it would participate only if it could maintain its independence, and at no point did it signal any willingness to negotiate monetary policy through the MED. Likewise, the representatives of ECOFIN mostly play a mediating role, leaving economic reports and recommendations for necessary actions to the European Commission. For its part, the Commission defines the expectations of fiscal and wage policy, but as a proponent of a rule-based approach, it too sees ECB monetary policy as sacrosanct and is hence unwilling to let it be called into question by MED participants.

In SGP fiscal policy, national governments impose rules on themselves. For wage policy, at least, employer and union representatives in the MED advocate a different approach. Employers want monetary and fiscal policy to be accepted as hard (rule-based) facts. So when it comes to keeping businesses competitive, employers want productivity to play the biggest role in determining competitive non-inflationary wage levels, and they push for decentralized wage negotiations (which, in their view, can best gauge the room for wage increases). At the same time, they demand that structural policies be included in macroeconomic discussions, as the organization of goods, service and labour markets decisively influence prices and productivity, and, by extension, wage policy. Accordingly, employers do not see the necessity of wage policy coordination on the EU level, and are pessimistic about the likelihood of receiving a mandate for such coordination from professional associations on the national level.

By contrast, unions have never accepted the rule-based policy approach on the EU level, seeing it as an obstacle for necessary countercyclical economic measures. (This attitude can be seen in their views about basic economic policy and the SGP.) In the eyes of the unions, unified currency, clear guidelines for ECB price stability and SGP self-restriction of fiscal policy leave wage policy bearing the entire brunt of external shocks. This necessarily hurts wages, as can be seen by continually sinking wage share in recent years. In response to these developments, the European Trade Union Confederation (ETUC) has demanded that the ECB stop fixating solely on price stability and allow more leeway for countercyclical measures in the SGP.

At the same time, the ETUC fears a "race to the bottom" resulting from decentralized wage negotiations, as national unions can gain a competitive or employment advantage over other EMU participants through wage restraint. Consequently, the ETUC has pushed for wage policy coordination on the EU level since the introduction of the EMU in an effort to circumvent downward wage pressure via "joint wage formulas" (i.e. productivity growth plus a target inflation rate).

In sum, then, the practical problems and conflicting interests associated with the MED do not make it the ideal forum for cross-policy coordination. The diversity of involved interests, the differing expectations of the participants and the collision between it and other institutions (SGP, ECB) limit the suitability of the MED considerably.

4.1.3 The Luxembourg Process

Full employment has always been one of the Community's key goals. Yet a unified EU wage policy does not exist; for the foreseeable future wages will continue to be negotiated on different levels within member states. Nevertheless, the Luxembourg Process, like union coordination efforts, represents an effort to make wage policy more Europeanized for the medium term. At the so-called Luxembourg Jobs Summit (in November 1997), the European Council launched the European Employment Strategy – also known as the Luxembourg Process – aimed at strengthening the coordination of national employment policies and at significantly reducing unemployment at the European level. Unlike union wage coordination, the Luxembourg Process does not focus directly on wage level policy.

The employment strategy of the Luxembourg Process aims to improve national labour markets.[10] Through reports, conciliation proceedings and the recommendations of the minister council, it seeks to give EU countries new ideas for advancing labour force training and for making the labour market flexible in the face of economic change. Prepared by the EU Commission and approved by the Council of Ministers, the Luxembourg Process's employment guidelines and employment recommendations are sent annually to EU countries. The employment policy guidelines aim primarily at the structural changes of the labour market and promote work flexibility, incentives for taking up work and better training. Its programme is defined by neoclassical labour market principles, which seek to eliminate rigidity wherever possible. For the area of macroeconomic employment policy, the guidelines advocate decentralized labour markets that stabilize inflation and seek to avoid fiscal deficits. The reason is that in decentralized labour markets unions have less influence on wage prices than that of unions in centralized ones, and their ability to push through uniform rules across broad areas is decreasing. This is why the trend has been towards fewer wage increases and more heterogeneity among wage agreements.

The Luxembourg Process is restricted to labour market policy and focuses on the improvement of national labour markets. Accordingly, it is a form of soft, cross-border coordination. Though there is no direct coordination between member states, the uniform labour market approach used by the EU for its recommendations generates a coordinating effect between national labour market policies.

The employment strategy of the Luxemburg Process is non-binding, which is also the reason why its effectiveness is doubtful. The EU has no harmonization within its employment strategy. Instead, it relies on the subsidiarity principle, which assigns the main responsibility to member states. Its employment strategy is characterized by deliberative and consensual coordination of joint targets, ethical competition, the fostering of learning processes and provision of incentives through target-based actions. It has no clear definitions and enforces no sanctions for infractions. The only penalty for deviation from the neoclassical position is peer pressure. Some have criticized the decentralized implementation on the national level (via national action plans) and its monitoring and surveillance as insufficient. In many policy areas there is a lack of comparable, reliable and meaningful indicators, not least because member states cannot always make available the necessary data.

4.2 Forms of hard coordination within the EU

Previously, I defined hard coordination as characterizing a commitment to binding rules. Furthermore, non-compliance generally triggers sanctions. The SGP, which coordinates the fiscal policy of the EU's member states, is an example of hard coordination, as it demands adjustment measures from EU states based on concrete fiscal targets and provides for sanctions in the event of non-compliance.

4.2.1 The SGP: a hard, cross-border form of coordination

The SGP is commonly referred to as the major building block of the EMU.[11] The SGP consists of the so-called two arms.[12] The preventive arm is related to strengthening surveillance of budgetary positions and coordination of economic policies. The corrective arm is related to speeding up and streamlining the implementation of the Excessive Deficit Procedure of the Treaty. Thus, the Pact is supposed to dissuade member states from adopting polices which inflict negative externalities on fellow EU member states or which cause the quality of the collective goods in the EMU to deteriorate.[13]

The principle purpose of the SGP is to ensure and maintain fiscal discipline within the EMU, safeguarding sound government finances as a means to strengthening conditions for price stability and for strong and sustainable growth conducive to employment creation.[14] It was also recognized that the loss of the exchange rate instrument in the EMU would imply a greater role for automatic fiscal stabilizers at the national level to help economies adjust to asymmetric shocks. The role of automatic stabilizers is part of the debate on the conduct of fiscal policy in the EMU – suggesting either a more active use of fiscal policy in the euro area or its limitation to enabling the full operation of automatic stabilizers.

In general, the member states have to comply with budgetary discipline by respecting two criteria: a deficit-to-GDP ratio and a debt-to-GDP ratio not exceeding a reference value of 3 per cent and 60 per cent, respectively. In practice, however, since the launch of the EMU the attention has been paid particularly to the reference value for general government deficit. In addition to the deficit and debt criteria, the member states are obliged to respect the medium-term budgetary objective of positions "close to balance or in surplus". Balanced budgets are supposed to allow the member states to deal with cyclical fluctuations, since they offer states more scope of action for a fiscal stimulus without breaching the SGP when growth slows. Apart from the nominal targets, the Pact defines a formal procedure for monitoring national policies, for issuing warnings to non-compliant member states and for sanctioning them if they do not correct their fiscal policies.

The basic rationale for the numerical rules for budget deficits and a multilateral surveillance of budgetary performance as laid down in the Stability and Growth Pact is to respond to two dilemmas resulting from the combination of a centralized monetary policy and a decentralized fiscal regime in the EMU. In the presence of incomplete capital markets, member states – particularly those which favoured a stable currency and sound public finances – wanted rules to guard against negative externalities caused by the unsound fiscal policies of some member states and the resulting threats to the collective goods shared by all members of the monetary union. The fiscal rules are first supposed to prevent negative externalities as moral hazard problems may arise with the decentralized setting of fiscal policy in EMU. As the member states share a common currency and therefore a common degree of price stability, the inflationary impact of expansionary fiscal policies in one EMU member state will influence the common price level and hence all EMU member countries, and it can harm economic stability in other EMU countries via the traditional channels of goods and capital markets.

The rules also respond to a collective action problem of providing collective goods shared by the members of a monetary union.[15] The existence of collective goods in the EMU, such as the common price level and low financing costs, creates new channels of externalities among the member states. In order to avoid such scenarios, fiscal rules and sanction mechanisms impose costs on the EMU member which put the collective goods of the EMU at risk. Short- and medium-term risk reduction is the most important driving force behind rule-guided coordination in the EMU. The fact that the nominal EU rules are stricter than the solutions adopted in some member states reflects the heterogeneity of the EU economies and the perceived need to rapidly build up the stability-oriented reputation of EMU.

Table 4.1 illustrates the SGP's position in a matrix of coordination methods. As we can see, the SGP only governs the cross-border coordination in fiscal policy. There are no rule-based obligations and there is no coordination of wage and monetary policy.

4.2.2 Weaknesses of fiscal coordination in the eurozone

Since its introduction, the SGP has been the subject of criticism. Below I discuss the weaknesses pointed out by critics and explain the reform measures taken in response. Building on experience with the SGP, I then present some ideas about the coordination of fiscal policy based on alternate macroeconomic parameters within the scope of a cross-policy coordination regime.

The SGP has been criticized at both the institutional and conceptual level. The former criticisms have cast doubt on whether the SGP is suited to internalize cross-border fiscal policy externalities (see Section 3.3.1.1). This internalization only works if regulations have been designed correctly, especially with regard to the relationship between violations and sanctions, which determine the incentives for adhering to the SGP. Criticisms at the conceptual level have questioned whether the SGP's focus on public debt can achieve its desired effect.

4.2.2.1 The SGP and the internalization of external effects

As I have shown, the primary externality of concern arises when expansive fiscal policy affects the stability of community goods (e.g. the exchange rates, inflation, interest rates) to the detriment of other countries. In a monetary union, the costs of higher government debt levels and interest costs are carried by all member countries, thus leading to a reduction in costs for individual debtor countries and, by extension, increasing incentives for allowing excessive debt to accumulate.

Table 4.1 Classification of coordination

		Horizontal coordination	
		Cross-border coordination	Cross-policy coordination (fiscal, monetary, wages)
Vertical coordination	Soft coordination		
	Hard coordination	Stability and Growth Pact	
	Centralized coordination		

Source: author's description.

The strongest version of this externality occurs when new debt piles up, forcing one state to declare bankruptcy and the others to assume part of the payment obligation. Article 125 of the TFEU expressly frees the community of liability for the debt of its member countries. However, the effectiveness of this statute depends less on its legal codification than on its credibility. And as the events of the government-debt crisis have shown, this credibility is doubtful.

The SGP cannot be considered an efficient institutional regulation when it manages to prevent bailouts. The economic criticism of the SGP is largely sparked by its one-size-fits-all approach for preventing excessive debt. The SGP primarily obliges all member states to follow the 3 per cent criterion, regardless of country-specific circumstances. But this criterion does not reflect the entire likelihood of state bankruptcy. The risk of state bankruptcy also depends on the reason for debt (investment or consumption, say) and on whether the debt is financed primarily by foreigners or by nationals. Hence, the 3 per cent criterion is ill-suited for correctly internalizing externalities that result from bailouts. Indeed, an economy's long-term financial solvency does not rely on the relationship between new debt and the GDP; the crucial issue is intertemporal budget equilibrium – and on this issue, the SGP says nothing explicit.[16]

The crises of recent years have shown the SGP's inability to prevent an impending state bankruptcy alone through debt limits for the public sector. For example, Spain and Ireland did not run excessive deficits or have outsized public debt levels before the financial crisis broke; on the contrary, they had better budgetary numbers than Germany. Their problems manifested elsewhere, namely in macroeconomic imbalances. Spain's imbalances could be traced back to the introduction of the euro and the eurozone money market, which caused interest rates to decline in EU countries, especially those in the south. Both governments and private debtors profited from this development, and were able to take advantage of a negative real interest rate caused by higher-than-average inflation rates, leading to a rise in consumption. In Greece, low interest rates increased government debt; in Spain, by contrast, they triggered a construction boom, and, later, a real estate bubble. When the bubble burst, Spain was left with heavy fiscal burdens. But the SGP does not account for the effects of bubbles in real estate or capital markets, nor for rapidly rising private debt, all of which can bring with them considerable fiscal difficulties. In this way, the SGP also lacks precision.[17]

The compatibility of the SGP with sustainable debt levels has been the subject of debate. It is frequently asserted that the SGP does not permit a distinction between good and bad debt. Government debt is acceptable when it is used to finance investments that bring higher tax revenues in the future, so that investment pays for itself. In cases like these, the government acts like a business that borrows money to invest. If a government investment increases public capital stock, the resulting debt is offset by new benefits, leaving the government's asset position unchanged. When future generations stand to profit it also makes sense to take on debt for government-provided benefits and services. However, there are two important observations to make about this "pay-as-you-use approach":

on the one hand, future gains are hard to predict; on the other, present generations cannot know the preferences of future ones. The SGP design tries to
accommodate the notion of sustainable debt levels by allowing some deficit
spending. Furthermore, by distinguishing between structural and cyclical deficits, the SGP enables debt accumulation during economic downturns. The economic justification is simple: during slumps the potential returns from
debt-financed expenditures are larger than in boom times thanks to the enhanced
fiscal effect of countercyclical spending.

4.2.2.2 The SGP and the time inconsistency problem

If the time inconsistency problem is the source of a fiscal cross-border externality (as I argue Section 3.3.1.1), then the pursuit of stability through economic
and fiscal policy will lack credibility from the start. This is because EU states
have an incentive to run short-term deficits by using expansive debt-financed
fiscal policy for increasing output and employment. This time inconsistency
problem looks worse when we take into account the economic arguments.[18]
Insufficient incentives for sustainable budgetary policy tend to encourage expansive policies – with negative consequences for other monetary union members.

   If the SGP were a purely rule-based mechanism, it could theoretically reduce
the time inconsistency problem. Any member state that ran excessive deficits
would be immediately and effectively sanctioned, which would eat up any short-
term benefits gained from debt spending. In reality, though, the SGP has a number
of institutional weaknesses, hence its poor results in achieving balanced budgets.[19]

   The first shortcoming is the lack of binding regulation for preventing structural deficits. The SGP consists of preventive and corrective components for
restricting the public debts of EU member states. The preventive component
obliges member states to pursue a medium-term budget target. This target must
have a structural deficit of no more than 1 per cent over the course of the economic cycle and encourage a balanced budget. The corrective component uses
the threat of the Excessive Deficit Procedure to make sure member states move
quickly to cut deficits when they occur. The prevention of structural deficits was
and continues to be SGP's true budget objective. A 3 per cent deficit is supposed
to be the exception for member states, but experience shows it's the rule, and the
medium-term budget target is rarely heeded. One reason is that the preventive
component is not backed with financial sanctions. Currently, the only option for
the European Council is to issue warnings when the medium-term target has not
been reached.

   The second shortcoming is the lengthy time between breach and sanction,
which reduces state incentive to eliminate debt. Unlike the preventive component, the corrective component *can* sanction member states when their deficits
are too high, but in the current system important sanctions do not occur until
late. Indeed, up to nine years can elapse between the identification of excessive
deficits and the enforcement of sanctions (provided a state fully exploits its room
for legal manoeuvre during the Excessive Deficit Procedure).[20] By that time, the

member state in question can be in such fiscal difficulties that additional fines make little sense, as they would only worsen the situation. Another problem with the delay is that sanctions can be suspended in retrospect if a state reduces its deficit below the 3 per cent maximum for two years or more. It does not matter whether the structural deficit is in the proximity of a balanced budget.[21] Accordingly, it might be the case that economic effects alone end up lowering the deficit below the threshold, which does not encourage states to develop more sustainable budget policies.

Sometimes sanctions are not just late; they are not enforced even when they apply. This is the third SGP shortcoming. It exists because the European Council, the organization that makes the decisions, rarely issues sanctions. Its hesitant stance is attributable to the fact that the majority of member states have repeatedly breached SGP guidelines and are already facing sanctions. As country representatives in the Council must pass judgement on other countries for sins they themselves have committed, there's little political will to hand out sanctions.[22] Political bartering is used in these situations to organize majorities. For instance, the sanctions issued to Germany and France for running excessive deficits were suspended in 2003 by the Economic and Financial Affairs Council. The European Court of Justice later declared this decision to be null and void as it occurred outside the required framework (C-27/04). Despite this clear decision, the credibility of the SGP was irreparably damaged.[23] The strong position of the European Council made it difficult to implement the SGP effectively. The ECOFIN Council is the key institution in the EU's process for coordinating economic policies. The Council's weakness is that many of its decisions are obviously motivated by political considerations rather than sound economic analysis. Furthermore, while the European Commission is entrusted with the supervision, it does not have sufficient legal means to perform this task in an authoritative way, because its warnings and recommendations have to be endorsed by the ECOFIN Council. The likelihood of implementing recommendations is accordingly diminished. So while countries must sanction fellow member states for excessive deficits, as democratically elected governments, they are themselves inclined, for domestic political reasons, to engage in deficit spending in order to achieve higher employment and growth. Numerous reform proposals to solve this institutional problem have been put forth since the SGP's creation, and especially since the start of EMU.[24]

4.3 Monetary policy: centralized coordination

The monetary policy coordination carried out by the ECB is a special form of centralized coordination. National monetary decisions are institutionalized on a supranational level, with the ECB serving as an autonomous organization that sets the means for controlling monetary policy. The ECB can make and implement its own decisions through direct, centralized control.

The problem with centralized monetary policy is that it follows uniform parameters based on average eurozone values, and does not consider the specific conditions in member states. In particular, centralized monetary policy is not geared towards national inflation and employment rates. When these important parameters take disparate paths, the pressure on a single, uniform monetary policy increases. The greater the heterogeneity of the economic structures in the eurozone, the more difficult uniform monetary policy is to implement. Heterogeneity comes in a variety of forms. First, there is real economic divergence, which, as I showed above, is legion in the eurozone and adversely affects the accuracy of monetary policy measures. Second, there is divergence in the transmission of monetary stimulus. This includes the effects of the money supply on the real economy (production, employment) and on the monetary sector (inflation rate). Third, there is inflation divergence, which leads to different real interest rates and, as a result, varying impacts on investment demand.

In a certain sense, the SGP facilitates the cross-policy coordination of monetary policy, although this does not take the form of direct coordination. Under the SGP, fiscal policy freedom is limited to achieving greater monetary policy freedom. SGP debt regulations were introduced to prevent the negative spillover of national debt policy on community goods (e.g. inflation rates, the common currency) and on the effectiveness of monetary policy. In this way, rule-based arrangements ensure that fiscal policy is of secondary importance to the price-stability targets of monetary policy. Similarly, whenever wage policy focuses on productivity, it becomes linked to monetary policy. And when wage policy is linked to ECB-controlled inflation, monetary policy ceases to have a coordination function. The monetary policy enjoys priority over wage policy in that wage policy must accept inflation as a fact. For this reason, I later discuss cross-policy coordination with the scope of a productivity-oriented wage policy (see Section 3.3.1.1).

4.4 The failure of coordination during the financial crisis

The European debt crisis did not come out of nowhere. It is the continuation of a cascade of crises. It began, at the latest, with the bursting of the tech bubble in 2000. The next crisis was the housing bubble, which ballooned in the United States and in several EU countries before cracks appeared in 2006, with full-scale deflation soon following. The housing crisis quickly led to a financial crisis because of the massive securitization of mortgage debt. Risk premiums rose steeply, the global economy plunged into recession, governments had to bailout banks and ratify stimulus packages and government debt increased drastically. The euro crisis erupted when heavily indebted EMU member states faced being shut out of credit markets. Hence, it was less a currency crisis in the classic sense than another chapter in an ongoing financial crisis.[25]

In essence, the shortcomings in governance over the EMU occurred because member states were not ready to relinquish their national responsibilities over certain regulatory areas, and without centralization (or, at least, coordination), the monetary union could not operate harmoniously. This led to an institutional vacuum in which grave macroeconomic imbalances arose within the eurozone, but they received no economic corrective. The outbreak of the financial crisis revealed the fragility of the institutional architecture of the EMU, in which institutional deficits led to grave macroeconomic instability.

4.4.1 Economic developments in the EMU before the crisis

Since the introduction of the euro, economic policy and economic developments in the EMU have escaped the control of the aforementioned regulatory mechanisms in important areas, revealing grave deficits in existing systems of governance. On the one hand, SGP rules were breached multiple times without any form of punishment, and in 2005 the Pact itself was revised. On the other hand, in the first half of the last decade the exchange-rate value of the euro increased considerably. During the same period, the nominal value of the euro increased even more. Ultimately, nominal unit labour costs and inflation rates between the member states began to markedly diverge. While cost levels in Germany remained the same, Europe's margins saw a 25–35 per cent rise. This bifurcation was also reflected in the price of goods. Such differences existed before the monetary union, but they could be balanced out through adjustments to national exchange rates. Once the euro was introduced, however, varying growth trends in unit labour prices substantially shifted competitiveness in Germany's favour.

On average, ECB price targets in the eurozone were nearly achieved, but for individual member states they overshot and undershot the mark.[26] This resulted in divergences between member states, both in real interest rates and in price competitiveness. The decisive thing was that the divergences had a persistent effect in the same direction, so that the smooth, market-based adjustment that many thought would occur never did. For countries like Spain, a lower-than-average real interest rate had a positive effect on domestic growth but a cumulative negative effect on price competitiveness. For countries like Germany, the opposite was the case. Accordingly, growth patterns were also different. Spain saw strong nominal and domestic growth but a negative trade balance due to an increasing current account deficit. By contrast, Germany showed weak domestic growth but a rising current account surplus. Because the share of domestic demand in both countries was considerably higher than the trade balance, real growth and employment in Spain (as in other countries on Europe's periphery) seemed noticeably stronger than in Germany. As to be expected with such differences in real interest rates, new construction investment in Spain had a markedly positive effect on growth in the first half of the aughts, while new construction investment in Germany had a markedly negative effect during the same period (as did unification-related adjustments). Also as expected, government account balances took divergent courses. Strong real and nominal domestic growth allowed Spain to stay under the 3 per cent threshold, with frequent budget surpluses and markedly improved public debt ratio. Germany, by contrast, violated the Maastricht criterion for years. At the end of 2007, it increased its value-added tax by three percentage points to bring its deficit ratio back above zero, a move that tended to weaken domestic growth. At the same time, the partial use of revenue to reduce supplemental wage costs for employers distorted price competitiveness upwards. For all the differences between the two countries, however, the income distribution between labour and capital worsened in both Spain and Germany at the expense of labour, leading to a declining wage share. In Spain unit labour costs were above the eurozone average; in Germany they were below. The effects of these distribution changes merit a separate investigation – that is, how they affected private consumption (a key determinant of domestic demand), savings, capital exports and growth in general (even outside the eurozone), along with their contribution to the financial crisis.[27]

4.4.2 Deficits in existing systems of eurozone governance

My discussion of economic trends in the eurozone has uncovered grave regulatory shortcomings. I have analysed some of these weaknesses already. SGP regulations were often ignored and violations were neither prevented nor corrected or sanctioned. This shortcoming (which is a failure to adhere to self-imposed norms) exists independently of whether one sees the SGP or its reforms as adequate. But when it comes to the appropriateness of the SGP, we notice that nominal budget deficits over time represent a residual parameter (towards which "end-of-pipe" policies are geared). Moreover, the relationship between budget balances and total economic price stability – one of the motivating factors behind the SGP – is by no means close. Budget balances are heavily influenced by general price growth. In a strongly inflationary environment, especially when taxes are progressive, it is easier to meet budget deficit thresholds through higher revenues (directly via a higher deflator and indirectly via its effect on real interest rates and real growth) than when prices fall below ECB targets. When the SGP was being amended, Germany tried to make prices a more direct and more important part of the deficit assessment process (though without insistence and without success).

The cardinal error was that, from a macroeconomic perspective, the regulatory mechanisms in place for coordination were concerned almost exclusively with residual budget balances. At the same time, the regulatory mechanisms ignored macroeconomic parameters that are especially relevant in a monetary union, or left the regulation of these parameters to individual member states. The widely held view that the EMU crisis started out as a government debt crisis is false. With the exception of Greece – a country with small economic significance but a large influence on the public perception of the crisis – the credit expansion took place in the private sector, where it fed a housing bubble. Only after the bubble burst did the excessive debt migrate from the private sector to the public sector. Accordingly, a consistent implementation of the debt threshold stipulated by the SGP would not have prevented the crisis. Still, an effective limitation of public debt in a monetary union is necessary – not only to prevent problem cases from occurring (like that of Greece's), but also to make otherwise solvent countries less susceptible to speculation-driven liquidity crises.

In addition to these problems, the implementation of the Lisbon Strategy in both its original and revised forms was too one-sided in its exclusive focus on structural reforms. It preferred voluntary, "open" coordination methods such as peer review, peer pressure and "best practice" discussions among member states. The original Lisbon Strategy explicitly provided for macroeconomic components along with its social policy targets, but it was not until the introduction of the Macroeconomic Dialogue, in 1999, that the coordination of macroeconomic growth and stability was conceived on an institutional level.

Yet, as discussed above, neither the Lisbon Strategy nor the Macroeconomic Dialogue saw their recommendations fulfilled. Fiscal policy was implemented exclusively on a national level and was for the most part procyclical. On the demand side, this contributed to the solidification and amplification of excessive divergence in the eurozone. A countercyclical fiscal policy would have narrowed (not expanded) latitude for wages, costs and prices. Instead, a restrictive, discretionary fiscal policy slowed growth and prices where they were weak already.

Costs were the main reason for excessive price divergence. Nominal wage costs and nominal unit labour costs ran permanently and persistently in opposite directions between member states. And both were drivers of prices and driven by prices. What is more, exogenous price shocks such as oil price increases caused wages to vary among member states, further amplifying divergence. Even before the formation of the EMU, economic policy called on member states to advocate a framework for determining wages (keeping in mind the role of labour and unions), so that nominal wages and labour costs would harmonize with price stability and medium-term productivity while taking into account differences in worker educational attainment and labour market conditions. Even more than with the SGP, these norms – set by state and government leaders and crucial for EMU functioning – were breached each year without consequences, despite the abundance of warnings from the beginning.

The fact that all this was overlooked or ignored is a failure of both contractual governance and governance in practice at the EMU and national levels.[28]

4.5 Interim findings

The EMU's macroeconomic governance has been characterized by yawning institutional deficits, especially during the financial crisis:

- The externalities identified in Chapter 3 as the rationale for coordination cannot be sufficiently internalized by the means of coordination institutionalized before the government-debt crisis. With an excessive focus on public sector debt creation, the SGP fails to consider other reasons for negative cross-policy externalities and bailout risks. Nevertheless, the SGP manages to solve the time inconsistency problem, despite the lack of credible, effective implementation and of sufficient sanctions. All things considered, however, the SGP was unable to internalize cross-policy fiscal externalities in the period before the government debt crisis.

- The same applies for other forms of coordination, which are either cross-border (BEPG, Luxembourg Process) or cross-policy (MD) in nature, but which are all soft forms of coordination. We must also keep in mind that in the coordination of national economic policies up to the outbreak of the crisis in 2009, there were strong asymmetries between economic-policy institutions and actors within the EU. Table 4.2 illustrates the forms of coordination in the EU already discussed. On the one hand, an autonomous central bank bears the entire responsibility for fiscal policy; on the other hand, procedures for all other policy areas are mostly "hard" and usually remain limited to a single area of policy (e.g. the SGP, monetary policy, the Luxembourg Process). The forms of coordination that actually engage in cross-policy coordination (MD) rely on a pure exchange of viewpoints – the softest form of coordination.

The neoclassical assignment approach can be clearly recognized in EU economic policy mechanisms. Each of the targets named in the key areas of EU economic policy (budget consolidation, productivity-based wages, price-based monetary policy, flexibility-based structural policy) is supposed to be pursued in isolation; negative side-effects on other targets are ignored. Hence, EU fiscal policy is not made to depend on monetary policy or wage policy or the speed of structural reforms. Positive effects on potential growth are promised from all measures, including synergistic effects between areas. Every policy area is supposed to contribute to more growth and employment through the pursuit of assigned targets.

The next step in my investigation will show that the originally strict separation between policy areas (in line with "assignment approach") underwent significant change over the course of the debt crisis. The first step in that change was the newly established Macroeconomic Imbalance Procedure – a form of hard cross-policy coordination. This regulatory measure is accompanied by various forms of soft cross-policy coordination, such as the Europe 2020 strategy or the European Semester. Finally, monetary policy has been given a fiscal policy dimension through the EU's purchase of member state government bonds – a measure that current reforms intend to continue through the ESM.

Table 4.2 Classification of coordination

		Horizontal coordination	
		Cross-border coordination	*Cross-policy coordination (fiscal, monetary, wages)*
Vertical coordination	Soft coordination	Macroeconomic dialogue; BEPG; Luxembourg Process	
	Hard coordination	SGP	
	Centralized coordination	Monetary policy	

Source: author's description.

Notes

1 Article 119 of the TFEU.
2 Article 282 of the TFEU.
3 See Hodson and Maher (2001) and Linsenmann and Meyer (2002).
4 Hodson (2011, 80ff.).
5 See Broad Economic Policy Guidelines (2003, p. 67).
6 See Boss *et al.* (2004, p. 74).
7 ECB (2000, p. 54).
8 ECB (2000, p. 54).
9 For the following, see Huemer (2009).
10 For the following, see Niechoj (2004, p. 14).
11 For the following, see Szelag (2007, p. 21).
12 The original Pact consists of two regulations and a Council resolution that specify the Treaty provisions on the Excessive Deficit Procedure (EDP). See Article 126 of the TFEU.
13 For an econometric analysis on the relationship between sovereign yields spreads and fiscal variables, see Maltritz (2012).
14 See Szelag (2007, p. 21); Hodson (2011, p. 60).
15 This observation follows from Schwarzer (2007, p. 20).
16 See Schmidt (2011, p. 60).
17 See Dietrich *et al.* (2010, p. 371).
18 See Schmidt (2011, p. 57) and Alesina and Perotti (1995, p. 1).
19 For the following, see Kullas and Koch (2010, pp. 7ff.) and Schmidt (2011, pp. 62f.).
20 See Kullas and Koch (2010, pp. 7ff) and Calmfors (2006, p. 22).
21 Sachverständigenrat (2009, p. 87).
22 See Kullas and Koch (2010, pp. 7ff).
23 See Kullas and Koch (2010, pp. 7ff).
24 For the recommendations submitted by economists, see Collignon (2003), Casella (2002) and Jacquet and Pisani-Ferry (2001).
25 See Landmann (2012).
26 For the following, see Koll (2011).
27 See Koll (2011).
28 See Koll (2011).

5 The expansion of coordination in the EU

The foregoing analysis has shown that the EU's existing coordination instruments only give limited consideration to cross-border externalities and interdependencies between policy areas. As a result, fiscal policy coordination and soft coordination efforts in the areas of general economic and macroeconomic policy have been unable to internalize externalities or bring about macroeconomic convergence.

Building on the previous chapter's findings, the current chapter discusses farther-reaching forms of coordination. In the area of fiscal policy coordination, I begin with an analysis of the expansion of the SGP. This expansion was undertaken as a reaction to the euro crisis. The goal was to improve the health of government balance sheets by more effectively internalizing the externalities of national fiscal policy. I then examine farther-reaching forms of coordination in view of alternate liability arrangements, comparing the incentives offered for debt accumulation within both federal and union state systems. I conclude with an assessment of specific farther-reaching forms of fiscal coordination, including Eurobonds, debt brakes and state insolvency procedures.

Beyond discussing fiscal policy coordination, I will show that the reforms of recent years represent a marked trend towards more coordination across policy areas – and a rejection of the strict assignment approach. The only area of macroeconomic policy that continues to resist coordination is wage policy. This chapter will identify the problems and opportunities presented by the implementation of a national or cross-border productivity-oriented wage policy. The chapter ends with a discussion of the new role the ECB has assumed during the crisis in the area of coordinated fiscal and monetary policy.

5.1 Reform of cross-border fiscal policy coordination

As described above, the SGP is a key instrument of fiscal policy coordination featuring binding rules and sanction mechanisms (i.e. hard coordination). But a number of conceptual and institutional weaknesses undermine its effectiveness. Until recently, the SGP was restricted to a specific area of fiscal action – namely, limiting deficits. In 2011, the EU enacted a major reform of the SGP because the existing regulations had failed to prevent national debt in most member states from continuing to rise. The problem was that many member states had made little or no effort to balance budgets even in good economic times. The public debt levels in member states had also risen dramatically due to the financial and economic crisis. The reforms therefore strengthened both the preventive and corrective components of the SGP. The goal was to force member states to quickly reduce their debt loads and keep them low over the long term, initially through tighter supervision.

5.1.1 Reform of fiscal policy coordination since the outbreak of the sovereign debt crisis

In the following section, the reforms to the SGP that have been undertaken are described and then assessed in terms of their effectiveness in correcting the SGP's shortcomings.

The reform process began with the appointment of a task force under the direction of the President of the European Council, van Rompuy. The task force was instructed to submit proposals for improving the crisis resolution framework and enforcing greater budgetary discipline. In September 2010, the Van Rompuy Working Group presented the first draft of its final report. In parallel, the commission formally introduced a package of six proposed rules (the so-called Sixpack). The package's proposals were aimed at improving budgetary monitoring as well as the monitoring and coordination of economic policies. The package also included a separate proposal for avoiding and correcting macroeconomic asymmetries. Finally, the commission introduced the "European Semester" to strengthen coordination in general, and to enhance the impact of existing and new EU regulations on the national implementation of budgetary and economic policy (see Section 5.2.3).

5.1.1.1 Reform of the preventive components of the SGP

The preventive components intend to prevent excessive deficits. The measures require member states to commit to medium-term, structural deficit objectives.[1] States are also required to present stability and convergence programmes each year, demonstrating to the Commission and the Council that they are capable of meeting their middle-term objectives, and are making efforts to balance their budgets.[2] The underlying idea is to prevent deficits from growing too large in the first place. The reforms increased the requirements placed on the programmes to be presented each year. Member states are now obligated to disclose information about government spending and the debt-to-GDP ratio, among other things. The stability programmes are compared with the Commission's macroeconomic and budgetary forecasts. The Council determines whether the member states have achieved their medium-term budgetary objective or are on a path to achieving it. In addition, the structural deficit must fall by at least 0.5 per cent of GDP per year. A new feature of the reform is that the Council also tracks government spending. If a member state falls short of its medium-term budgetary objective, then the annual growth in expenditures must be less than the potential GDP growth rate. Any reduction in government revenues must be matched by cuts in government spending or an increase in other government revenues. With a qualified majority, the Council can determine whether a member state has deviated significantly from its stability and convergence programme. Another new feature of the reform is that the Commission (instead of the Council) may now issue the offending member state a warning. With a qualified majority the Council may then accept the Commission's recommended corrective measures and pass them on to the member state. On the recommendation of the Commission and with a qualified majority the Council can also determine that a member state has undertaken no or insufficient steps to implement these recommendations, and add new ones on top of them. Under the reform of the SGP, failure by a eurozone country to implement these additional recommendations can result in the imposition of sanctions in the form of an interest-bearing deposit of 0.2 per cent of the previous year's GDP – that is, unless the Council opposes it. The final new feature of the reform is that on the Commission's recommendation and with a qualified majority, the Council may also impose a fine amounting to a maximum of 0.2 per cent of GDP on non-compliant euro member states if they have intentionally or by gross negligence provided false deficit or debt data.[3]

5.1.1.2 Assessment of the reformed preventive components

The "medium-term budgetary objective" is the budgetary objective that a member state must work to achieve in order to ensure their debt is sustainable over the long term.[4] A deficit of 3 per cent is acceptable only in rare cases. Yet member states have clearly shown that they do not view exceeding the 3 per cent limit as exceptional. In fact, they pay little attention to their medium-term budgetary objectives. The fiscal consequences of this attitude are alarming.[5] For example, if a member state has an annual deficit of 3 per cent, a real economic growth rate of 1 per cent and an inflation rate of 2 per cent, then national debt will over the long-term approach 100 per cent of GDP. That level of debt is a risk to economic growth. The preventive components have attracted more attention from policymakers and the public since they were armed with sanctions. But the actual concern is whether the sanctions (interest-bearing deposits) go far enough, since they put only slight financial pressure on the member states sanctioned. It would make more sense to add even tougher sanctions at this stage, sending a clear message that non-compliant eurozone countries must put their house in order. One possibility would be to force a country that falls short of its "medium-term budgetary goals" to make a non-interest bearing deposit instead of an interest-bearing deposit. If the country continues to be in violation, the deposit could be incrementally converted into a fine. The deposit (but not the fine) would be refunded once the national budget is brought back in line with regulations.

The new spending regulations are a positive development because they ensure that unexpectedly higher revenues will be used to reduce the debt load, while allowing for automatic stabilizers and other acceptable debts. But the disadvantage of the new regulations is that they make the already difficult existing regulations of the preventive components even more complicated and hard to understand. The increasing complexity of the preventive components makes them even less popular with policymakers and the public than before.[6] Furthermore, the preventive components now take into account the level of national debt. That is a significant improvement since the experience of recent years has proven that national debt levels cannot be controlled by means of deficits alone. In addition, high levels of national debt negatively impact economic growth. The euro crisis has also demonstrated that capital markets can lose confidence in member states with high levels of debt, even if they have their deficits under control. And if a country with a high level of debt loses access to capital markets, the risk of an international banking crisis is many times higher than if a member state with a high deficit but a low level of debt loses that access.

The reform provision allowing the Commission to issue a warning is based on the Treaty of Lisbon, meaning it is secondary legislation modifying the original law.[7] The modification is an improvement because it increases the likelihood a warning will be issued in the future. The Council has issued such a warning only once before (in 2003 to France), many times ignoring the Commission's recommendation to do so. But the benefits of the reform are undercut by the stipulation that the Council must first determine wrongdoing. Past experience has shown that the Council usually uses any influence it has to protect member states from negative consequences. The second step in the process (assessing budgetary goals) is also vulnerable to political manipulation, because the Council can only demand that a stability and convergence programme be revised with a qualified majority. This increases the risk that the Council will accept a stability and convergence programme that does not in fact fulfil the requirements. A better approach would be to make the revision of a stability or convergence programme virtually automatic by forbidding the Council from rejecting the Commission's recommendation for revision except with a qualified majority. An additional problem is that no sanctions are provided for a eurozone country that presents an inadequate stability or convergence programme for a second time. There is also some concern eurozone countries will seldom be required to actually pay the newly introduced interest-bearing deposits. Although the reform has the advantage of making the payment of interest-bearing deposits virtually automatic, the problem remains that the Council can reject the Commission's recommendation to impose the sanction with a simple majority. The reform would be more effective if the European Parliament had gotten through its original proposal that the Council could reject the Commission's recommendation to take a deposit only with a qualified majority. The regulation actually put in place allows other member states threatened by interest-bearing deposits to use their votes for political purposes. They can still form a blocking minority, especially if the larger member states are involved. Therefore, doubt remains whether the payment of deposits will really be "almost automatic."[8]

5.1.1.3 Reform of the corrective components

The corrective components of the SGP apply when the Commission's assessment of a country's budget policy determines that government deficit and debt indicators have exceeded specific levels.[9] If the preventive measures have not been successful, the corrective measures provide for an Excessive Deficit Procedure, which intends to force member states to reduce their deficits. An excessive debt procedure is initiated when the budget deficit exceeds 3 per cent of GDP, or if the total public debt exceeds 60 per cent of GDP. The reform now defines a sufficiently diminishing gap between the actual debt level and the 60 per cent threshold as an annual reduction of at least 5 per cent of GDP over the previous three years. If the gap is sufficiently diminishing, then the debt level requirement is viewed as fulfilled. If a member state fails to meet the deficit or debt level requirements, then the commission is required to produce a report on the state of the country's economy and medium-term economic position, as well as the factors affecting them. As is the case with the preventive components, a eurozone member state that provides false data may be sanctioned. With a qualified majority, the Council can determine based on the report that a member state has an excessive deficit. Under the reform of the SGP, a sanction is imposed in the form of a non-interest bearing deposit of 0.2 per cent of the previous year's GDP – unless the Council opposes it. With a qualified majority the Council then decides on recommended corrective measures. If on the recommendation of the Commission the Council determines that a member state has undertaken no effective measures to reduce its excessive deficit, as long as the country is a eurozone member state, the non-interest bearing deposit can be converted into a fine – but again only if the Council does not oppose it. After that the Council can issue a deadline to the member state. If nevertheless the country still does not implement any measures to reduce its deficit in the following four months, with a qualified majority and on the Commission's recommendation the Council can determine and impose sanctions on the member state. The final new feature of the reform is that these sanctions are now fines remitted to the EFSF or ESM.

5.1.1.4 Assessment of the reformed reactive components

We should welcome the fact that a debt level of more than 60 per cent of GDP can now trigger an Excessive Deficit Procedure. Before the reform, the SGP emphasized deficits over public debt on economic grounds. To illustrate this reasoning: if a member state has an annual deficit of 3 per cent, a real economic growth rate of 3 per cent and an inflation rate of 2 per cent, then the level of national debt will over the long-term approach the 60 per cent threshold. This demonstrates that, assuming these conditions, it is not necessary to track the debt level if the deficit is watched carefully. This is because the deficit is a dynamic rate and the debt level is an absolute amount. As a result, careful monitoring of the inflow and outflow of debt can be used to effectively control debt levels. The experience of recent years, however, has proven otherwise. One problem is that the deficit limit of 3 per cent is set too high. Many member states do not typically have a real economic growth rate of 3 per cent. Instead it is usually closer to 1 per cent. Using this lower rate, it follows that the average deficit can only amount to 1.8 per cent of GDP – that is, if we want the national debt over the long-term to sink to the 60 per cent threshold. Yet there may also be legal problems with the debt level requirement. The EU treaties take legal precedence over regulations. So long as Article 126 of the TFEU still refers to an "Excessive Deficit Procedure", any Excessive Deficit Procedure initiated against a country for disregarding its debt level requirement violates EU treaties with legal precedence and leaves the member nation the option of taking legal action.[10]

Strengthening monitoring and making the level of national debt a factor in triggering the Excessive Deficit Procedure is, from an economic point of view, an excellent idea, for a high level of national debt is a serious threat to economic growth. The negative consequences of a high level of national debt are primarily caused by disproportionally increasing interest payments on the rising debt. High interest payments limit government funds available for investment or education, which in turn negatively impacts economic growth over the long term. Simultaneously raising taxes to service the debt encourages tax avoidance, reducing efficiency. In addition, rising interest payments increase the risk of falling into a debt spiral. This risk is particularly large if a member state cannot pay the interest on existing debts without new taxes. Finally, a high level of national debt jeopardizes a country's ability to react effectively to economic shocks and other crises.

As discussed in the section on the preventive components, the euro crisis has demonstrated that member states with high levels of national debt can become a burden to other member states. If these states lose the confidence of the capital market, an international banking crisis could follow. Using the level of national debt as a trigger for the Excessive Deficit Procedure therefore makes good sense. But there is also a downside to closer monitoring of debt levels. Suddenly reducing the debt levels of many member states at once could endanger Europe's economic development. Nevertheless, the overall advantages of reducing the levels of national debt far outweigh the disadvantages. Another positive aspect of the reform is the quick-acting regime of sanctions, allowing eurozone member states to be sanctioned significantly earlier than before. That means the SGP's corrective components are a stronger deterrent. Monetary sanctions have a greater impact at earlier stages as well, because non-compliant member states' ability to pay is then significantly reduced by the end of a drawn-out excessive debt procedure. But some question remains on whether the level of sanctions is high enough to effectively force member states to maintain budgetary discipline. To meet the new debt level requirements, many member states have to make cutbacks that greatly exceed the possible sanctions.[11]

The reform has also failed to improve the Excessive Deficit Procedure's efficiency. Moving to the next step of the procedure still requires a Council decision with a qualified majority. The same applies for determining that a deficit is excessive[12] or that no effective consolidation measures have been taken.[13] Yet these decisions must be made before the "virtually automatic" sanctions are triggered. That means the Council of Ministers are still like judges who are also guilty of the offences they are supposed to be judging. Even if the member state specifically targeted by the Excessive Deficit Procedure is not allowed to vote, the reform allows other member states who are also either potential or actual deficit violators plenty of opportunity to use their votes for political purposes. They can still easily form a blocking minority to prevent the vote passing with a qualified majority, especially if the larger member states are involved. A better approach would be to make deficit determination and sanctioning automatic once a member state has exceeded the SGP's objective targets. But that would require amending the original laws. Accordingly, doubt remains as to whether the new sanction mechanism will actually be effective, since the steps of the procedure that entail sanctions still require a Council decision with a qualified majority. In addition, some questions remain concerning whether the level of sanctions is high enough to effectively force member states to continue to reduce their debt levels.

5.1.2   *Farther-reaching forms of fiscal policy coordination*

The SGP is the eurozone's key instrument of fiscal policy coordination. In addition to further strengthening the SGP's enforcement regime, in recent years a number of other, farther-reaching forms of fiscal policy coordination to control government debt have been discussed. Debt brakes, state insolvency procedures and Eurobonds are the most commonly considered.

The organization of the political union in question plays a decisive role in determining whether different forms of coordination should be introduced. The key question here is how federal states and union states differ in the incentives they offer for debt consolidation. The following analysis examines the different incentives for debt accumulation in federal states and union states. The conclusions will then be used to determine whether farther-reaching forms of fiscal policy coordination within the eurozone beyond the SGP are appropriate.

5.1.2.1   *Fiscal policy coordination incentive structures in different constitutional settings*

Incentives for debt accumulation are critical in determining whether a specific form of fiscal policy coordination is appropriate. These incentives are in turn determined by the regulations governing regional debt liability. Two kinds of political organizations with different forms of regional debt liability are *federal states* and *union states*.[14] The primary difference between these two types of organization is the central government's liability for the individual member regions' debts. In federal states there is no joint liability, meaning each individual member region is liable for its own debts. In union states the member regions can still take on their own debts, and those debts are first and foremost their own liability. But as a guarantee, the centralized government is secondarily liable for the member regions' debts. So whatever the regional governments do, they can rely on the other members of the union to pick up the pieces afterwards.[15]

INCENTIVES FOR DEBT ACCUMULATION IN FEDERAL STATES

In federal states, the regional member governments are entirely liable for the debts they take on. In contrast with union states, in federal states the central government is not liable to the regional governments' lenders (i.e. the "no bailout" principle applies). Instead, the lenders must themselves work with their debtors to assess their risk exposure. As a result, interest rates for the refinancing of government debt in a federal state are determined by the financial resources of the debtors and the rating assessments of lenders. The most important issue here is that the lenders' policies match the individual regional governments' propensity to incur debt. This is because individual regional member governments' demand curves diverge from one another due to such factors as different demographics or debt accumulation tendencies. In a federal state, lenders determine demand curves that reflect the individual regional governments' likelihood to incur debt. Unlike in a union state, in a federal state the regional governments' financing costs rise together with their individual levels of debt, creating a direct incentive not to pile up more debts. In other words, regional governments that add debt are confronted with a rising interest rate curve. More debt means a higher risk premium and therefore higher financing costs, which in turn reduces the demand for debt. This is the key difference between a federal state and a union state: in a union state shared liability and risk taken on by the central government can lead to a higher level of total debt without increasing the regional governments' financing costs. The incentives for debt accumulation are defined by the central government's total debt level, not by regional government debt levels. Since in a union state the regional governments share their risk, the total demand for debt is actually larger than the sum of the regional governments' demand for debt.

To take an example from history, the German Empire with its 26 sovereign states and around 40,000 municipalities was a federal state.[16] The states and municipalities had considerable spending and financial autonomy. There was no horizontal or vertical fiscal equalization, and, as a result, no shared liability among the regional governments. The state was organized under the principle of institutional congruence, meaning the circle of beneficiaries, of policymakers and of taxpayers in every regional jurisdiction and on every level always perfectly overlapped. No one could live at the expense of their neighbours or could be forced to support their neighbours.

Today, the United States is an example of the incentives offered by a federal state. Instead of sharing liability as in a union state system, the central government offers no such safety net. Instead there is a great deal of uncertainty. For example, in the summer of 2010 California's request for a bailout from the United States government was rejected. There is also an orderly insolvency procedure for regional governments that entails a certain amount of risk for investors in government bonds if payments fall short. This is still true even today despite the extensive debt taken over (in fact or implicitly) by the Fed and the US government in the course of the bailouts. But it should be noted that the United States uses fiscal transfers to absorb asymmetrical shocks. Unemployment insurance in the United States is actually also one method of fiscal transfer. A high level of unemployment increases the number of workers receiving benefits in states with low growth, while low unemployment reduces the number of workers receiving benefits in states with high growth. The eurozone has no balancing mechanisms like these except contributions to and receipts from the EU budget in rudimentary forms (e.g. the Structural Fund and the Cohesion Fund).[17]

Joint liability for debt means that the costs paid by regional member states in Germany's union system remain largely independent of their level of debt. But each state in the United States pays debt costs in line with its individual level of debt. To guard against debt costs rising too high, many states in the United States have on their own initiative amended their constitutions to include debt limits of various kinds. The levels of government debt among the states in the United States illustrate the results. Even in the crisis year of 2009 the levels of debt among the states was between about only 8 and 27 per cent, with California having a level of only about 23 per cent after making drastic budget cuts. That stands in stark contrast to Germany, a union state, where the level of debt ranged from about 7 per cent in Bavaria to almost 70 per cent of GDP in Berlin.[18]

In theory, there is no risk of a bailout in a federal currency zone. Given functioning capital markets and a credible no-bailout provision, debt levels should be prevented from rising in the first place. In practice this is not the case, however. The United States is an example of a federal currency zone with a mix of strict legal debt limits, state insolvency proceedings, fiscal transfers and credible no-bailout provisions: aside from Vermont, all states in the United States are required either by their laws or their constitutions to have a balanced (operative) budget.[19] Carrying forward a deficit from one budgetary year to the next is in general not allowed, though there are a wide variety of ways that the individual states comply with this requirement within their budgetary and legal frameworks. Debts can only be taken on to finance investment. In principle, the central government can never be liable for the debts of the regional governments. There is no horizontal fiscal equalization as in the German system. However, there is vertical financial assistance. About 30 per cent of the states' expenditures (including Medicaid) consist of federal grants. 40 per cent of local government revenues come from the state governments (state grants). The states in the United States are required to balance their budgets each year and cannot simply carry forward deficits from year to year. Instead, they must either present a programme for short-term budget cuts or raise taxes. Since the balanced budget provisions were introduced at the state level, not one US state has failed to comply with the provisions (which is equivalent to not meeting the Maastricht deficit criterion).

There is no explicit procedure for US states in financial distress. Federal law does not allow US states to file for bankruptcy. But US municipalities can file for insolvency. Chapter 9 of the US Bankruptcy Code states that individuals and municipalities can file for bankruptcy. Certain regional governments, departments and institutions in a state can qualify as municipalities, while the state itself cannot. There have been many cases of insolvency on the municipal level. A notable example was New York City (though not the State of New York). Domestic and international pressure resulted in New York City finally receiving a loan with harsh conditions from the federal government in Washington, DC. Normally the US Federal Reserve can also buy municipal bonds on the market as long they mature in under six months. However, the Fed is forbidden by law from giving financial assistance to insolvent debtors. That means the Fed is not permitted to bailout individual municipalities, and the Fed does not consider it. Only financing instruments equally accessible to all are available.

INCENTIVES FOR DEBT ACCUMULATION IN UNION STATES

In union states there is a different system. Usually member regions can take on their own debts, and those debts are first and foremost their own liability. But as a guarantee, the centralized government is secondarily liable for the member regions' debts. So whatever the regional governments do, they can rely on the other members of a union state to pick up the pieces afterwards.

Another crucial difference between a union state and a federal state is the status of the lender.[20] In a union state, the central government above all protects the lender. Although that incentivizes debtors to take on excessive debt and lenders to keep providing them with new credit, the lender is always protected. In a federal state each regional government takes on debts according to its individual debt demand curve. Lenders, in turn, set their lending conditions based on each regional government's likelihood to honour debts. In a union state, a pooling of the demand curves leads to a greater risk of default among the individual regional governments. As noted above, this is because in a union state the regional governments share their risk, making the total demand for debt actually larger than the sum of the regional governments' demand for debt.[21] The incentive for debt accumulation is increased because the financing costs are defined by the central government's total debt level, not by regional government debt levels. This also makes consolidation more difficult, because each regional government's minimum contribution is relatively small and can only have a limited effect on reducing financing costs. In sum, pooling increases moral hazard.

This is the precise situation in Germany (particularly before the constitutional debt limitation came into effect). Regional governments in Germany have no risk in the case of insolvency and can always count on a bailout from the central government. In a decision from 27 May 1992, the German Federal Constitutional Court (FCC) declared that the central government and the regional governments in Germany are bound by a kind of community solidarity and are obligated to support one another.[22] As a result, the court decided that the central government and regional governments must help and contribute aid when any member of the community is in an extreme budget crisis. At the time, the judgement was criticized for incentivizing regional governments to deliberately precipitate a budget crisis in order to force other members to pay for their fiscal policy mistakes.[23] The FCC's decision resulted in the regional state governments of Bremen and Saarland receiving extensive aid from 1994 and 2004. In 2004, Bremen's debt level was still higher than that of any other regional state government. In Saarland as well, budget cuts had not had a long-lasting positive effect. But the FCC's decision of 1992 had clearly established that the central government and regional governments were jointly liable for each other's debts. So any time the central government or a regional government finds themselves in an extreme budget crisis, the rest of the community is obliged to help.

The rating agencies' scoring of the local state governments proves that shared liability decisively influences the assessments of market participants. The FCC confirmed the liability of the federal state as ultima ratio in its "Berlin decision" of 19 October 2006. However, the FCC sought to strengthen the regional state governments' responsibility by requiring a high level of budgetary emergency and proof that the regional government cannot solve its budgetary problems on its own, which would normally be by expenditure cuts. Notwithstanding high preconditions for the solidarity principle to apply, the rating agencies gave both the central government and the regional state governments their highest rating, indicating that regional states ultimately enjoy a bailout option.

For the regional state governments, shared liability significantly increased their refinancing options. Since ultimately any regional state government that enters insolvency can always count on a bailout from the central government and the other state governments, even states with extremely high levels of debt retain access to the credit market over a long period. They also receive loans with conditions that are practically the same as for all the state governments. So unless the joint credit rating of the central government and state governments as a whole falls, the refinancing interest rate does not function as a means of enforcing fiscal discipline.[24]

The result is that regional state governments in Germany are inconsistent in how responsibly they manage their budgets. There are some that fail to undertake structural consolidation, have persistently excessive level of debts and require long-term support from the central government. Saarland, Schleswig-Holstein, Bremen and Berlin are the primary examples. The different levels of debt vary far more than in the United States, a federal state system.[25]

5.1.2.2 Incentives for debt consolidation in federal and union states

Two approaches for strengthening debt consolidation incentives have been identified by observing historical trends. These two approaches are derived from the OECD's comparative study of the fiscal relationships among various levels of government in over 30 nations.[26] Both approaches are equally valid for the federal and union state systems.

The first approach is a maximum debt ceiling enforced by sanctions or a requirement to first seek permission from the central government before taking on any debt. The second approach is credible uncertainty that regional governments will be bailed out, with the financial markets realistically assessing the regional governments' debt instruments and sanctioning them with higher rates of interest if they pile up too much debt.

The first approach limits regional governments' ability to take on debt. This is achieved through statutory regulation. In contrast, the second approach is aimed at reducing the debtor governments' appetite for debt. This is a market-based strategy that uses the risk of insolvency to link the cost of credit as closely as possible to the risk of default. A no-bailout provision can only be effective in reducing the incentive to take on debt if the credit markets are efficient. But before the 2008 currency crisis, financial markets paid little attention to budget deficits and levels of national debt. After the crisis, markets became supersensitive to the levels of debt among EU member states.[27]

Unlike market-based methods of reducing the incentives to take on debt (such as using market interest rates to enforce discipline), debt limits rely on discretionary regulation. That means maximum debt ceilings are not determined by the market's actual response to debt levels. Instead they are determined by a decision of the government. Statutory debt ceilings may try to reflect economically sustainable debt levels, but they cannot reliably represent the market's concrete verdict in every case.

Figure 5.1 shows forms of fiscal policy according to the relevant principle of state organization and market orientation. On the left are the two state organization principles distinguished by shared liability. On the top are the two approaches to reducing debt distinguished by their market orientation. These categories will be used in what follows to discuss the two different approaches to reducing debt, i.e. national debt brakes and government insolvency procedures.

The suitability of each approach depends on the form of state organization that prevails. A credible no-bailout provision and government insolvency procedure are better suited to a federal state with a market economy, where regional governments' ability to take on debts is determined by their likelihood to honour them. These market-based approaches could of course be implemented in a union state, where shared liability determines the regional governments' ability to take on debt. But market-based approaches are less effective in union states, because shared

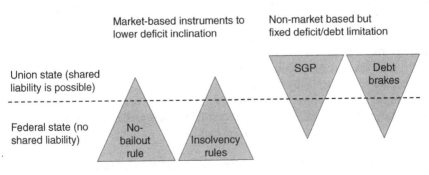

Figure 5.1 Fiscal policy arrangements.

liability produces such an outsized incentive to take on debt. So in a union state, debt limits (such as the SGP) and debt brakes are the wisest approach.

NATIONAL DEBT BRAKES

National debt brakes are not necessarily a means of coordinating fiscal policy, since each country on its own determines whether to implement debt brakes and of what kind. They can only be implemented in national law, because no international legal framework exists for implementing debt brakes. Yet the financial crisis has made the implementation of debt brakes a focus of fiscal coordination efforts. As discussed above, the Euro-Plus Pact of 11 March 2011 called for national debt brakes to coordinate fiscal policy, and demanded their implementation by member states for the first time. In the pact, the eurozone member states committed themselves

> to translating EU fiscal rules as set out in the Stability and Growth Pact into national legislation. Member states will retain the choice of the specific national legal vehicle to be used, but will make sure that it has a sufficiently strong binding and durable nature (e.g. constitution or framework law).[28]

The signing of the Treaty on Stability, Coordination and Governance in the EMU (the so-called "Fiscal Compact") made the members' commitment to implementing the debt rules in their national law even more concrete. Twenty-five EU member states have now committed themselves to adopting uniform and permanently binding budgetary rules in their national law. Although the actual implementation has been left up to the member nations, debt brakes are increasingly viewed as an appropriate method for avoiding negative fiscal policy spill-overs in the eurozone.

The development and spread of national debt brakes   National rules for limiting government debt adopted into the constitutions of the eurozone countries could complement the regulations of the SGP. There are already a great number of national rules in the eurozone that are intended to cap government debt.[29] Since the early 1990s, the popularity of fiscal rules has grown rapidly. In the beginning of the 1990s only 15 fiscal rules had been implemented. By the end of 2008, the number had risen to 67. A closer analysis of the rules shows that government spending rules were also strengthened beginning in the mid-1990s, with revenue rules following somewhat later. Still, the largest number of implemented rules are budget and debt limits.[30]

In almost all eurozone countries, however, these rules are simply normal legislation. Only Germany and Spain have added debt brakes to their constitutions.

The existing rules differ widely. They include:[31]

- expenditure rules limiting government spending (in Belgium, Finland, France, Ireland, Italy, Luxembourg, Holland, Austria and Slovakia);

- debt rules that limit the total debt level (in Poland, Luxembourg and Slovenia); and
- budget rules that limit the annual deficit (in Germany, Finland, Austria and Spain). Deficit regulations are also divided among rules that set a deficit ceiling regardless of economic conditions; zero-deficit rules that permit only balanced or surplus budgets; and cyclically adjusted deficit rules that allow higher deficits during an economic downturn.

The rules differ in how they take into account current economic conditions, in their depth (how many fiscal levels they limit), and in their breadth (how many areas of government finance, public companies and entitlements they cover). They also differ in terms of their legal foundations and implementation mechanisms. The variety of approaches here is enormous. The rules range from constitutional amendments to simple political agreements. The implementation mechanisms commonly use automatic sanctions and link budget planning with budget implementation.

Germany's budget rule is often used as an example of a debt brake. German lawmakers addressed the high incentives for debt accumulation in their union state by amending the constitution in 2009 with a debt brake. At that time, two alternatives for stabilizing debt levels were discussed: the federal state approach or the unitary state approach. In the end, a centralized approach using debt limits and debt brakes was adopted.[32] The goal was not to reduce the incentives for debt accumulation, but to limit access to credit. This approach followed historical precedent, from the Prussian State Debt Law of 1820 and the constitutional regulations of 1871, to the Weimar Republic's Article 115 and the run-up and aftermath of the 1969 finance reform. The rule resembles the SGP. Since the constitutional amendment created a binding debt limit set by the central government, it essentially brought Germany closer to a unitary state system.

The German constitutional regulations set out in Article 109, paragraph 3 and Article 115, paragraph 2 of the German Basic Law (the constitution) require that the budgets of the central and regional state governments be "in principal structurally balanced". The German regional states are not permitted to have budget deficits. The central government is permitted to annually take on new debts of up to 0.35 per cent of GDP.

If economic conditions are not "normal," the central government can take on a higher level of debt. In periods of downturn, stimulus packages financed by loans can be implemented to boost the economy (i.e. through deficit spending). It is expected that these new debts will then be entirely erased by surpluses during the next upturn. For this purpose, a control account is established that tracks when deficits over (or under) the 0.35 per cent of GDP limit are added (or subtracted). If the net balance of the control account falls below more than 1 per cent of GDP, then the excess debt must be eliminated "considering economic conditions" – meaning only during an upturn. The absolute maximum the control account is permitted to fall below is 1.5 per cent of GDP. Financial transactions (such as privatization proceeds) cannot be applied to maintaining the debt limits.

Germany's federal government must fully comply with the debt limit rules starting in 2016, with the regional state governments following in 2020. In general, there are no sanctions for violating the German debt brake (so long as there is no violation of the SGP). The laws establish a Stability Council to monitor adherence to the regulations (Article 109a of the German Basic Law). If the Council determines there is the threat of a budget emergency, it can agree on consolidation measures with a regional state government or the central government. But implementation of these measures is not binding, and inadequate implementation of them does not incur any penalties.

Table 5.1 provides an overview of debt brakes among eurozone member states. A number of countries were required to adjust their debt brakes to comply with the Fiscal Compact. In the beginning of September 2011, Spain amended its constitution with a similar debt brake in the form of a budget rule. The Spanish rules set the maximum structural deficit at 0.4 per cent of GDP, with the central government allowed 0.26 per cent of GDP and the regional governments 0.14 per cent of GDP. The exact deficit limits are not determined by the constitution. They are set by an implementation law instead. At the end of 2011 Slovakia amended its constitution with a debt brake that set the maximum national debt at 60 per cent of GDP. In 2012 Italy and France passed legislation to introduce debt brakes, as foreseen by the Fiscal Compact. France additionally implemented a "golden rule" (i.e. balanced budget requirement).

There are also countries in Europe outside the eurozone that have debt brakes.[33] Switzerland amended its constitution with a debt brake in the form of a spending regulation in 2003. The amendment was first passed in a 2001 popular referendum, winning 85 per cent of the vote. This spending regulation targets total expenditures. According to the rule, the maximum "total expenditures that can be approved" must be aligned with "expected revenues under current economic conditions". As in Germany, a control account is used to track deviations from the rule. The Swiss spending regulation has proven quite effective. Since the debt brake was put in place to control the national debt, the debt level sank from 28 per cent in 2003 to 21 per cent in 2010. Poland amended its constitution in 1997, forbidding the government from taking on debt over 60 per cent of GDP (debt rule) and requiring it to take consolidation measures before reaching the maximum limit. But this debt rule has only been moderately successful. Government debt in Poland rose from 37 per cent in 2001 to 55 per cent in 2010. Bulgaria amended its constitution in August 2011 with a debt brake. The measures consist of a combination of debt and budget rules and took effect in 2012. They require that the debt level not exceed 40 per cent of GDP and the budget deficit not exceed two per cent of GDP. In the beginning of 2011 in Hungary, the government adopted a new constitution, including a debt brake prohibiting the debt-to-GDP level to rise, and requiring it to be reduced if it exceeds 50 per cent. The debt-to-GDP is, however, allowed to rise if there is a lasting and significant economic downturn.

In the United States, Article 1, Section 8 of the Constitution gives Congress alone the power to take on debts in the name of the United States. Until 1917, each new loan had to be passed by both chambers of Congress. Due to the high level of new debt taken on during the First World War, the procedure was simplified by a law that authorized the Treasury Department to issue government bonds up to a specific maximum amount. But the issue of government bonds is still subject first to the budget passed by congress.

Economic consequences of debt brakes on incentives for debt accumulation   A critical question is to what extent these regulations have affected fiscal indicators such as deficit and debt levels. Several scientific studies have been published on the US states, the Swiss cantons, the EU member states and the OECD.[34] Current studies of the United States show that revenue, expenditure, budget and debt limits have significantly affected various fiscal indicators, particularly deficit levels. The same holds true for the US states. Although EU member states introduced fiscal rules comparatively late, studies show they have also had a significant effect. The effect of budget rules on primary deficits is particularly apparent.

Besides a general trend towards lower debt-to-GDP levels, empirical studies also point to a number of other relevant factors. Countries with debt brakes spend noticeably less than countries without limit rules, but only if the regulations are adopted in the constitution.[35] Other studies show that a combination of a strong finance minister and a weak parliament,[36] as well as popular referendums, lead to lower debt-to-GDP levels.[37] The same holds true for debt brakes adopted in the constitution (instead of formulated as simple laws) and approved by politically independent courts.[38] In addition, providing unreliable fiscal data using "creative bookkeeping" incurs higher risk premiums. The studies also show that countries that adopt strict budget and expenditure rules incur lower risk premiums, and are less likely to be "punished" by the markets with higher returns for a single budget deficit. This indicates that countries with strict fiscal rules inspire more confidence among market participants and investors. It should, however, be kept in mind that the strength and strictness of fiscal rules among the EU nations vary considerably. But dramatic steps have been taken by many countries to make fiscal rules stricter, mainly due to the Fiscal Compact. These include Italy and France (2012), Spain and Slovakia (2011), Spain again (2002 and 2003), the United Kingdom (1997), Sweden (1996 and 2000) and Holland (1994).[39]

According to the German Federal Ministry of Finance, studies across the world provide extensive evidence that establishing numerical fiscal rules can promote sustainable budget policy – and that capital markets have faith in their effectiveness. But the fiscal effectiveness of debt rules relies on credibly excluding bailout mechanisms. In this regard, the effectiveness of the German debt brake is questionable. A problem with the German debt brake is that it changes nothing about the underlying incentive structure created by the shared liability between the central government and the regional state governments. The regional state governments must balance their budgets by 2020. But deciding how that will actually happen has been left entirely up to them. There are no sanctions

Table 5.1 National budget rules in the eurozone

Country	State level	Design of rules	Since	Bindingness	Sanctions	Monitoring	Exceptions
Belgium	Region	Zero deficit	<1990	PA	Y	II	N
	Municipal	Zero deficit	<1990	LA	Y	II	N
	Social insurance	Spending limit	1992	LA	Y	II and MF	N
Germany	Federal	Cyclical deficit rule	2009	LA (constitution)	N	II	Y
	Region	Zero deficit	2009	LA (constitution)	N	II	Y
	Municipal	Deficit	<1990	LA	Y	II of Regions	N
Ireland	Federal	Spending limit	2004	LA	Y	MF	N
	Municipal	Deficit	2004	PA	Y	MF	N
Spain	Federal, region, municipal	Cyclical deficit rule	2011	LA (constitution)	Y	II	Y
	Region	Debt limitation	1980	LA, PA	Y	MF	N
	Municipal	Zero deficit	1988	LA	Y	MF	N
France	Federal, region, municipal	Cyclical deficit rule	2012	LA	Y	II	Y
	Municipal	Debt limitation	1983	LA	Y	II	N
	Social insurance	Debt limitation	2008	LA	Y	P	N
Italy	Federal, region, municipal	Cyclical deficit rule	2012	LA (constitution)	Y	II	Y
	Region	Spending limit, deficit rule	2007	LA	Y	II, MF	Y/N
	Municipal	Deficit	2001	LA	Y	II	N

Luxembourg	Federal	Debt and spending limit	1990	CA	N	No	Y
	Social insurance	Deficit	1999	PA, LA	N	MF	N
Netherlands	Federal, region, municipal	Deficit	1994	CA	N	MF	N
Austria	Federal, region, municipal	Deficit, spending limit	2005	LA	Y	Gov	Y
Portugal	Federal	Zero deficit	2002	LA	Y	MF	N
	Regions	Deficit	2007	LA	Y	MF, II	N
	Municipal	Deficit	2007	LA	Y	MF	N
Slovenia	Federal, region	Debt limitation	2000	CA	Y	MF	N
	Municipal	Debt limitation	1990	LA	Y	MF, II	N
Slovakia	Federal	Debt limitation	2011	LA (constitution)	N	II	Y
	Region, municipal	Debt limitation	2002	LA	Y	II, MF	N
Finland	Federal	Deficit, spending limit	2003, 2007	PA	Y	MF, P	N
	Region	Deficit	2001	LA	N	MF	Y
	Municipal	Deficit	1999	LA	Y	II	N

Source: Deutsche Bank Research (2010); own description; September 2012; no information available for Greece.

Notes
PA = Political agreement; LA = Legal act; CA = Coalition agreement; II = Independent institution; MF = Ministry of Finance; P = Parliament; Gov = government.

except the possibility of a suit brought by the opposition against an unconstitutional budget.[40] So the problem of enforceability remains an issue. In addition, the central government continues to be obligated to aid regional state governments with extremely high debt levels, as the FCC's 2006 decision on Berlin's budget crisis confirmed. The fact is that the central government and the regional state governments still share liability.

Moreover, the establishment of the Stability Council has not put an end to shared liability. The Stability Council will monitor the budgets of the regional and central governments until consolidation transfers begin in 2020. If a regional state government or the central government is threatened by a budget emergency, the Stability Council and the government affected agree on a consolidation programme. The programme is usually for five years. Regional governments present a report to the Stability Council every six months and work with the Council to implement other measures. Despite these reports and the regional governments' accountability to the Council, the Council cannot impose sanctions on the regional state governments. Council decisions pertaining to the regional state governments must be upheld by the central government's vote and a two-thirds majority of the regional state governments. The bottom line is that regional governments can simply ignore the ban on debt, precipitate a budget crisis and then ask for aid from the central government. The only way to counter this incentive is to end shared liability between the central government and the regional state governments, and make individual governments solely responsible, as they are in a federal state.

In conclusion, debt brakes would not be necessary if the eurozone had a credible no-bailout provision or effective budget control. But it has neither. As discussed above, the SGP has failed to produce sustainable, long-term results in budget policy. The reaction of the European bond market during the financial crisis shows that investors also continue to be sceptical about budget controls. The various rescue packages offered during the financial crisis cast serious doubt on the no-bailout provision. Finally, the efficiency of the markets (necessary for a no-bailout provision to be effective) is far from certain: at least before the crisis, bond prices responded comparatively little to budget deficits.

Debt brakes function in a way that more closely resembles the SGP than a no-bailout provision. A no-bailout provision uses market incentives to put pressure on governments to take on less debt. Debt rules and the SGP are freely chosen maximum debt limits. The analysis above has shown that market incentives relying on a no-bailout provision are weaker in a union state than in a federal state. That is because in a union state, it is assumed that liability will always be taken over by other governments in the union. Given a no-bailout provision that lacks credibility and an ineffective SGP, debt brakes are a reasonable alternative.

The European Fiscal Compact requires its signatories to introduce limits on new debt into their national law. But simply introducing debt brakes is no guarantee that a responsible fiscal policy will result. The experience with the SGP casts doubt on how credibly effective national debt brakes can be. The failure of the SGP – which is European law and therefore has precedence over national law – illustrates how essential political considerations are in determining whether a legal or constitutional norm is really binding. The SGP's failure was partially caused by the lack of an independent monitoring body. This created a political and economic incentive in the Council of Ministers to protect their mutual interest. The Fiscal Compact's regulations require that adherence to the debt brakes be enforced by an independent body.

INSOLVENCY PROCEDURES FOR STATES

Another form of fiscal policy coordination is an insolvency procedure for states. As Figure 5.1 shows, insolvency procedures are conceivable under a union state and a federal state system. Yet as a market-based mechanism, the insolvency procedure is better suited to the "market-oriented" federal state.

Debt limits seek to cap debt; a credible no-bailout policy aims to reduce a state's tendency to accrue debt. Disincentives to accrue debt are assured by several means: a non-guarantee of bailout for debtor countries; the realistic assessment of member state debt risks by financial markets; and interest premiums on excessive debt. In this purely market-based incentive structure, the existence of an insolvency procedure is essential, for without the assumption of liability by the highest fiscal authority, a procedure is needed for when debt becomes unsustainable. In this sense, the insolvency procedure is a market-based supplement to the no-bailout clause.

The insolvency of countries that belong to today's eurozone is nothing new. Since 1824, Austria, Greece, Germany, Portugal and Spain have been unable to pay their debts to creditors at least once. Greece alone has had to restructure its debts five times since its founding (1826, 1843, 1860, 1893 and 1932).[41] Most instances of de facto insolvency occurred during the time of the gold standard. Similar to the current situation in the eurozone, it was difficult for states to pay off their debts with the traditional tools of national monetary policy, including currency devaluation.

So while there have been many cases of government insolvency, Europe has yet to enact insolvency regulations for countries. The United States is the only country with a formal insolvency procedure for its territorial entities. Chapter 9 of the US Bankruptcy Code lays down an insolvency procedure for municipalities and counties. The idea of an insolvency procedure for states is not new, of course; it's been used repeatedly since the late 1970s, mostly by non-governmental organizations and churches.[42] The aim of the state insolvency procedure is to pay back creditors and unburden the debtor state, giving it the opportunity to reorganize itself economically. In addition, the procedure can increase the transparency and legitimacy of the restructuring process. Moreover, an insolvency procedure can have a clear deterrent effect, and thus help to discipline the budgetary behaviour of other states. Since an insolvency procedure forces all creditors of a debtor state to participate in debt restructuring, it can help prevent taxpayers from having to bear most of the debt (whether in the form of higher taxes or bailout packages).[43]

One of the first proposals for a state insolvency procedure to find a political and international audience was submitted by Krueger of the IMF in 2002. The IMF's Sovereign Debt Restructuring Mechanism (SDRM) posits a framework for a country with unsustainable debt to pay off its obligations in a regulated manner. According to the proposal, countries no longer able to service their debts and at risk of losing creditworthiness would submit themselves to the SDRM. While the optional nature of the SDRM ensures national sovereignty, it is designed to prevent debtor countries from postponing restructuring measures, which creates additional costs for creditors. If the SDRM is initiated, a majority of experienced creditors – grouped by type of borrowed capital – decide about the servicing of individual creditor groups. The remaining creditors are then bound by the decision of the majority. The SDRM stipulates the following terms for protecting the remaining capital of the debtor country and its creditors:

1   A temporary debt moratorium, preventing loss of capital during debt restructuring talks.
2   Creditor protection, ensuring that no individual creditor receives preferential treatment in debt servicing.
3   Separate creditor status for new capital acquisitions; restructuring measures are ultimately determined by majority decision.
4   Administration of the SDRM by the Sovereign Debt Dispute Forum, created by the modified statutes of the IMF; the Forum mediates between the debtor state and the creditors and monitors the propriety of majority decisions.[44]

The IMF proposal met with broad disapproval in the United Kingdom, United States and large parts of the private sector in 2003. It was initially viewed as a failure.[45]

State insolvency procedures differ significantly from insolvency procedures for a private company. First, the state insolvency procedure must preserve the sovereignty of the debtor country, i.e. only the debtor country should be authorized to initiate the procedure. Despite this constraint, debtor countries should have an interest in undergoing the procedure, for it allows them to recover their economic health and international standing. The second difference to a private insolvency is that the state as public debtor cannot be liquidated. Indeed, due to the challenges of assessing non-marketable infrastructure, for example, it is nearly impossible to determine the net assets of a debtor state. Third, in a state insolvency procedure, creditors may not focus on maximizing debt recovery. Instead, it must be assured that the state has a solid basis for restructuring its finances and restoring its economic health. During restructuring negotiations, for example, the debtor may not be placed under the absolute authority of a trustee (who, say, can intervene in the tax sovereignty of the country or cut public services), as this would contradict the principals of democracy and subsidiarity. Moreover, the debtor country is usually better informed than outsiders about the deficits in existing social insurance and tax systems, and should thus have a significant voice in any restructuring process. Another important prerequisite is the presence of a legal mechanism and an institution to mediate and monitor the propriety of decisions. The IMF and others have made specific recommendations in this regard.

At the end of November 2010 the Eurogroup issued a statement[46] in which it made several recommendations for the design of a state insolvency procedure. The European Council endorsed these recommendations.[47] In its statement, the Eurogroup proposed that starting in 2013, all newly issued government bonds should come with a Collective Action Clause (CAC) (i.e. a standardized and identical restructuring clause). It was foreseen that this clause would be included in the contractual language of newly issued bonds. In accordance with the ESM Treaty (Article 12, Paragraph 3) the CAC model became mandatory in all new eurozone government securities with a maturity above one year issued on 1 January 2013. The goal of the CAC is to force the private sector to bear part of the burden when restructuring government debt is necessary. During restructuring negotiations, private creditors can agree by majority decision to extend maturity dates or cut the debt owed; these decisions are then binding for the remaining creditors. Without CAC, a creditor can block a restructuring negotiation with a dissenting vote. The CAC addresses this problem. Yet in addition to regulating the restructuring, the CAC sends out a signal: creditors must now "officially" take the potential insolvency of a country into account.

State insolvency procedures have been criticized for their potential to affect a nation's entire financial system – or, as in the case of Greece, to affect all of Europe. The Advisory Council of the German government has argued against this view, pointing out that the existence of an insolvency procedure would force investors to factor in a state's potential insolvency when purchasing government bonds, either by demanding higher interest rates or reducing their exposure. The Advisory Council has also rejected the criticism that banks of an insolvent country would suffer undue difficulty in obtaining credit from the ECB. If the ECB adheres to its mandate and does not buy government bonds or only does so by demanding a risk premium, then the banks affected by an insolvent country would reduce their bond holdings. As the demand for bonds from high-debt countries decreases and the demand for bonds from countries with solid finances increases, the interest rate would once again assume its natural function on the market and create transparency between good and bad risks. This alone already serves as an incentive for countries to pursue sustainable economic activity.[48] Hence, an insolvency procedure offers a debt relief option that can have a disciplining effect on the budgetary policies of other member states, and it ensures both public and private investors are on board.

For the purposes of this study, we must keep in mind the following: state insolvency procedures are a market-based instrument of fiscal policy coordination for strengthening budgetary discipline. But they are only effective in a system in which there is no shared liability, because this is the very thing insolvency is supposed to preclude. The insolvency procedure is best suited for a federal system in which every state is responsible for itself and lending is based on each country's ability to bear debt. The insolvency procedure should be viewed as a supplement to the no-bailout rule, and as a market-based instrument for limiting incentives to accrue debt, as opposed to the SGP and debt brakes, which reduce options – but not incentives – for taking on debt.

An insolvency statute for the member states of the EU can provide a building block for fiscal policy coordination, making clear that no member state can rely on financial support from partners to protect them from insolvency. This should encourage governments to make greater efforts to achieve sound budgetary policies and avoid excessive debt. An insolvency statute would also send an important signal to investors that they must take the risk of government insolvency (and the partial loss of creditor claims) seriously. In this sense, the mere existence of an insolvency statute would have a positive effect on the budget activities of member states.

FISCAL COORDINATION THROUGH EUROBONDS

Another way of strengthening fiscal-policy coordination is the creation of a pan-EMU bond market. In the course of the government debt crisis, various Eurobond models were discussed. Frequently, the arguments for and against the Eurobonds followed political lines. The models introduced by Delpla and von Weizsäcker and the German Council of Economic Experts have achieved special prominence.[49]

Depending on their structure, Eurobonds can be more or less consistent with market incentives. My analysis will show that the most prominent Eurobond models under consideration try to maintain market incentives and establish a form of shared liability. As the categories presented in Figure 5.1 show, eurobond models contain a mixture of variable instruments that are determined by the market and fixed instruments that are determined by the sovereign state. Yet at their root, Eurobonds are better suited to a union state than a federal state system, for in the latter, the kind of collective liability provided by Eurobonds is foreign to its very essence.

The Eurobond model   Initially, the idea of Eurobonds was posited by Nauschnigg.[50] De Grauwe and Moesen have also proposed the issuance of EU-wide bonds.[51] Delpla and von Weizsäcker have presented the most elaborate scheme thus far, which features the partial joint funding of European budget deficits.[52] Yet common to all proposals is that debt liability should no longer reside exclusively with the state that assumes debt. Rather, debt obligations are shifted in whole or in part to the EMU.

The proposal tendered by Delpla and von Weizsäcker tries to dissipate concerns about the collectivization of borrowing. The aim of collective bonds, they argue, is:

1   to permit the organized return to fiscal stability despite high levels of state debt and looming crisis;

2   to encourage the effective financing of existing debts so as to avoid debt crises in economically weaker countries that are at risk of debt traps due to increasing risk premiums.

According to Delpla and von Weizsäcker, a new common debt instrument known as "blue bonds" should be created, allowing EU states to emit up to 60 per cent of their GDPs in a bond for which all member states are liable. As such bonds would carry a low interest rate, refinancing costs for EU states would fall. This new instrument would presumably be secure and solvent. The market for blue bonds would be comparable in depth to the market for US Treasury bills. Furthermore, blue bonds would guarantee member states similarly low refinancing costs. Thanks to good market liquidity and high investment security, blue-bond interest rates would likely be below current eurozone averages, yet higher than current interest rates on German bonds.[53] This prediction, however, presupposes that investors have sufficient trust in the governance mechanisms of the eurozone.

According to the proposal, for debt beyond 60 per cent of GDP, eurozone countries would issue bonds for which they alone are liable. The holders of these bonds – known as "red bonds" – would have a secondary claim to repayment behind blue bond holders. This would make red bonds more risky and more expensive than blue bonds, and their cost would be likely to increase with rising debt levels. Hence, member states would have a clear incentive to stay below the 60 per cent GDP threshold. Red bonds would be clearly associated with the possibility of government insolvency. Furthermore, in the event of such insolvency, creditors would be represented collectively (thanks to CACs), enabling debt restructuring and (partial) debt relief to be pushed through.[54]

According to the proponents of this proposal, the introduction of blue and red bonds would not only reduce the financing costs of debt levels below 60 per cent of GDP, but also create a useful instrument for encouraging member states to practise greater budgetary discipline. The higher interest rates associated with red bonds would create an incentive for states to keep their debt levels low. The disciplining force exerted by red bonds is what distinguishes this plan from proposals for a eurobond for all state debts. In the midterm, the introduction of community blue bonds would lead to lower costs for those states that would be forced to bear the brunt of a possible bailout. The division of debt into blue and red bonds would also help avoid self-fulfilling financial crises. As a spike of mistrust on financial markets would primarily increase returns on red bonds, but not on blue bonds, the speed with which a country is driven into insolvency would be slower than is currently the case.

To ensure that the low interest rates of Eurobonds are not misused for irresponsible budgetary policies, the emission of blue bonds for debt levels above 60 per cent of GDP would be forbidden. Delpla and von Weizsäcker argue that an independent Stability Council should be created that would submit to participating countries a non-negotiable proposal for emission of blue bonds for the coming year, which national parliaments would then ratify. This ratification would be necessary, since member states collectively guarantee debt. Countries that pursue a negligent budgetary policy could be pushed out of the system by limiting the amount of blue bonds they receive. What's more, this system could be outfitted with a mechanism to reward financially solid countries: if a country voluntarily does not issue blue bonds for several years, then it would not be liable for the debts of others.

One alternative to the setting of blue bond emission limits by a Stability Council would be the automatic issuance of blue bonds up to the Maastricht limit and without additional monitoring beyond the budgetary and economic policy coordination already in place. The advantage would be an avoidance of discretionary decisions about blue bonds limits, which might be politicized and lead to conflict within the eurozone. Automatic issuance makes sense in light of concerns as to whether the Stability Council would really act independently, or whether it could be influenced by individual member states.

During the introduction of the new eurobond system, the outstanding bonds of member states could be traded for blue and red bonds. Independent of the current debt level of each member state, every investor would receive blue and red bonds, such that the sum of outstanding blue bonds after exchange would be equal to 60 per cent of the member state's GDP. This bond exchange would likely be neutral or even positive in its effects for creditors, because the riskier securities (red bonds) would be counterbalanced by safer securities (blue bonds). And since blue bonds would be especially secure due to the shared liability of EU states, the overall level of risk is likely to improve, such that all investors could be expected to give their consent. The willingness of investors to approve the exchange could be expected to be particularly high in the case of old government bonds with a subordinate claim to repayment. If an investor refused the exchange, then all of his bonds would be converted into red bonds.

The European Redemption Pact In its 2011/2012 Annual Report, the German Council of Economic Experts proposed a European Redemption Pact (ERP) that takes an alternative approach to the issuance of Eurobonds.[55] The main feature of the proposed redemption fund is the temporary collective financing of state debt in EMU member countries with debt levels in excess of 60 per cent of GDP. The ERP stipulates that participating countries would receive collective financing for a period of five years (during a so-called roll-in phase). This financing would be made possible by collectively guaranteed debt securities that would be sold on financial markets. The funds obtained from issuing these securities would be channelled to the participating countries. The credit line would be predetermined before the issuance of securities, and would be based on the distance between national debt levels and the 60 per cent GDP threshold prescribed in the SGP. For instance, Italy could transfer around half of its current debt to collectively guaranteed debt over a period of five years (with liability for the rest remaining at the national level). This corresponds to just about half of the debt assumption that would be possible via the Redemption Fund (based on Italy's debt level in 2011). Other participant countries that stand to receive considerable financing would be Germany and France. The Redemption Fund proposal foresees debt repayment by participating countries at a rate based on the amount of debt taken on. The envisioned repayment period is 20–25 years, which is enough time to make the adjustment path bearable for participating member states. Given the establishment of the necessary institutional structures, the ERP promises to significantly lower interest rates on collectively guaranteed debt as compared to the interest rates that prevail on markets today.

In its proposal, the German Council of Economic Experts emphasizes that collectively guaranteed debt should not create incentives for member states to pass on debt to other member states. The proposal formulates five criteria that must be fulfilled before the funds from Eurobonds can be accessed:

1   The introduction of national debt brakes to ensure the reduction of state debt, thus eliminating incentives to speculate against EMU member states. A monitoring system should also be established to ensure national adherence to debt limits. Violations would trigger the requirement of immediate payment.

2   National debt consolidation and growth strategies to establish and support medium-term paths for debt reduction.

3   Termination of the roll-in if a country does not meet its obligations under point 2 during the roll-in.

4   A surcharge levied by participating countries on value-added tax and/or income tax that goes directly to the repayment of the Redemption Fund. Potentially, primary repayment of the Redemption Fund debt could be written into state constitutions.

5   The partial pledging of national foreign exchange reserves (20 per cent of assumed debt).

Criteria 1 and 3 are designed to oblige participating countries to lay the groundwork for long-term budget consolidation in the roll-in phase. Criteria 4 and 5 are designed to provide additional funds for covering debt repayment, thus further limiting liability risk.

According to the proposal, the interest-rate lowering effect comes from multiple sources:

1   Collective borrowing would allow for a more liquid market. Due to their larger market volume, collective debt securities would be easier for investors to trade, which would tend to lower interest rates.[56] The breadth of the market could also be increased by issuing some securities for less than the entire 25-year period of the ERP. If the maturity period is limited to ten years, as is the case with most government bonds, the breadth of the market would roughly double. A repayment over 25 years would still be possible, however: when the shorter-term securities mature, new ones would simply be issued.

2   The collective guarantee of debt in the Redemption Fund by weaker coun-
     tries and countries with high solvency (such as Germany and the Nether-
     lands) would reduce the risk of loan default compared with nationally
     guaranteed debt (e.g. of Spain or Italy alone).
3   The primary servicing of collective debt (as formulated in the criteria) and
     the pledging of foreign exchange reserves and central bank profit margins as
     collateral would also lower interest rates, further reducing the risk of default
     on collective debts.

Criticism of Eurobonds   The question of whether or not to introduce
Eurobonds or a Redemption Fund has ignited heated debate. The basic issue
concerns the extent to which the collectivization of state debt is acceptable in the
eurozone. Aside from political considerations, there are also central economic
questions related to their technical implementation and incentive effects. For
example, the model proposed by Delpla and von Weizsäcker poses numerous
technical questions related to ranking of the blue and red bonds. The establishment of an order of repayment is common in international financial markets,[57]
usually within the same issuance (e.g. with structured securities) but also with
other obligations (e.g. subordinated bonds issued by banks).[58] However, the
management of two large debt amounts with different ranks distributed over
multiple countries in accordance with the joint liability of blue bonds creates
new technical problems, including the proper demarcation of domestic debt in
the debtor state. Whether it is even possible to implement and monitor a risk
classification system for such bonds remains uncertain.

It is also clear that every collectivization of member state debt weakens the
principle that countries should be responsible for their own debts, even if collectivization provides incentives to adhere to stability criteria.[59] The collective liability
established by blue bonds in the eurozone would be similar to the current collective liability for debts between the federal states of Germany. The collectivization of debtor solvency within the eurozone would bring negative incentive effects.
Creditors would lose interest in monitoring individual euro states for solvency and
focus instead only on the solvency of the eurozone in general. And markets would
lose most of their disciplining effect when excessive debt is no longer punished
with higher interest rates. Member states in the eurozone would be able to pass off
most of the costs of additional debt to the other member states. Debt would not
primarily burden their own solvency, but the solvency of the entire eurozone.

In addition, a debt collectivization mechanism does not change the reasons
for macroeconomic imbalances. This problem is caused by the hybrid nature of
the EU, which has created a single monetary union for divergent, independent
sovereign states with their own economies, budgetary regulations and interests.
There is a divergence of economic interests regarding the transfers produced by
collectivizing external debt and liability, and such collectivization would mean
the further undermining of market mechanisms.

To repeat, Eurobonds are foreign to the liability arrangements of a federal
system, as each member state is responsible for its own debt, yet Eurobonds

collectivize a significant part of that debt. Eurobonds do make sense in a union state system, however. Indeed, the structure of the eurobond system resembles the German system, according to which the *Bund* must guarantee the debts of the *Länder*. The EU is not yet a union state, only an association of states; a central fiscal policy authority does not exist in the EU. The organs of the EU do not possess sufficient autonomous and independent budgetary or tax policy authority. In addition, the Federal Constitutional Court of Germany has come to the conclusion on multiple occasions that a transfer of authority to the EU, especially when budgetary law is concerned, is not authorized by the German constitution. Accordingly, the introduction of Eurobonds seems to depend on the existence of a fiscal union in which the EU becomes a central authority with power to determine budgetary and tax law.

The central institutional weakness of the Debt Redemption Pact arises from uncertainty as to whether its rules will be strictly adhered to over the next 20–25 years. After several years countries are likely to deviate from their debt repayment schedules or see a relaxing of the repayment terms, which would diminish the institutional credibility of the pact. Yet at the same time, fixing a binding and inflexible repayment path for the next 20 years is out of the question, as economic trends may make adjustments to repayment schedules necessary. But the problem remains that it cannot be guaranteed that countries will adhere to their repayment schedules. What is more, the implementation of the ERP seems problematic, especially with regard to mandatory tax increases, as current EU agreements do not provide for central tax collection.

5.1.2.3 Fiscal policy coordination for economic stabilization

Within the countries of the eurozone, neither monetary policy nor exchange rate policy are available as stabilization tools to counteract asymmetric shocks. The only available tool for stabilizing business cycles is national fiscal policy. The experience of recent years has shown, however, that national fiscal policy is inadequate as a stabilizing mechanism. Governments tend to pursue procyclical fiscal policies, and thus tend to intensify economic cycles on the national level rather than mitigate them. In addition, the uniform interest rate policy of the ECB further strengthens and prolongs fluctuations and divergence in economic trends between member states.[60]

In the EU there are already transfer payments between the member states that are financed by the EU budget. Yet the EU only has a budget equal to 1 per cent of GDP – a relatively low figure – and the current configuration of transfer payments between EU member countries is less aimed at offsetting economic fluctuations than offsetting long-term income discrepancies. In the United States, by contrast, the vertical financing relationships between the federal, state and municipal levels create a fiscal instrument that operates like an optimum currency area. In the United States, around 30 per cent of the expenditures of the states (including Medicaid) are made up of federal grants. Moreover, 40 per cent of revenues from local municipalities come from the states in the form of state grants.[61] A look at the monetary regimes of successful federal systems – such as the United States and Germany – shows that all use different forms of intertemporal and cross-border financial policy instruments to offset asymmetric regional shocks.[62]

A transfer system for the eurozone based on economic trends could help to even out cyclical imbalances between member countries.[63] The idea is to implement financial transfers from booming countries to those that are in recession. If a country is growing above the euro area average, that country is a net contributor which means it receives fewer payments than it pays into the compensation system. However, if a country has an unfavourable economic climate compared to the other member states, then it is a net recipient. As a result, in the former case the economy is dampened, and in the latter case it is stimulated. It is important to emphasize that the goal of this type of equalization payment is to harmonize business cycles and not to equalize the general income and prosperity of individual countries.[64]

Two versions of this economic transfer mechanism have been considered so far: direct fiscal transfer payments and indirect fiscal transfer payment through establishing Europe-wide social and unemployment insurance.

With direct fiscal transfer payments, countries would pay a part of their tax revenues that responds strongly to the business cycle (such as the revenues from value-added tax) into a collective European fund. These payments would then be distributed to member countries in proportion to their per capita potential growth rate. Countries that have a gap between real output and output potential – the so-called output gap – that is less than the average output gap in the eurozone receive more than they transfer. Countries that have an output gap that is higher than the average output gap in the eurozone transfer more than they receive. The more the economies of the member states are in sync, the fewer transfer payments are made.[65]

The advantage of such a mechanism is that it supports a countercyclical financial policy that is in harmony with the SGP. Countries that are experiencing an economic downturn – countries that receive more than they pay – can increase their fiscal expenditures without burdening their national budgets. But a problem with the direct fiscal transfer mechanism is that the determination of the output gaps and the output potentials is usually imprecise and the figures are often revised over time. For instance, the EU Commission or the OECD regularly issues forecasts about output gaps, but their calculations are always strongly corrected later.[66] Hence, transfer payments could fall short of their stabilizing and synchronizing aim, or politicians could abuse the system. Moreover, it is unclear whether stabilization fund payments to national governments can really meet demand in time. Usually, public expenditures have long planning and implementation horizons. As a result, it is almost impossible to rechannel transfers from Brussels quickly into new state expenditures or public investments. This problem can possibly be defused by obligating countries to use transfer revenues for social insurance or for debt repayment.

An alternative to direct fiscal transfer is the introduction of social and unemployment insurance at the European level, introduced parallel to national insurance systems. Assuming that unemployment has a close relationship to the economic situation of the country, a European insurance system would generate payments between member states of the monetary union in a manner similar to a direct fiscal transfer system, only in this case households – and not governments – would receive the transfers.[67]

In this system, employees pay a part of their wages into a European unemployment insurance fund; should they become unemployed they receive support from the same fund. The payments are for a limited time period and are based on earnings before unemployment. The payments should only cover *short-term* unemployment, and should be limited, say, to one year.

In contrast to the direct fiscal transfer system, a European system for social insurance and unemployment insurance has the advantage that transfer payments are fixed promptly and almost automatically and thus do not need to be calculated and negotiated. As a result, there is less room for arbitrary political decisions. The most important objection against the introduction of a European unemployment insurance fund is that it is superfluous: all member states already have welfare systems and support for the unemployed. These existing systems cushion the consequences of economic downturn on the national level and thus help synchronize economic developments in the eurozone. It is argued that if a European unemployment insurance fund were merely to replace the existing systems without creating an additional compensatory effect, it would offer no advancement over the previous system of national insurance.

Like all national social security systems, the European unemployment insurance fund has regional equalization effects. Areas with a relatively high share of people eligible for benefits receive more money than they pay into the insurance system, while regions with a relatively low share of people eligible for benefits receive less than they pay in.[68] In the start phase of this new European institution, wealth would have to be redistributed considerably – to the detriment of premium payers in countries with a lower-than-average number of short-term unemployed. There are many details about the introduction of a European unemployment insurance fund that would need to be worked out first. In particular, a mechanism must exist to guarantee the comparability of the benefit coverage and equal access across states.

We thus find that a fiscal mechanism to synchronize national economic situations in the EMU would be fundamentally desirable. For clearly, such a mechanism would represent an adjustment instrument, promoting a more perfect currency area. As discussed above, there are to date no adjustment instruments in the EMU (e.g. labour mobility, wage flexibility, fiscal transfer). An equalization mechanism could even-out economic divergences within the eurozone and, in this way, improve the effectiveness of monetary policy. In practice, however, the implementation of a fiscal equalization mechanism faces considerable challenges.

5.1.2.4 Interim findings

Incentive structures related to the handling of debt liability in a political union show that as a state's responsibility increases, the incentives for taking on debt fall and budgetary discipline increases. This is because as responsibility increases, each member state goes into debt based on its individual demand curve, while creditors set loan terms according to the likelihood a country will default. Accordingly, the incentive structure for assuming debt varies between the federal state and the union state systems. In the union state system, the priority lies in creditor protection by the community of states. In the federal state system, every member assumes debt based on its own demand curve, while creditors base their loan terms on the individual likelihood that a country will default. In the union state system demand and default likelihood are pooled together, with the risk shared among all the states, which is why the aggregate demand for credit is higher than the sum that would otherwise be individually demanded.

The degree to which instruments for reducing debt are viable and useful depends on the specific incentive structures native to the federal and union state systems. When it comes to budget consolidation, the incentivizing tools are identical in both systems: limiting the possibility of taking on debt through debt brakes or authorization requirements; as well as reducing the tendency to assume debt through a credible bailout insurance for debtor countries, a realistic risk assessment of member state debt instruments by financial markets, and sanctions for excessive debt through interest rate increases.

Against this backdrop, the fiscal forms of budgetary consolidation show varying levels of suitability as incentive instruments. The best-suited fiscal form also depends on which liability model applies. The introduction of Eurobonds and shared liability would undermine the no-bailout principle that is so central to the federal system. Eurobonds fit better with the shared-liability incentive structure of the union state system, which pools demand curves. Incentive instruments such as national debt limits, by contrast, are conceivable both under the union state and federal state systems. Yet their effectiveness depends on their binding force, especially in a union state system. Indeed, in a union state system, binding national debt limits are the only way to prevent the highest fiscal authority from assuming liability for member state debts. Here, too, debt limits are not a market-based incentive mechanism; they are set by state actors.

On a general level, insolvency procedures for states are suited for aligning the creation of debt with liability for its repayment. If the debtor is not liable for the full debt – i.e. if the debt is partly externalized – then the debtor has a greater incentive to assume debt. A formal procedure would make sense for dealing with the debt crises of territorial entities, as it ensures a credible no-bailout scenario. The American experience with Chapter 9 of its Bankruptcy Code shows that a formalized insolvency procedure provides an incentive for consolidating budgets.

My analysis has shown that different forms of fiscal policy coordination need to be discussed in connection with how liability for debts is managed. This is because the appropriateness of fiscal policy coordination depends on the organization of fiscal liability (Figure 5.1). In a union state system, shared liability is not only possible; creditors expect it. In a federal state system, shared liability is precluded. National debt limits have been imposed on all eurozone members by the Fiscal Compact and have been introduced or reformed in numerous countries. Like the SGP, the debt limit is an instrument that does not use market incentives for budgetary discipline but restricts debt through limits fixed and administered by state actors. The SGP and debt limits are thus better suited to a union state system than to the market-based federal system. The same applies to Eurobonds. Even if they try to maintain market pressure, they ultimately involve some sort of collectivization, and thus work better in a union state system.

A credible no-bailout rule and the state insolvency procedure are coordination forms that aim to create preventive market incentives for debt reduction. The insolvency procedure establishes legal certainty for debtors and creditors and provides incentives for creditors to verify debtor solvency. With its market-based incentives, the insolvency procedure is better suited for the federal state system.

Nevertheless, the utility of these findings for developing concrete recommendations for action is limited in two senses. First, the instruments I discuss fit better with either one form of state organization or the other, but they can still be used in both. For instance, the SGP and national debt limits also make sense in a system without shared liability when financial markets are inefficient and a credible no-bailout clause has no effect. Conversely, an insolvency procedure in a collectivized union state system can also provide market-based incentives for budgetary discipline. Second, the EU or the eurozone cannot be clearly assigned to either of the two forms of state organization due to its structure. In a formal legal sense, the EU is a federal state system without collectivization because of the no-bailout clause anchored in its primary law. Yet in practice the EU deviates from this principle, as the bailouts and other interventions show. Hence, all instruments of fiscal policy coordination can potentially be used in the EU, for it combines elements of the federal and union state systems.

Fiscal policy coordination instruments that aim to improve state budgets should be distinguished from coordination instruments that aim to create economic homogeneity between countries. In the first chapter I noted that the preconditions of an OCA do not apply to the EU and, due to the EU's lack of fiscal transfer, cannot be met. Given the importance of cross-border fiscal transfers in the United States, a lowering of economic heterogeneity is also desirable in Europe; indeed, it is a precondition for effective monetary policy. But the most prominent instruments – a fiscal compensatory mechanism and a Europe-wide unemployment insurance fund – encounter considerable problems with implementation.

5.2 The expansion of cross-policy coordination through macroeconomic monitoring

Until 2011 the SGP was a coordination instrument limited exclusively to the fiscal policy metric of government debt. Over the course of the government-debt crisis, however, it became clear that this narrow focus would not suffice, as the weak fiscal positions of many eurozone members are not merely attributable to excessive public debt. In 2007, for example, Ireland and Spain ran fiscal surpluses (equal to 0.3 per cent and 1.9 per cent of GDP, respectively) and had relatively low public debt-to-GDP ratios (25 per cent and 36 per cent, respectively). Nevertheless, these two states have been hard hit by the crisis. This indicates that standard fiscal indicators are not sufficient. Furthermore, more restrictive fiscal policies can sometimes help, but they are not a panacea for macroeconomic imbalances. The crises in Greece, Spain and Ireland have clearly shown that macroeconomic imbalances can lead to tensions that come to a sudden head, placing enormous strain on member state budgets. When these countries are no longer able to service their debts, financial institutes may collapse. Macroeconomic imbalances can result from, among other things, current account imbalances (such as when the value of imports exceeds the value of exports for prolonged periods) or from movements on capital markets (such as when bubbles form on real estate or stock markets).

Before 2011, neither the eurozone nor the EU in general monitored macroeconomic developments in and between member states.[69] This changed in 2011. The EU Commission now has the task of conducting systematic monitoring in order to identify and correct excessive imbalances in and between member states. Its aim is to prevent negative effects for the fiscal policy of other member states or for the economic and monetary union. The monitoring procedure will involve the regular assessment of economic imbalance based on a scoreboard that consists of several indicators, including indicators of the external position of the economy (e.g. current accounts, external debt, real effective exchange rates) and of its internal situation (e.g. private and public sector debt).

Macroeconomic monitoring in the EU is based on two regulations: the first regulation concerns the avoidance and correction of macroeconomic imbalances; the second regulation concerns implementation of measures for correcting excessive macroeconomic imbalances in the eurozone. Specific guidelines concerning macroeconomic monitoring are contained in the first regulation. Through the systematic monitoring of macroeconomic parameters, the aim is to identify and prevent excessive imbalances in and between members states. Macroeconomic imbalances are defined as "all tendencies that lead to macroeconomic developments that have or could have a negative effect on the function of the economy of the member state or the economic and monetary union in general".[70] The second regulation lays out sanctions that may be taken against eurozone states that run excessive macroeconomic imbalances and that have not taken or do not intend to take the proper corrective measures.

5.2.1 The techniques of macroeconomic monitoring

5.2.1.1 Warning mechanism

The macroeconomic monitoring procedure has two stages. The first consists of a warning mechanism to detect signs of macroeconomic imbalances early on. The second consists of a procedure for handling excessive macroeconomic imbalance that already exists in, or poses a risk for, a member state. This procedure is designed to reduce excessive imbalances or stop them from arising in the first place. During the second step, financial sanction can be imposed on member states.

The basic steps of the warning mechanism are as follows:

1   The Commission issues an annual report based on a scoreboard.[71] The report identifies the member states that are affected or are at risk of macro-economic imbalances. The ECOFIN Council discusses the report and under-takes a general assessment.[72] The Eurogroup discusses the report when it concerns euro states. The Eurogroup is an informal committee, but never-theless important. Its job is to coordinate the tax and economic policy of euro countries.

2   The Commission takes into consideration the assessments of the Council and the Eurogroup and then implements a detailed review of the member states that they believe are affected by or at risk of imbalances.[73] The full review is then published.

3   If the Commission concludes that an excessive imbalance exists, it initiates a procedure for excessive imbalance. The Commission defines excessive imbalances as "grave" imbalances, including those that endanger the "orderly function of the economy and the monetary union".[74] If the Com-mission concludes that the imbalance is not excessive, then the Council (at the Commission's recommendation) can submit recommendations for pre-ventive measures to the affected member states.[75] It is at the discretion of the Council to issue such recommendations.

5.2.1.2 Procedure for excessive imbalance

If the threshold values have been exceeded, the Council can – based on the recommendation of the Commission – identify excessive imbalance and demand that the member state submit a plan for corrective action. If these measures are not deemed to be effective, the Council can demand a new plan. If the Council rejects this second draft, the member state can – at the recommendation of the Commission – be sanctioned with a fine equal to 0.1 per cent of the previous year's GDP. The Council can reject this recommendation with a qualified majority. The proceeds from the fine go to the EFSF or the ESM. After the cor-rective action plan is approved, the Commission and the Council monitor its implementation. Euro states that fail to fully implement corrective actions must make an interest-bearing deposit equal to 0.1 per cent of the previous year's GDP, unless the Council rejects this Committee recommendation with a quali-fied majority. (This reversal mechanism by majority decision applies to all sanc-tion procedures. The affected member states themselves have no vote in the Council.) If the member state still fails to fully implement the corrective actions by the next deadline, then the interest-bearing deposit becomes a fine – again, unless the Council objects – the proceeds of which flow into the EFSF or the

ESM. By contrast, if the member state implements the corrective action plan, the procedure is halted.

5.2.1.3 Indicator selection for macroeconomic scoreboards

In the scoreboard approach, indicators assume key importance as parameters for healthy economic development. Borrowing from the recommendations of the Commission and ECB, I discuss six indicators below: (1) current account balance, (2) net foreign position, (3) real effective exchange rate based on unit labour costs, (4) real rises in housing prices, (5) public debt and (6) private sector debt. I investigate to what extent the indicators are sufficiently meaningful for macroeconomic stability and to what extent the criteria should be integrated into the binding rules and sanctions of the SGP.

ACCOUNT IMBALANCES

The current account balance describes the flow of foreign economic transactions made by a country over a single year and is considered one of the simplest indicators for determining competitiveness. The more competitive a country is, the more goods and services it exports. Economists are in disagreement about the maximum sustainable size of a current account deficit. A "sustainable" current account deficit is one that does not trigger long-term changes in the behaviour of economic subjects domestically or abroad.

Account deficits can have a variety of causes and need not be negative per se. For instance, high investment profitability in countries that are catching up in real economic terms – through interest rate differences or a higher productivity, say – can generate account deficits.[76] Developing countries with low income levels can display a "healthy" account deficit as they accrue capital for long-term profitable investment, which supports economic convergence. In such an environment, above-average output growth permits above-average wage increases. For instance, account deficits are not a problem if the financing of the current account balance occurs via so-called greenfield foreign direct investment (FDI) in the export sector. With FDI, foreigners invest in new businesses whose production serves the export sector. The export revenues then ensure debt servicing of the current account deficit. The deficit occurs because investing firms import machines and materials. By contrast, large foreign deficits that do not accompany an investment boom in the export sector are associated with a permanent rise in foreign debt.

One possible explanation for current account deficits is higher consumption, since the budgets of catch-up economies tend to consume more in the present in expectation of higher growth in the future.[77] Closely linked to this idea is the hypothesis that the account deficit depends on different business cycles – and hence, like output gaps, changes relative to the main trading partners. If this is the case, a current account deficit can only be sustained when the anticipated growth occurs early.

If one looks at eurozone data over the last decade, one can conclude that the higher inflow of capital into deficit countries that accompanies growing account deficits can hardly be explained by the increase of investment in productive capital. Even in cases when an increase in investment levels can be observed, this is small relative to the increase of capital inflow. Instead, capital inflows appear first and foremost to have financed investment in residential construction and consumption.

The CEP Default Index is a good measure to express this development.[78] The CEP assumes that net borrowing should not be used for consumer expenditure, but instead to increase physical capital stock. In other words, foreign credit should be used for capital formation, so that the returns on this capital can be used to pay off the credit's interest and principal. The index assesses the net lending and net borrowing of the total economy (NTE), and the resources used to increase the physical capital stock for a certain period. Countries like Germany, which has a current account surplus, export capital and are thus net lenders. As they do not need any foreign credits, they are not at risk of insolvency. Countries with current account deficits need foreign capital and therefore are net borrowers. To determine their medium-term creditworthiness, it is vital to know whether or not they are using the borrowed capital to increase their capital stock or for consumption. In the former case, capital returns are generated which can be used to pay back external credits. In the latter case, however, external credits are simply eliminated through consumption.

Table 5.2 and Figure 5.2 illustrate the situation in Greece and Portugal. While these countries have used their net foreign lending to increase their capital stock, in every year since 2000 the increase in capital stock has been lower than net borrowing, which means that the difference has been used for unsustainable consumption. By contrast, Germany has been a persistent net lender and, in addition, has increased its capital stock. In sum, examining net lending and borrowing as well as the use of the money borrowed from abroad yields a pattern similar to that for current account balances (Figure 5.3).

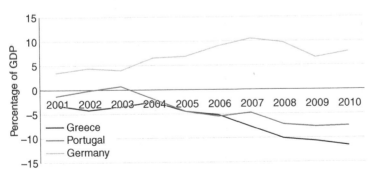

Figure 5.2 CEP Default Index: Greece, Portugal, Germany (source: Gerken and Kullas, 2011).

Table 5.2 CEP Default Index

	2001	2002	2003	2004	2005	2006	2007	2008	2009	2010
Greece										
NTE, as percentage of GDP	-10.1	-11.6	-10.8	-9	-9.4	-10.4	-13.4	-15	-12.9	-10.1
Investments increasing physical capital stock, as percentage of GDP	6.9	7.4	7.3	6.5	4.9	5.2	5.7	4.9	2.2	-1.5
CEP Default Index, as percentage of GDP	-3.2	-4.2	-3.5	-2.5	-4.5	-5.2	-7.7	-10.1	-10.7	-11.6
Portugal										
NTE, as percentage of GDP	-9.1	-6.7	-4.4	-6.7	-8.9	-9.5	-9	-11.3	-9.6	-8.4
Investments increasing physical capital stock, as percentage of GDP	7.8	6.5	5.1	4.8	4.4	4	4.2	4.1	1.9	0.9
CEP Default Index, as percentage of GDP	-1.3	-0.2	0.7	-1.9	-4.5	-5.5	-4.8	-7.2	-7.7	-7.5
Germany										
NTE, as percentage of GDP	0	2.1	2	4.8	5.2	6.6	7.7	6.7	5	5.2
Investments increasing physical capital stock, as percentage of GDP	3.5	2.3	2	1.8	1.7	2.4	2.8	3	1.6	2.6
CEP Default Index, as percentage of GDP	3.5	4.4	4	6.6	6.9	9	10.5	9.7	6.6	7.8

Source: Gerken and Kullas (2011).

Note
NTE = net lending or net borrowing of the total economy.

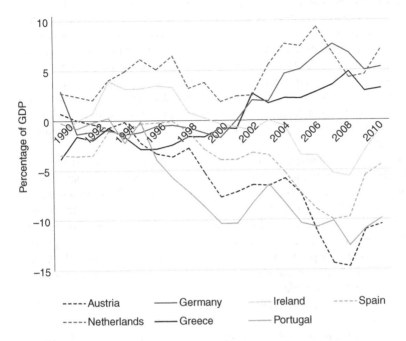

Figure 5.3 Current account imbalances (source: Eurostat).

On the other hand, a current account surplus is not necessarily positive. Increased savings in the present improve a country's foreign asset position, which can cushion future pressures from demographic change, such as in Germany or Japan. The investment of these savings abroad enables domestic savers to diversify their asset risk and to profit from higher returns in rapidly growing catch-up economies experiencing different demographic trends.[79] As mentioned, a current account surplus can be induced by capital exports, as when caused by a lack of attractive domestic investment opportunity. Accordingly, one measure to reduce surpluses that are induced by capital exports is to improve domestic investment opportunities.

In this context, we have to ask about symmetry in current account balance monitoring – whether, in other words, both surplus and deficit countries should be addressed. Also unclear is whether threshold values, as in the SGP, should be introduced, and, if so, the degree to which they should be binding. This approach fails to recognize that account imbalances are always the result of the economic policy of several countries, not just one. In the eurozone the account imbalances are the result of a highly uneven development of different demand aspects. In countries like Spain, Portugal and Greece, economic development feeds on economic growth, which in past years has been primarily due to consumption and construction. This has boosted imports, which, in turn, has contributed to a rapid rise in account deficits. In Germany, by contrast, private consumption has remained mostly stagnant. Practically speaking, its growth is driven almost exclusively by exports. As in other countries with weak domestic demand, the high growth of foreign demand has led to increasing surpluses. In part, the developments are a clear consequence of national economic policy. In Spain, for instance, real-estate tax policy fostered the construction boom. In Germany, labour market reforms and wage restraint improved competitiveness and strengthened exports while weakening consumer demand. Given these considerations, it seems best to take a symmetric approach to analysing current account balances that investigates the causes of surpluses and deficits without automatic sanctions.

As can be seen in the first annual growth report of the Commission from 2011 and 2012, the Commission appears to believe that both current account deficits and surpluses are a negative phenomenon.[80] The Commission has proposed that countries with a higher account deficit pin wages to productivity growth, as this would support competitiveness and foster structural reforms that lead to greater output. It still needs to be investigated whether and to what extent wage policy coordination based on a productivity orientation is institutionally possible. Conversely, states with high account surpluses should liberalize their service sectors and network-bounded industries.

Dullien and Schwarzer have proposed an "External Stability Pact" for the purpose of avoiding current account imbalances. According to their proposal, as soon as account deficits or surpluses exceed a threshold of 3 per cent of GDP, a procedure would be initiated comparable to the deficit procedure of the SGP – namely, warning, reduction plan, sanctions.[81] They argue that the reduction of account imbalances should remain a national responsibility. Under the proposal, sanctions (including fines or exclusion from EU projects financed by the European Social Fund or the European Fund for Regional Development) should be monitored on the European level by the European Commission (e.g. as part of the SGP procedure), but sanctions should occur automatically. The External Stability Pact does not just aim to reduce structural EMU imbalances, but also incentivize stronger economic policy coordination in the EMU and foster a stronger awareness of "common interest" without excessively restricting national authority.

The advantage of the proposal made by Dullien and Schwarz is that it reduces long-term structural problems in the EMU and its beggar-thy-neighbour conduct. What is problematic is that the legal implementation of the pact would have to be highly binding, even though account imbalances are not necessarily a negative phenomenon. Indeed, the factors that have contributed to an account imbalance are not always clear. Deficits can be a sign of economic catch-up when FDI is high, or the result of adverse unit labour prices trends. As there are many possible causes of account imbalances, the analysis that occurs when the warning threshold is exceeded must take into account a broad spectrum of factors, including real-estate sector growth, investment levels, private debt and unit labour prices. Yet in general, there is insufficient theoretical understanding of the causes and effects of imbalance. Case studies, therefore, are the best way to identify the reasons for account imbalances when the symmetric threshold values have been exceeded. This is why the EU stipulates that economic policy recommendations should be issued only after probing analysis of the country in question.[82]

A larger problem with macroeconomic monitoring is the potentially restricted room for manoeuvre at the national level for fixing the imbalance. Within the context of the SGP this limited room for manoeuvre is no problem, as the state has clear instruments at its disposal for increasing revenues and reducing expenditures. The situation is different with current account imbalances, however, as the state has few corrective instruments available, and the available instruments are often ineffective or hard to control. Tariff autonomy has mostly deprived the state of wage policy as a decisive lever for improving competitiveness. Steps to foster output occur in companies and can hardly be influenced by the state. At most the state can have an indirect effect. So, for instance, the liberalization of service markets can strengthen domestic demand, and the resulting fiscal effects can increase imports. The effect of these measures, however, may be limited or politically impossible to implement. This calls into question the punitive force of macroeconomic monitoring. How should a state be sanctioned when it is not able to influence the result? Because of the restricted options for influencing current account balances, sanctions due to current account imbalances are likely to occur considerably less frequently than is the case with the SGP.

NET FOREIGN POSITION

The net foreign position records the balance of assets that national agents (state, companies, private individuals) have abroad and all assets that foreigners have domestically.

A negative net foreign position is not necessarily a bad thing. It can occur when foreign businesses have made large direct investments in a country – similar to what can occur with current account deficits. However, the growing foreign debt of a eurozone country can be a significant problem when this debt is owed by the government. While in normal cases governments can improve their debt position by increasing taxes, if a country has a high foreign debt, this option does not apply. The country as a whole lacks the net assets to pay off its obligations.

It is also unclear whether the monitoring of net foreign position should be symmetric or asymmetric. An asymmetric threshold – i.e. a minimum negative net foreign position below which debt is unsustainable – has the advantage that a positive net foreign position usually presents no problems for the net creditor country. However, high foreign asset levels can expose creditor countries to the risk of exogenous shocks, such as economic crises in its main trading partners. This increases the risk of an economic contagion. Furthermore, a high positive net foreign position can mean a high deficit in another euro country. All these factors speak for a symmetric monitoring approach.

The risks of high net foreign borrowing have been shown empirically. As illustrated in Figure 5.4, countries that have had a high level of net foreign

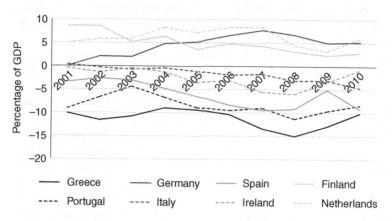

Figure 5.4 Net lending/borrowing (source: Gerken and Kullas, 2011).

borrowing in the past decade have also had difficulties refinancing in the wake of the government debt crisis. Greece, Portugal, Spain and Italy are the countries with the highest levels of net foreign borrowing in the past ten years.

This assessment stays the same even when one considers that the loans were used to expand capital stock. Above we saw the importance of a country's net foreign position, as illustrated by the CEP Default Index. In countries like Greece, Portugal, Spain and Italy, the net foreign position is problematic because foreign loans have only partly been used for investment that increases capacity (Figure 5.5). The data show that in the four crisis countries, the net borrowing position vis-à-vis foreign creditors constitutes a severe risk. A negative value in the CEP Default Index indicates that net borrowing exceeds the net additions to physical capital. Accordingly, these countries are not only consuming 100 per cent of their domestic income, but also part of their net borrowing. Such a trend

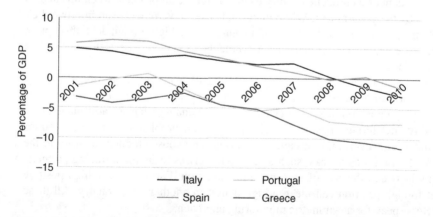

Figure 5.5 CEP Default Index: Italy, Spain, Portugal, Greece (source: Gerken and Kullas, 2011).

threatens solvency. Although there are differences between eurozone countries – net borrowing in Portugal and Greece is greater than in Italy and Spain, for example – the latter also have experienced declining competitiveness over the last ten years.

Since all four countries that have been experiencing problems on financial markets (Spain, Italy, Greece, Portugal) all have a negative value in the CEP Default Index, the net borrowing position would appear to be an indicator worthy of consideration under a macroeconomic surveillance regime.

REAL EFFECTIVE EXCHANGE RATE BASED ON UNIT LABOUR COSTS

The nominal exchange rate within the eurozone is fixed by a uniform currency: the euro. Hence, the real effective exchange rate serves as a helpful parameter for determining a country's competitiveness. This fictive exchange rate compares the prices of a consumer basket for a selection of countries. The nominal development of unit labour costs is then used to assess price development.

Eurostat calculates the real effective exchange rate for the main trading partners in the eurozone. Especially for countries of the EMU, the real effective exchange rate is an important instrument for representing relative competitiveness and its change over time. It can serve to uncover aberrations in national output or in wage levels.

The real effective exchange rate (REER) aims to assess a country's (or currency area's) price or cost competitiveness relative to its principal competitors in the euro area. Changes in cost and price competitiveness depend not only on exchange rate movements, but also on cost and price trends. The specific REER for the Excessive Imbalance Procedure scoreboard is deflated by the price index (for the total economy) against the euro area partners. A rise in the index value means a loss of competitiveness.

Figure 5.6 presents the REER since 1997. Comparable imbalances can be identified by the current account balance history. What is striking is the improvement of Greece's REER up to 2000. This likely reflects the country's efforts to meet the criteria for membership in the eurozone by 2001. In subsequent years, Greece's REER worsened. Until 2008 Ireland and Portugal showed a positive, though constantly worsening, REER. Since 2009, Ireland has been able to improve its competitiveness by running a negative REER. The competitiveness of Spain has worsened continuously. By contrast, Germany showed a negative REER, meaning it was able to consistently improve its competitiveness.

REER trends are also reflected in the growth of nominal unit labour costs (NULCs) (Figure 5.7). The NULC is defined as the ratio of total compensation of employees divided by GDP as a ratio of total number of persons employed.

Since the REER reflects the relative competitiveness of eurozone countries, an asymmetric, relative approach is advised when drawing on this parameter to assess economic development. A symmetric approach would hinder institutional competition between countries, restricting their ability to improve their relative competitiveness. Thus, a reasonable option would be to set an asymmetric

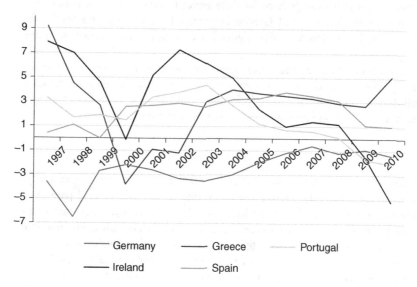

Figure 5.6 Real effective exchange rate (source: Directorate General for Economic and Financial Affairs (DG ECFIN), 16 trading partners (euro area): three-year percentage change).

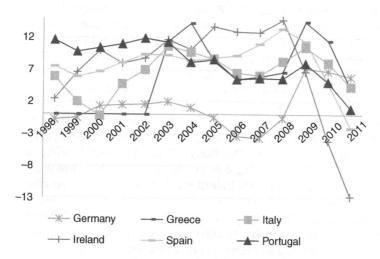

Figure 5.7 Nominal unit labour costs (source: Eurostat; figures for Greece available from 2003 only).

maximum threshold based on the inflation criteria defined in the Maastricht Treaty. Under the Maastricht Treaty, the inflation rate in a country seeking euro-zone membership may be no higher than 1.5 percentage points above the average of the three EU countries with the lowest inflation rates. A similar threshold value could be applied to REERs with the following rule: the REER should be no higher than 1.5 percentage points above the annual European-wide growth in NULCs.[83]

However, in terms of the suitability of the criterion for triggering sanctions, considerations similar to that for current account imbalances apply. Since labour costs are the main determinant of the REER, governments have only very limited influence over the REER. Wage policy is determined by unions and employers, even though governments may express their political desire for certain changes in wage trends. But there is no direct way for the government to alter the REER. Therefore, this criterion may be useful to identify certain developments and differences in competitiveness, but it is not an appropriate parameter for triggering sanctions against a country.

REAL RISES IN HOUSING PRICES

In the scoreboard, housing prices are measured as the change in prices in housing markets relative to the change of the final consumption expenditures of households and non-profit institutions serving households. A positive value means that housing prices are growing faster than the growth in consumer spending.

As the crises in Spain and Ireland have shown, economic bubbles can cause account imbalances in financial and real estate markets. In the case of a real estate bubble, housing prices increase disproportionately, and added value growth shifts from the tradable sector to the non-tradable sector. For this reason, it is advisable to include this indicator in the macroeconomic scoreboard. The correction in the housing market over the past years is illustrated by Figure 5.8. In Greece, Spain, Ireland and Denmark, housing prices have decreased significantly.

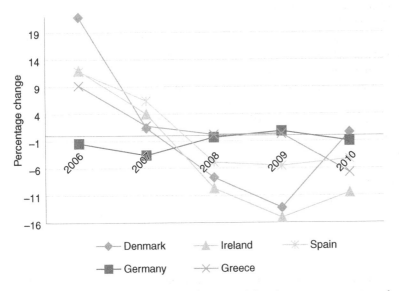

Figure 5.8 House price index (source: Eurostat, deflated, one-year percentage change).

Yet it remains unclear if a threshold value for real estate price growth can be effectively defined, beyond which harmful effects can be assumed to necessarily occur. Researchers have proposed a maximum annual price increase of 6 per cent,[84] but any specific upper limit is arbitrary, as the clear identification of price bubbles in real estate markets or other capital markets is fraught by difficulty. Economists have been trying for some time to develop metrics for the identification of excessive real estate prices, but the impossibility of determining the "true" price for a product mean their prospects for success are virtually nil. More so than with other indicators, a variety of supplemental factors must be taken into consideration when assessing real estate prices, including the geographic scope of housing price increases (regional or general?), the market for real estate construction financing and construction permit application activity. A preliminary database for the analysis of real estate price trends has been compiled, but the entire euro area has yet to be covered.[85]

PUBLIC SECTOR DEBT

Public debt is the only indicator used for fiscal monitoring under the SGP. Public debt is usually set in relation to economic output. High levels of public debt can adversely affect competitiveness and prospects for growth. In addition to an increased tax burden for households and business, high levels of public debt mean higher interest payments, which increasingly undercut the government's ability to invest in projects that promote growth (e.g. infrastructure, education). Moreover, higher public debt loads can depress private sector investment, as government borrowing leads to a crowding out of investment. Furthermore, public debt can depress consumption if consumers anticipate that debt levels will lead to higher future tax rates or depressed growth.[86]

To assess whether a public debt indicator is useful, it makes sense to ask whether it would have given warning of the most recent crisis. While trends in other areas (e.g. net foreign liabilities, trade deficits, housing prices) foreshadowed the current crisis, for public debt this is not the case. As Figure 5.9 clearly shows, government debts did not begin to rise until the financial crisis erupted and the government began to take over private debt. The prime examples are Ireland and Spain, which until 2007 had exemplary performance under the criteria of the SGP, with sinking public debt levels. Thus, as discussed above, public debt levels alone are not a sufficient indicator for representing imbalances within Europe.

Nevertheless, it makes sense to use a symmetric, absolute threshold value in the case of public debt. The discussion about threshold values has been discontinued because the Maastricht Treaty already prescribes a limit of 60 per cent of GDP.

PRIVATE DEBT

This indicator measures the debt held by households and businesses. Usually, private debt is measured relative to GDP. Private saving rates and debt levels

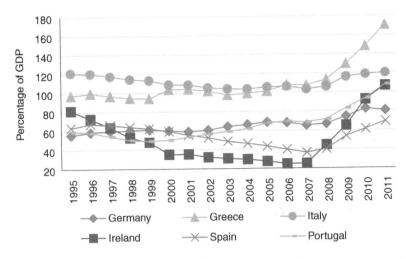

Figure 5.9 General government gross debt (source: Eurostat).

vary from country to country in the EMU and are determined, in part, by historical circumstances. In any event, an excessive level of private debt over time and/or in comparison to other countries is generally a good indicator of the misallocation of capital. Excessive debt frequently indicates that a country's interest rate in previous years was low, promoting debt accumulation. One consequence of low interest rates may be overspeculation in capital and real estate markets, creating high risks for the financial sector and, ultimately, for public coffers.

Figures 5.10 and 5.11 show rising private debt levels over the past decade. In almost all EU states except Germany, private debt has risen since 2001. Between 2001 and 2007, private debt levels increased in Greece by 65 per cent, in Spain by 62 per cent and in Ireland by 44 per cent. When the bank crisis erupted, private debt increased even more.

Considering the foregoing observations regarding current account imbalances and net foreign liabilities, one must conclude that the higher capital influx into high-deficit countries that accompanied growing trade deficits can hardly be explained by increased capital investment. Even in cases where an increase in capital investment can be observed, the rise is small relative to the overall increase in capital flows. Thus, capital flows to high-deficit countries seem to have primarily financed investment in housing construction and consumption. Yet the enormous growth of real estate investment – which could not be sustained and fell abruptly with the onset of the economic crisis – must be seen in retrospect as wholly negative. For one, the real estate boom caused enormous problems in the banking sectors of the affected countries. For another, resources and labour went into the construction of housing units that now stand vacant. And since it is difficult to retrain construction workers for other careers, structural unemployment has risen sharply. The cause of the construction boom was

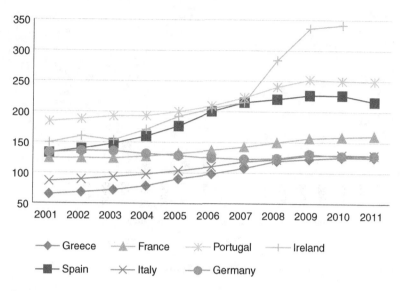

Figure 5.10 Private debt as a percentage of GDP (source: Eurostat).

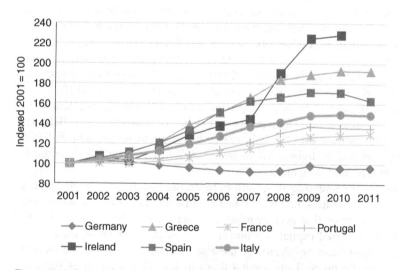

Figure 5.11 Private debt index (source: Eurostat).

not rational decisions about saving and investment, but hyperinflated housing prices, which stimulated new construction. The housing market bubble was thus an important source for some of the imbalances, at least in some of the high-deficit countries. Ultimately, the low real interest rates were responsible for increased consumption and housing investments, both of which drove up private debt.

Yet as an indicator private sector debt levels are by definition backward looking. For this reason it is advisable to examine the growth of private debt over time instead of merely its current level. Debt growth tends to correlate procyclically with economic growth. A threshold criterion for private sector debt should thus take nominal GDP growth into consideration, and not just current debt levels. Accordingly, an asymmetric and relative upper limit is advisable.

Yet it is unclear how a relative threshold based on quartiles could be implemented. In the approach proposed by the Commission in June 2010, quartiles result from the totality of growth rates of all countries over a prolonged period. The upper quartile value – 75 per cent of the distribution – represents a relative, asymmetric maximum value. A preliminary assessment of debt growth in the private sector (budgets, non-financial companies and non-profit organizations) for all euro countries since 2000 yields a value of just over 10 per cent for the upper quartile of the distribution.[87]

While this value is far above the nominal growth trend for euro countries, it need not be seen as excessive in all cases. A country-specific analysis would be needed to determine the exact causes of excessive credit expansion. For instance, if debt growth is due to real economic catch-up processes or financial deepening in individual countries, a high level of debt growth could be considered sustainable. However, if the growth is due to a generally low interest rate level or an asset price bubble, this assessment would not apply. Conversely, a low level of debt growth can be caused either by low domestic demand or by export-driven growth.

These remarks show that the quartile method proposed by the Commission – with relative threshold values – must give more consideration to country-specific and context-related factors than to indicators based on absolute threshold values. Especially problematic with regard to the quartile method is that past aberrations can lead to a misaligned threshold. If the growth trend demonstrated by the indicator is excessive, then the quartile approach tends to underestimate potential risks. One alternative would be to compare long-term average nominal growth with long-term average debt growth. But this would also miss the mark, since it would make a medium-term reaction to undesirable trends more difficult. To determine the exact maximum threshold level, further analysis is required, but such work lies behind the scope of this book.

5.2.1.4 Assessing the indicator approach for macroeconomic monitoring

In general, the tensions that arise from macroeconomic imbalances in the eurozone can be approached in three ways. The first approach (1) seeks to finance macroeconomic imbalances in the long term. By contrast, the other two approaches (2 and 3), seek to reduce macroeconomic imbalances. These approaches differ, however, on whether the market or government policy should coordinate the reduction:

1   Member states could agree to cement macroeconomic imbalances instead of reducing them. An unwillingness to undertake the necessary reforms is one clear reason for pursuing this option. The need to reduce macroeconomic imbalances can be circumvented if Europe becomes a "transfer union". Accordingly, countries with account surpluses would finance consumption in countries with account deficits. The decisive question is whether such an arrangement would be accepted by the richer countries that have to finance these transfers.

2   Member states that want to reduce macroeconomic imbalance could let markets do the necessary work. In this case, far-reaching reforms would be needed, as macroeconomic imbalances in the eurozone can be reduced only via reforms on product, capital and labour markets, or by reducing loan availability through higher interest rates in states with excessive debt levels. But as the examples of Greece, Spain and Ireland show, reforms and cost-cutting measures can lead to excessive burdens being placed on the populace, and trigger considerable political instability. From a political and economic perspective, this is highly problematic. Affected member states can only alleviate the burdens posed by needed reforms by reverting back to national currencies, as adjustments to the exchange could partially replace the need for real reform. Yet the political decisions made since 2010 for supporting ailing euro states have made a return to national currencies unrealistic at this time.

3   Macroeconomic imbalances can also be reduced by policy coordination, as proposed by the Commission as part of its macroeconomic monitoring regime. This method also requires reforms to the product, capital and labour markets, but it has two advantages over market-based coordination alone (approach 2). First, the necessary burdens for reducing macroeconomic imbalances can be distributed over multiple member states. This is possible since macroeconomic imbalances often occur in two or more member states (e.g. a trade deficit in one country almost inevitably means a related trade surplus in another). Accordingly, the reduction of macroeconomic imbalances can take place in both countries at once. The advantage here is that the burden of reducing macroeconomic imbalances can be shared by several countries. Countries with account deficits would need to improve their competitiveness, while countries with account surpluses would need to strengthen their domestic demand by liberalizing their service sector and increasing consumption. In this way, the burdens of reducing macroeconomic imbalances could be divvied up. With purely market-based coordination, by contrast, the countries with a current account deficit must carry the entire reform burden alone.

Thus, removing macroeconomic imbalances through the new mechanism appears to offer the advantage of allowing the burden of adjustment to be split between surplus and deficit countries. The political logic here is that an onerous need for adjustment in one country can be avoided.

However, the foregoing analysis has demonstrated that the macroeconomic imbalance procedure has a number of shortcomings, particularly from the perspective of institutional economics. First, the country subject to recommendations and sanctions may not be the same country that caused the imbalances. Furthermore, a country's balance of payments and relative exchange rates (i.e. key parameters for the competitiveness of the economy) cannot be effectively managed by the government. Sanctioning a country for negative trends in these parameters thus does not appear to be appropriate.

Second, the perspective of institutional economics also tells us that efforts to assure symmetry in these parameters would reduce the ability of economies to compete with one another. A current account surplus may be caused by a number of factors, including wage trends and private sector innovation. Incentives for improving competitiveness would be reduced by regulations to ensure symmetry between countries in these areas.

Third, it is doubtful whether the scoreboard can accurately identify macroeconomic imbalances. This is particularly true with a view to price bubbles on real estate or other capital markets. Economists have been trying for some time to develop metrics to identify excessive real estate prices, but the impossibility of determining the "true" price for a product mean their prospects for success are virtually nil.

Fourth, macroeconomic imbalances are not negative per se; every imbalance requires subsequent interpretation. Economies – especially catch-up economies – can show account deficits when they import investment goods and finance these through foreign exchange deficits. Developed economies are usually ready to grant loans, since catch-up economies offer high growth rates and, with them, high yields. In many cases, such imbalances pose a risk for a country's fiscal policy. For this reason, it is right that the Commission does not base the determination of macroeconomic imbalance on the scoreboard alone. Rather, it first subjects the member state in question to a more detailed analysis. This analysis can have a considerable impact on the Commission's recommendations. For example, if Germany's longstanding account surplus was attributed to the fact that its relative competitiveness is markedly higher than countries with account deficits, then the Council would direct its recommendations to countries with account deficits, calling on them to increase their competitiveness by suppressing wages. A current account surplus is always accompanied by capital exports, since countries with account deficits must finance the import surplus with foreign loans, i.e. with the import of capital. Accordingly, Germany's current account surplus might also be attributable to capital exports, i.e. due to a lack of attractive investment opportunities in Germany. Thus, if the Commission believes that account imbalances have been induced by capital exports, then its reform recommendations would be directed at Germany, instead, with a call to improve domestic investment opportunities. In such a case, countries with low competitiveness would not need to undertake reform measures.

Because of uncertainty about the source of imbalance, it would seem to make sense for the Commission to refrain from the "automatic" interpretation of the scoreboard. Instead, it should consider all data in context and as part of a comprehensive analysis, regardless whether specific metrics are part of the scoreboard or not.[88]

Fifth, scoreboard approaches are per se backward looking. As the product of historical developments, macroeconomic tensions are an endogenous factor in scoreboard design. This endogeneity distorts the objective assessment of the ability of monitoring instruments to identify negative trends. Another limiting factor is the long time span between indicator analysis, policy recommendation, imbalance correction and sanction. For this reason, effective economic policy management is possible at most over the longer term.

All in all, the macroeconomic imbalance procedure is the first form of binding cross-policy coordination in the EU that includes cross-border coordination (see Figure 5.12). As such, it is a useful complement to the SGP, which is limited to fiscal parameters alone. Nevertheless, the scoreboard is in need of improvement. Specifically, the warning thresholds and manner with which scoreboards are implemented into existing processes of economic policy coordination must be defined more precisely. In an ideal case, the scoreboard would complement the implicit coordination brought about by capital market pressure. Recent years have shown that capital markets do not always react rationally. A macroeconomic scoreboard can increase transparency and thus help markets to take appropriate action (e.g. increased risk premiums). Yet it would appear that the proposed scoreboard approach can influence member state economic policies over the medium term at best. The scoreboard could be a good way to create information transparency and exert political pressure. Moreover, it would be a convincing sign that eurozone countries will take their coordination more seriously in the future.

5.2.2 *The Europe 2020 strategy*

The EU's Europe 2020 strategy represents a new type of economic policy coordination. The successor to the Lisbon Strategy, Europe 2020 is "based on

		Horizontal coordination	
		Cross-border coordination	**Cross-policy coordination (fiscal, monetary, wages)**
Vertical coordination	**Soft coordination**	Macroeconomic dialogue; BEPG; Luxembourg Process	
	Hard coordination	**Macroeconomic imbalance procedure**	
		SGP	
	Centralized coordination	Monetary policy	Bonds purchases by ECB or ESM

Figure 5.12 Fiscal policy arrangements.

initiatives aimed at intelligent, sustainable, and inclusive growth in the European Union" by increasing "employment, productivity, and social cohesion". The Commission defines five core objects to be achieved by 2020:

- to raise the labour participation rate of the population aged 20–65 from the current 69 per cent to at least 75 per cent;
- to increase investment in R&D to 3 per cent of GDP;
- to reduce greenhouse gas emissions by at least 20 per cent, increase the share of renewable energy in final energy consumption to 20 per cent and achieve a 20 per cent increase in energy efficiency;
- to increase the share of the population having completed tertiary education to at least 40 per cent and to reduce the share of early school leavers to 10 per cent; and
- to reduce the number of Europeans living below national poverty lines by 20 million people.

Given the aim of this study, it is reasonable to ask whether these objectives require EU-level coordination. I have argued that such coordination should be employed when an isolated national economic policy leads to external effects, or when economies of scale justify EU-wide coordination. For four of the five core objectives – in the fields of labour policy, R&D, education and poverty – the need for coordination based on these criteria is weak. There are neither appreciable external effects nor economies of scale that would justify Europe-wide coordination. The area of education policy shows this most plainly. The lack of need for uniform coordination in demonstrated by the German national case: educational policy is decided at the state, and not the federal level. Less clear is the question of whether the EU should issue uniform targets for R&D spending. In the area of basic research one might argue that some member states benefit from the discoveries of other member states without contributing to them financially. Yet institutions that conduct basic research generally only contribute to the innovation efforts of companies in the immediate region. Accordingly, the incentives for countries to "freeride" off others are generally low. As a result, a Europe-wide R&D spending target makes little sense.

Particularly in the absence of external effects and economies of scale, coordination regimes threaten to ignore the preferences of individual member states, and restrict institutional competition. Thus, instead of fixing uniform targets for all member states, it would appear better to encourage information exchange and mutual learning between member states based on existing channels of communication. The only area in which EU-wide coordination should be little cause for concern is environmental policy. This is because the positive externalities generated by national environmental protection efforts to reduce greenhouse gases are not sufficiently incentivized. It is unnecessary, however, to stipulate that a certain share of energy be produced by renewables. For efficient environmental policy, it is enough to cap greenhouse gas emissions. And the market should be responsible for choosing how best to do it.

As part of the Europe 2020 strategy, every EU state has been asked to translate the strategy's objectives into national goals, allowing for due consideration of each country's particular circumstances. The Integrated Guidelines for Economic and Employment Policies requires that every member state identify critical areas and initiate appropriate action through national reform programmes. The Commission can issue policy recommendations, though these are non-binding. What is more, the Europe 2020 strategy is now coordinated with the budgetary aims of the European Semester, as I explain in the next section.

5.2.3 The European Semester

The European Semester is another form of coordination. Put into force on 1 January 2011, the European Semester grew out of the Europe 2020 strategy and the reform of the SGP. The goal of this measure is to coordinate and monitor the budgetary and economic policy of member states more proactively. The European Semester was created to identify and correct macroeconomic imbalances, especially differences in competitiveness and debt, and to ensure that member state reforms serve the ends of Europe 2020. For instance, the European Semester temporally aligns the annual coordination cycles of the SGP with Europe 2020, even as they remain formally and legally separate. The integrated annual control cycle assembles multiple aspects of EU economic policy monitoring, including measures to ensure budgetary discipline, macroeconomic stability and growth promotion. Hence, the European Semester expands the coordination introduced by Europe 2020 for the five objectives named above by harnessing the budgetary monitoring procedure of the SGP. In this way, the Council can issue proactive recommendations that consider a variety of spheres and interdependencies.

The European Semester is designed to work as follows:

- In January the Commission submits an annual growth report presenting the economic challenges faced by the EU and the eurozone. In its first report, issued on 12 January 2011, the Commission presented ten priority measures to the EU's member states.[89] The report has three areas of focus: macroeconomic stability (particularly budgetary consolidation), labour market reforms and growth promotion. The wide range of economic policy measures taken into consideration underscores that the Commission is pursuing cross-policy coordination.
- By the end of February, the European Council must ratify the general guidelines formulated by the Commission. These guidelines must then be reviewed by member states when drafting Stability and Convergence Programmes and National Reform Programmes. The purpose is to guarantee the compatibility of member state economic policy plans.
- By mid-April, the member states must update their Stability and Convergence Programmes as well as their National Reform Programmes, with the former offering projections about budgetary plans for the following year. If the budgetary plans are inadequate, a revision can be recommended.

- At the beginning of July the Council ratifies the country-specific guidelines formulated by the Commission. The guideline recommendations are based on the Stability and Convergence Programmes, the National Reform Programmes and the results of macroeconomic and policy area monitoring.[90]
- Recommendations in the area of fiscal policy are then issued for the following year.
- Key reforms can be recommended, and deadlines set, for growth promotion and the reduction of macroeconomic imbalances.
- In the second half of the year, the member states finalize their budgetary plans for the following year.
- In the annual growth report from the subsequent year, the Commission assesses how well member states have followed guidelines.

The establishment of the European Semester has expanded the scope of economic policy coordination in the EU. First, it creates a link between the implementation of Europe 2020's aims and the fiscal policy requirements of the SGP, interweaving economic and social policy recommendations with fiscal policy recommendations. The recommendations address a variety of subjects, including public finances, structural renewal for tax policy and labour market questions (e.g. youth unemployment). Second, the EU is no longer restricted to issuing economic and fiscal policy aims. It now also advises national governments on specific measures to reach these aims. Regarding labour market policies in Germany, for example, the Commission expressed concern about the low

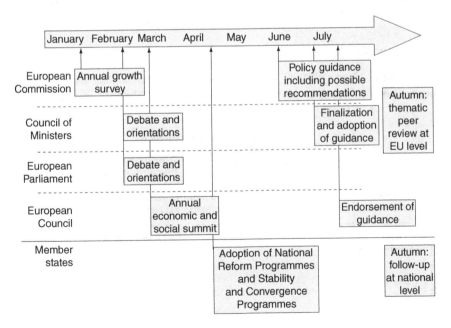

Figure 5.13 European Semester of policy coordination (source: European Commission).

full-time participation rate for women in the labour force. Fiscal disincentives for second earners and the lack of full-time childcare facilities and all-day schools hinder female labour market participation. Moreover, regarding tax policies the Commission stated that fiscal disincentives arise from a high tax wedge, which is particularly attributable to high social security contributions. This tax wedge leads to high unemployment, particularly among low-skilled workers.

We thus see a clear effort to consolidate, synchronize and expand existing forms of coordination. The avowed aim is to stop fiscal and economic policy isolation and align policies with each other. The European Semester is a form of coordination that is both cross-border and cross-policy (see Figure 5.14). It is cross-border in that the Commission centrally evaluates national policies and checks them for complementarity and, if needed, adjusts them. It is cross-policy in that it links economic policy recommendations with fiscal policy recommendations. Viewed vertically, the coordination can be categorized as "soft": its recommendations are non-binding; the only way it can force states to adhere to its recommendations is through peer pressure, i.e. "naming and shaming".

The linkage between the aims of the SGP and Europe 2020 can, however, adversely affect the consistent enforcement of SGP budgetary guidelines. This is because the political recommendations for budget planning no longer need to concentrate on adhering to stability criteria. The instrumentalization of member state budgetary planning for implementing the Europe 2020 strategy cannot be ruled out. The comingling of economic and fiscal policy recommendations could easily lead to a special status for certain budget outlays, potentially making the enforcement of stability criteria more difficult.

5.2.4 The Euro-Plus Pact

The Euro-Plus Pact (EPP) is a political control instrument that, unlike other coordination forms, has an intergovernmental character. The EPP covers almost

| | | Horizontal coordination | |
		Cross-border coordination	Cross-policy coordination (fiscal, monetary, wages)
Vertical coordination	Soft coordination	Macroeconomic dialogue; BEPG; Luxembourg Process; EU 2020 strategy; EU semester	
	Hard coordination	Macroeconomic imbalance procedure	
		SGP	
	Centralized coordination	Monetary policy	

Figure 5.14　Classification of coordination.

every area of economic policy. The member states are responsible for its implementation, and reports issued by the Commission provide for monitoring. While the EPP has many points of overlap with the other coordination initiatives, its binding force lies far behind the others; in truth it is nothing more than a "gentlemen's agreement" among government ministers.

The EPP was adopted at the EU-27 European Council meeting on 25 March 2011. Its membership includes 23 EU member states – 17 eurozone countries and six non-eurozone countries (Bulgaria, Denmark, Latvia, Lithuania, Poland and Romania). Hence the name "Euro Plus".

The EPP's general aim is to strengthen the economic pillars of the EMU. This new thrust to economic policy coordination is designed to improve competitiveness and promote business-cycle convergence. The EPP concentrates on areas that fall under member state authority and that are important for increasing competitiveness and avoiding harmful imbalances.

Despite these aims, the EPP fails to clearly demarcate itself from other forms of coordination. Furthermore, it fails to provide any clear extra value. The EPP begins by issuing guidelines intended to explain its relationship to other forms of coordination in the EU. First, it is stated that the EPP is in harmony with existing economic EU policy oversight (Europe 2020, the European Semester, BEPGs, SGP), and that it serves to strengthen them by providing additional utility. Second, it is stated that the EPP concentrates on the policy domains that are important for promoting competitiveness and convergence (e.g. wage policy). Third, a call is made for government ministers to commit themselves each year to fulfilling national obligations. EU government ministers are to monitor EPP goal fulfilment on the political level based on reports provided by the Commission.

The EPP specifies four concrete aims. The primary aim is the promotion of competitiveness. To this end, wage and productivity growth are to be assessed with a view to competitiveness. Furthermore, a productivity-oriented wage policy is to be sought that preserves the bargaining autonomy of management and labour (tariff autonomy). The EPP also endorses a wage policy of restraint in the public sector, and advocates increasing productivity by liberalizing protected sectors and increasing expenditures in education and research. The second avowed aim of the EPP is to promote higher employment through functional and flexible labour markets; the passage of reforms that lower taxes on labour; and the harmonization of corporate taxes. The third aim is to ensure the sustainability of public finances, especially the long-term funding of pensions, healthcare and welfare. It also calls for ensconcing SGP rules in national law, such as debt brakes (as already implemented in Germany). The EPP's fourth aim is to strengthen financial stability by, among other measures, carrying out bank stress tests and setting up effective financial market oversight.

As mentioned above, the intergovernmental and non-binding character of the EPP makes it a "soft" form of coordination that extends over a variety of policy areas (cross-policy coordination; see Figure 5.14). Because it lacks a sanction-based monitoring system, however, its scope and binding force is less than that of other forms of coordination. Nevertheless, it has much in common with them: increasing competitiveness is already part of the new macroeconomic monitoring system of the SGP; its employment aims can be found in Europe 2020; and ensuring the sustainability of public finances is already a part of the SGP.

5.2.5 Cross-policy coordination for credit lines with attached conditionality

The conditional credit lines extended to embattled eurozone states during the crisis represent a form of cross-policy coordination. Although the programme is designed to preserve a country's liquidity (or solvency, depending on the interpretation) and thus belongs to fiscal policy, its conditionality is not limited to measures for consolidating budgets; indeed, it extends to all areas of economic policy. In this way, the EU acknowledges that the causes of crisis in each country do not lie solely in fiscal policy, but are also connected to broader structural factors. The enumeration of measures offered below highlights the comprehensive reform approach pursued in the case of Greece.[91] Tax increases and expenditure cuts make up the fiscal policy core, and are directed towards budget consolidation. Yet additional measures aim to reform Greece's labour market, especially the wage-setting process, to encourage greater wage flexibility. The programme's reforms even extend to the public service sector, and seek to make administration more effective and transparent. The structural reforms contained in the programme include changes to the Greek pension and health insurance systems.

Attached conditionality for Greece's loan assistance programme

1   Budgetary measures

- Tax increases (value-added tax, gasoline tax, duties on alcohol, tobacco, gambling, fines on illegal construction and use) and spending cuts (wage cuts for public servants, reduction of pension entitlements, fewer investment expenditures), totalling €30 billion in annual savings, starting in 2014.

2   Labour market:

- Reform of the wage-setting process in the private sector: reform of tariff negotiations in the private sector; provisions for wages to rise more slowly in certain regions than agreed on for the sector as a whole; introduction of variable wage components so as to align wages more strongly with company productivity.
- Relaxing dismissal protections: extending the trial period for new employees to a year; reducing severance packages during lay-offs; increasing the minimum requirements for activating regulations that permit mass lay-offs, especially for larger companies; loosening rules for temporary labour contracts and part-time work.

- Reform of minimum wages: permitting below minimum wages for special groups such as new entrants to the labour force and the long-term unemployed; freezing minimum wages for three years.
- The flexibilization of working hours: introduction of annual working-hour accounts and the reduction of bonuses for overtime.
- Fighting under-the-table employment: tightening oversight, tightening rules for registering new employees.
- Ensuring welfare coverage: redistributing welfare to help those most in need.

3 Public services:

- Payment system: establishing a central payroll service; reforming the payment structure so as to better differentiate wages according to performance and responsibilities.
- Procurement: establishing an electronic platform for all sectors and levels for contract bidding/auctions.
- Transparency for all expenditures: online publication of all state expenditure decisions.
- Regional administration reform: transfer of responsibility and means via the proper authorities.
- Independent review of central government: external audit of its organization and operation.
- Better regulation: reducing administrative barriers.

4 Pension reform:

- Increasing legal age of retirement to 65 for all employees, even for those employed since before 1 January 1993, and for female public servants; stronger ties between benefits and contributions; pension amount to be calculated by the average wages for all years of pension contributions, not just the last five; price indexing of pensions; introduction of corrective factor for rising life expectancy; increasing the minimum years of contribution from 37 to 40 by 2015.

5 Healthcare reform:

- Complete reformation of the system: adding double-entry bookkeeping, operational oversight and the publication of audited annual reports.

6 Economic regulations:

- Loosening rules for start-ups; simplifying and accelerating the licensing of companies, industrial activities and professions; tax relief for mergers and acquisitions; implementing service guidelines for key sectors: tourism, retail and education; opening closed professions; liberalizing goods transport by road; train service reform; liberalizing the energy market; increasing the requests for EU money from the structure and cohesion fund.

These comprehensive reform conditions reflect the EU's continuing attempts to acknowledge the interdependencies between policy areas and to make them the basis for greater competitiveness. This approach is clearly evident in the Europe 2020 strategy and in the European Semester. Thanks to its strong bargaining position, the EU has been able to persuade recipient states to accept the reform requirements attached to credit extension.

The reform requirements associated with loan extension are an example of cross-policy coordination, as assistance (which is a fiscal policy measure) is directly linked to wage and structural policy reform. Yet it is also an example of cross-border coordination: the reform requirements are designed to reduce the negative spillovers affecting other countries. Budget stabilization and structural reforms seek to reduce negative effects on the stability of the euro, on the financial markets and on the general prospects for growth in the EU. Due to the conditionality of the credit extension, it can also be classified as a hard form of coordination (Figure 5.15).

5.3 Expanding wage policy coordination

My previous analysis has shown that wage policy generates cross-border externalities for other national economies (Section 3.3.1.2) and also exhibits interdependencies with monetary and fiscal policy (Section 3.3.2.2). Wage policy has cross-border effects on inflation, and thus on the common currency and on the ECB's interest rate policy. In addition, wage policy affects a member state's industrial competitiveness, and thereby has a direct effect on the competitiveness of producers in other countries. Expansive wage behaviour can set off cross-border effects on demand. Conversely, a restrictive wage policy may well strengthen one country's price competitiveness, but also can lead to lower aggregate demand in the EU as a whole.

		Horizontal coordination	
		Cross-border coordination	Cross-policy coordination (fiscal, monetary, wages)
Vertical coordination	Soft coordination	Macroeconomic dialogue; BEPG; Luxembourg Process; EU 2020 strategy; EU semester	
	Hard coordination	Macroeconomic imbalance procedure	
		SGP	
		Conditionality on rescue programmes	
	Centralized coordination	Monetary policy	

Figure 5.15 Classification of coordination.

Despite these interdependencies that exist between wage policy and other policy areas, the question of whether a horizontal form of coordination is needed in the form of an overarching policy of coordination between monetary and wage policy remains highly contentious. Neoclassical and Keynesian doctrines collide with each other in this area. Thus, in the following section I will first examine the need for wage policy coordination, and then explore possible ways to configure such coordination. First, I will show that wage and monetary policy are interdependent, and illuminate the inadequacy of the current level of inter-action between these two policy areas. Next, I will examine what options exist for coordination from the perspective of different schools of economic thought, and to what extent a productivity-oriented wage policy could meet the require-ments of both opponents and supporters of coordination. Subsequently, I will analyse the feasibility of implementing a productivity-oriented wage policy. In this connection, the effectiveness of existing coordination initiatives in the euro-zone will be examined. Finally, I will look at national wage negotiation systems and ask whether they would be compatible with European-wide policy coordin-ation. To what extent is the harmonization of wage negotiating systems neces-sary and feasible?

5.3.1 The problem of insufficient transparency on the part of wage and price policy actors in the eurozone

Monetary and wage policy are mutually interdependent. Indeed, the ECB emphasizes the impact of cost factors on inflation growth when analysing its direct inflation target (the so-called first pillar of monetary policy). By forecast-ing price trends over the next one to two years the ECB hopes to prevent infla-tion in consumer prices.[92] Since wage costs are the most significant element in overall macroeconomic costs, the ECB has an interest in seeing a wage policy that is compatible with its own inflation target. At the same time, wage policy actors also need transparency regarding the ECB's monetary policy targets. The theoretical assumption that unions and management can determine an optimal nominal wage simply by knowing the actual inflation rate is unrealistic, since it is based on the notion of perfect prescience. Instead, there is a need to explicitly include expectation formation on the part of unions and management in the ana-lysis. However, expectation formation has become much more problematic for the wage negotiating parties since the introduction of the euro. Before the intro-duction of the euro, the national central banks (NCB) and the national wage negotiating actors operated face-to-face; today, the ECB must confront the various national actors from all of the euro nations. These national actors are characterized by heterogeneous objectives, and differing degrees of coordination exist at the national level. Given this diffuse situation of conflicting interests, it is impossible to develop the kind of "intimate communication" that generally used to exist in Germany before the introduction of the euro. In those days, each side knew precisely what the other side was doing, and as a result, errors in expectations were relatively rare.[93]

The ECB has attempted to solve the information problem facing unions and management by letting the actors know in advance exactly how it will respond to their wage policy decisions. However, a consistently implemented rule-based monetary policy is inadequate to resolve the information problem that exists in the eurozone because, unlike the NCBs, the ECB's integrated monetary policy is directed at averaged figures and not at the specific changes taking place in each European nation. The wage policy negotiating parties need to know these averaged figures in order to predict the ECB's response. If the euro area was a homogeneous economy, this calculation would be no more difficult at the EU level than at the national level. However, since – as analysed above – the eurozone remains a heterogeneous area with respect to inflation rates, employment rates and so on, calculating these averages entails major difficulties. In fact, the actors have to anticipate the wage policy that other eurozone nations will pursue in order to predict the ECB's response. Since wage policy is poorly coordinated through the euro area, however, it is virtually impossible for the actors to accurately determine, say, how much inflationary pressure will result from wage policies in other nations as a way of deducing the ECB's probable response and determining the optimal strategy for their own interests.

Alongside informational deficits, the euro area must confront limitations in the ECB's options for action as a consequence of its integrated monetary policy, which entails misdirected incentives for wage policy and may even have a destabilizing effect in the heterogeneous union that is the eurozone. Before the introduction of the euro, the NCB could deliberately sanction wage negotiating parties in the event of undesirable developments in the wage bargaining process. The mere threat of sanctions could exert a disciplinary effect. For example, since the wage bargaining parties knew that the NCB would not compensate for wage increases that interfered with the nation's price competitiveness with an equivalent devaluation, they would not embark upon such increases in the first place. However, with the euro, the playing field has fundamentally changed for the national wage negotiating parties. The ECB will not respond to inflationary wage policies embarked upon in a single euro nation, but instead, will only respond if a number of euro nations take this step, thereby creating inflationary pressure throughout the eurozone. Individual nations thus have no reason to believe their actions alone will incite an ECB response. And when the ECB does respond, "collective sanctions" have the disadvantage of impacting all member nations more or less equally. This is not desirable from an allocative perspective. Countries that have pursued an inflation-free wage policy get no credit for having done so from the ECB, but instead, are sanctioned in exactly the same way as countries that have pursued an inflationary wage policy.

This kind of undifferentiated response by the ECB has a significant negative allocative effect, which is destabilizing. Countries with a restrained wage policy achieve low national inflation rates. Accordingly, the real interest rate is high in these countries, leading to weak investment demand. This, in turn, has an additional anti-inflationary effect and is associated with negative employment effects. The opposite situation presents itself in countries undertaking very large wage increases. The more divergent wage developments become, the more distorting the effects of an integrated monetary policy. Through its effects on real interest rates, an integrated monetary policy creates incentives for an inflation-lowering wage policy, leads to inflation-related poor investments, and aggravates divergence processes in the eurozone.

The foregoing discussion has shown that two problems arise in the interaction between the actors that determine monetary policy and wage policy: first, there are informational deficits, which is the result of insufficient transparency and predictability in the monetary and wage policy decisions made by the involved actors. This problem has been intensified by the creation of an integrated central bank for the entire eurozone. In addition, there is a second problem arising from the fact that the predictable dual interactional schema (action and reaction) that used to exist between national wage negotiating parties and national central banks has been disrupted and no longer exists. This creates disincentives for both sides and results in allocative inefficiencies.

5.3.2 Controversy on the need to coordinate wage and monetary policy

As we have seen, informational deficits are suffered by eurozone actors involved in monetary and wage policy, which can have negative effects on the real economy. This leads to the question of whether coordination between wage and monetary policy should occur and, if so, in what form. Classical and Keynesian economists have traditionally made very different recommendations for action in this area.

5.3.2.1 Neoclassical and Keynesian views about the role of coordination and monetary policy practice

Basically, the neoclassical "assignment" approach rejects every form of economic policy coordination. According to this approach, the best results will be achieved in a currency union when each actor is left alone to fulfil its designated task. The precondition for successful economic policy is thus to maintain a clear division of responsibilities (assignment), according to which the central bank should be exclusively responsible for the price level; the government for structural reforms, sound budgetary policy and reliable framework conditions; and the unions for the growth of employment.

Thus, we find that the assignment approach does not allow for the coordination of wage and monetary policies within the EU. In the context of a single monetary policy geared exclusively towards price stability and a fiscal policy committed to supercyclical budget consolidation, real wages are the key factor determining production and employment and for assimilating symmetrical and asymmetrical shocks. According to this view, the high level of unemployment in Europe can predominantly be ascribed to "structural" causes, and monetary integration is often seen as the catalyst for structural reforms.[94] This position is reiterated in the BEPGs as well as the annual employment guidelines under the Luxembourg Process.

To supplement their economic arguments based on neoclassical principles, opponents of coordinated monetary and wage policy fall back on their legal interpretation of the ECB's original mandate. The status and objectives of the ECB are set forth in the EU Treaty,[95] which defines the independence of the central bank in detail. According to the treaty, neither the ECB nor any NCB nor a member of any of their decision-making bodies may request or receive instructions from societal organs or institutions, member governments or other bodies. The governing bodies referred to are thereby obligated not to attempt to influence the ECB in performing its functions. According to the ECB, this definition "prescribes clear boundaries with respect to the collaboration between community organs and institutions on the one hand, and the ECB on the other".[96] With regard to collaboration in the area of economic policy, the ECB interprets these boundaries in such a way "that the relationships between the ECB and other economic policy decision-makers cannot go beyond non-binding dialogue". This interpretation would explicitly rule out any form of *ex ante* coordination of monetary policy with other policy areas. However, the legal argument is misguided, as policy coordination need not compromise the independence of the ECB. Indeed, economists and politicians who argue for the coordination of economic policy generally do not question that the ECB must be independent. The ECB's fundamental independence is also unaffected by recent changes that took place when the ECB began to purchase government debt on the bond market during the sovereign debt crisis in an effort to keep bond rates in embattled eurozone countries from rising too high. While the ECB's independence precludes it from receiving instructions, if deemed necessary, the central bank may certainly participate in a general coordination of macropolicies, so long as it can be assured that this does not compromise the central bank's ability to pursue its primary task, namely protecting the stability of price levels. Indeed, one could argue that the ECB's independence is what makes coordination possible in the first place. For if the central bank were dependent on community bodies or governments, this would mean that it would have to accept instructions and, accordingly, might be unable to honour its commitments. Indeed, only independent institutions are in a position to engage in the *ex ante* coordination of economic policy.

Yet even though neoclassical economists and European institutions may oppose cross-policy coordination of wage and monetary policy, they nevertheless acknowledge the information problem described above. For this reason, they agree to the need for coordination to the extent that it permits the ECB to obtain reliable information about production potential. Thus, from the neoclassical perspective, there is a need for the kind of coordination that would increase efficiency by providing improved access to information.[97] Neoclassicists recognize that an optimal monetary policy response depends significantly on the availability of reliable information about the actual expansion of production potential. The sooner a central bank can be assured that there will be an expansion in production potential, the sooner it will be prepared to take steps to assure expansion of aggregate demand by means of an expansive monetary policy. If wage policy can credibly demonstrate that it has embarked upon a long-term moderate course, and structural reforms are taking place concurrently in the labour market, the central bank can use this information in formulating monetary policy and embark on an expansive course sooner than it could justify without this information. Naturally, in a real-world setting, problems will always arise about the forecasted magnitude of the effects on production potential. Nevertheless, in a real-world setting as well, the fully credible determination of a moderate wage policy course would tend to move the central bank in the direction of an optimal, that is, an accommodative, monetary policy.

From a Keynesian perspective, the coordination of wage and monetary policy should be deepened.[98] Keynesian economists argue that an emphasis on the structural reform of labour markets and wage bargaining systems ignores the fact that these measures only have an impact on nominal wages, and not on real wages (if one assumes that in imperfect commodity markets, prices come about as a result of a mark-up being added to unit labour costs). Therefore, downward nominal wage differentiation and general wage restraint initially have an effect only on prices, and can only exert a possible influence on growth and employment if the ECB rewards this wages policy with a symmetrical and consequently more expansive monetary policy.[99] According to the Keynesian point of view, an employment and growth-oriented monetary policy that stimulates investment and effective demand is required in order to achieve a reduction in the non-accelerating inflation rate of unemployment (NAIRU), and not just reforms to the labour market.[100]

The Keynesian view asserts that the lack of coordinated wage policies and the trend towards national corporatist competitive structures are having negative repercussions on macroeconomic performance. In phases of rising employment, it is not possible to achieve the necessary nominal wage restraint. The ECB may as a result be forced to intervene and cause unemployment to rise. In phases of high unemployment, countries with a high degree of national wage bargaining coordination can exploit this advantage to strengthen their price competitiveness by means of nominal wage restraint. It is argued that such competitive corporatism poses a danger when it is pursued by several countries, especially large ones, since it causes deflationary pressure to be exerted on the eurozone as a whole.[101]

Accordingly, Keynesians favour a reorientation of monetary policy based on the coordination of monetary, fiscal and wage policy at various levels. In the envisioned new distribution of policy functions, both wage and fiscal policy need to assume some of the responsibility for ensuring stability in so far as the ECB becomes more involved in growth and employment policy. Thus, the Keynesian perspective goes much further than neoclassical doctrine, favouring coordination to improve the harmonization of wage increases and monetary policy measures. Yet such coordination would necessitate loosening the ECB's mandate to maintain price stability in order to encourage greater consideration for wage policy – something that is rigorously opposed by neoclassical proponents of the assignment approach.

Theoretical disputes about the scope of required coordination notwithstanding, the ECB is already pursuing a "soft" form of coordination in its monetary policy practices based on an exchange of information. The ECB regularly participates in discussions that take place at the EU level. For example, the Economic and Financial Ministers Council has become an important interlocutor for the ECB. Moreover, the ECB takes part in the Macroeconomic Dialogue. In this regard, it participates in an exchange of information about economic policy in the EU and in member states. However, from the ECB's perspective, the purpose of such dialogues is not to conclude binding agreements. Yet one could certainly anticipate that the ECB would take note of certain signals from employee and employer organizations and consider them when setting policies. If there were clear indications of an impending policy of wage restraint, the ECB could or might feel compelled to take this into consideration in setting its strategy, as wage restraint would lead to a more favourable prognosis for price development and for potential growth, which would have an impact on monetary policy measures. However, there are a number of reasons that such a situation might not result in an *ex ante* agreement. Thus, it is questionable how far-reaching or binding such notifications from the employee and employer organizations could actually be. Moreover, the ECB would reject making any strict commitment, arguing that risks for price level stability could arise from another quarter, which would require action that would run counter to the commitment made to industry and labour.[102] At the same time, the ECB is attempting to gain more influence on wage growth in Europe. The ECB regularly warns European unions against demanding excessively "steep" and supposedly inflationary wage increases, and exploits wage policy to justify its relatively restrictive monetary policy. In addition, the ECB frequently criticizes the "institutional rigidities" of national systems for reaching collective wage agreements, which prevent the rapid adjustment of wages to altered competitive conditions. The ECB explicitly favours dismantling the policy that continues to exist in a few European countries that indexes wages to inflation, and has voiced opposition to the establishment of minimum wages.[103]

5.3.2.2 Productivity-oriented wage policy as a consensus-building principle

Despite disagreements about the need for coordination, in the economic policy debate a consensus can be seen in broad-based calls for the implementation of productivity-oriented wage policy. A productivity-oriented wage policy can be classified as a form of vertical cross-policy coordination. This coordination is founded on the orientation of wage growth to other macroeconomic parameters (inflation and productivity). Basically, this approach is a one-sided form of coordination, since it only subjects the wage policy actors (unions and employers) to a guideline, but not the ECB.

Proponents of both the neoclassical and Keynesian views can agree upon the principle of a productivity-oriented wage policy. From a neoclassical perspective, wage agreements that exceed the sum of inflation and productivity growth have negative effects on competitiveness in the affected branches, and lead to negative employment effects. This interpretation regards wages as an instrument for influencing competitiveness. Seen in this way, a wage increase oriented to productivity would define the maximum acceptable level of wage increases. Collective wage agreements leading to little or no wage growth would lead to greater competitiveness, and thus to additional positive effects on employment. Some proponents of neoclassical economics would reject a productivity-oriented wage policy during times of underemployment. In the view of such economics, more employment requires wages that are oriented to the marginal productivity of labour, which is typically below average labour productivity. Therefore, they believe that increases in real wages should be kept below the rate of growth in aggregate labour productivity.[104] From the point of view of the classical assignment approach, a productivity-oriented wage policy is desirable because it subjects the wage agreement negotiators to unilateral regulation while protecting the decision-making scope of the ECB.

Similarly, according to the Keynesian view, macroeconomic wage externalities can be internalized more effectively when nominal wage growth rates are determined on the basis of the sum of long-term productivity growth for the economy as a whole and the central bank's inflation target.[105] Keynesians believe the effective coordination of wage bargaining would be able to reduce inflationary pressure when employment is rising, and, in doing so, lower the employment limit expressed in the NAIRU. Such an approach to wage policy would make it possible for the central bank to tolerate a higher level of employment while still meeting its inflation target.[106] However, unlike the neoclassical economists, Keynesians believe that the possibility for higher wages arising from inflation and productivity growth should at least be fully exhausted.

THE WELFARE EFFECTS OF COORDINATING MONETARY POLICY AND A PRODUCTIVITY-ORIENTED WAGE POLICY

A productivity-oriented wage policy would consider changes in wages in terms of both their cost effects and their effects on demand. It would assure that nominal claims to higher wages do not exceed the available real social product and that real wage costs remain the same. Theoretically, a wage policy structured in this way is neither inflationary nor deflationary.[107] Maintaining the orientation to productivity would favour real capital investments, economic growth and growth in employment.

Model-based studies confirm these theoretical predictions. They conclude that the coordination of wage and monetary policy based on a transparent and uniform wage policy trajectory could bring about welfare gains. Boss *et al.* compare three different scenarios using the NIGEM model developed by the National Institute of Economic and Social Research (NIESR). They compare a wage restraint by employers and unions in Germany without the coordination of monetary policy; wage restraint in Germany with the coordination of monetary policy; and wage restraint in the euro area with the coordination with monetary policy.[108] The starting point in each scenario is that the wage negotiating parties in Germany agree upon a policy of moderate wage increases and can credibly signal their commitment to the ECB of keeping German wage policy on a moderate course. The European scenario looks at the effects of a coordinated wage restraint policy implemented by the three largest nations in the eurozone (Germany, France and Italy). It is assumed that these countries can credibly portray to the ECB their commitment to a specific wage policy course. Because of this coordination, interest levels fall; monetary policy has a stimulatory effect on macroeconomic demand. Rising GDP has a positive effect on wage increases. Since monetary policy has a stimulating effect, and thus the positive effects of wage restraint on international price competitiveness for domestic products strengthens macroeconomic demand, the real GDP increases more than it would without coordination. When compared to coordination purely at the national level (that is, coordination between German wage policy and the ECB's monetary policy), European coordination has a larger effect. Since the wage moderation achieved in all three nations will result in greater potential growth in the eurozone, the ECB would have to increase its target goals for nominal GDP (or the reference value for the growth of the monetary supply) to a greater degree than in the other scenarios in order to keep the inflation rate on its target trajectory. Accordingly, interest rates would fall more, and this would amplify the stimulus on macroeconomic demand, the expansion of GDP and the positive effects on wage increases.

CONFIGURING THE WAGE AND PRODUCTIVITY FORMULA

However, the question naturally arises of how to best manage the parameters of a productivity-oriented wage policy. This management would pose no problems if the eurozone constituted an OCA with a homogeneous structure. However, no such homogeneity exists in the eurozone, either with respect to national productivity rates or national inflation rates. The non-homogeneity is especially notable with respect to divergences in unit labour costs, as described earlier. Therefore, there is a need to examine which standards for inflation and productivity should be applied so as to avoid negative effects on the real economy.

First, it is important to decide which inflation indicator should be used as a metric. Ideally, the wage formula should be configured in such a way that it has an anti-inflationary effect and reduces divergence in competitiveness in the eurozone. As the analysis in Section 2.2.2 has shown, significant differences in inflation continue to exist in the eurozone, and they have contributed to imbalances and widening differences in competitiveness due to their effects on real interest rates. For this reason, there is a need to foster greater convergence in inflation rates.

The wage formula could either be pegged to the national inflation rate, the European inflation rate or the ECB's target inflation rate. If inflation is measured by the actual national inflation rate, this has the clear advantage of not worsening the wage position of the labour force. However, the following problem arises: if national price increases (due to strong economic growth) are to be taken into consideration in wage increases (as envisaged in the wage formula), this will perpetuate inflationary trends as soon as they set in. The ultimate consequence is a loss in price competitiveness for a country with a booming economy. The reverse scenario takes place if the wage formula is broadly applied in an economy that is experiencing weakness, as was the case, for example, in Germany after 2000. In such a situation, the strict application of the wage formula would result in gains in price competitiveness.

Given these dynamics, the wage formula should be built around a European standard – either the average rate of price increases in the eurozone or the ECB's target inflation rate.[109] A wage formula of this kind would serve to reduce both deflationary and inflationary tendencies, while also reducing divergence in competitiveness. Yet orienting the wage formula to a European inflation standard is not without its own problems: it would make countries with above-average inflation rates lose their price competitive advantage, but would reward them with lower real interest rates. These would be offset by wage policy-related inflation rates. In this instance, the losers in the resource allocation battle would be the firms, due to rising unit labour costs. Precisely the opposite situation would occur in countries in the eurozone with below-average inflation rates.

Basing the wage formula on a European inflation standard is also problematic from a distributional perspective. If the actual inflation rate exceeds the target inflation rate, wage earners will experience losses, whereas companies will benefit from inflation. If, instead, workers laid full claim to wage increases for inflation, this would result in second-round effects, as described earlier, and the carousel of the wage–price spiral would simply continue to turn. In this situation, the unions would have a hard time persuading their membership to accept large losses in purchasing power. To deal with this situation, one might imagine a one-time compensatory payment to offset losses in purchasing power, or government compensation payments to workers financed by increased tax receipts from higher inflation-related earnings.

Another problem relates to the standards for measuring productivity. Should a productivity-oriented wage policy be oriented to sectoral or national changes in productivity? Large differences in sectoral productivity may arise in a sector-based wage negotiation policy. If wage increases of equal percentage are applied to all branches and operations, one should anticipate great resistance from those sectors with weaker productivity, and, not least, from employers in the public sector. To moderate such conflicts one might imagine implementing a lower overall wage increase as a lowest common denominator, while at the same time granting supplemental increases for high-productivity sectors or companies. Clearly, this would be a complex system to administer and could lead to lop-sided wage differences between sectors. In the extreme case, this could result in a dual labour market structure, where strong segments would pay production-oriented wages while wage development in the weaker segments would become broadly disconnected from productivity growth. Wages in these segments would tend to approach the minimum wage. In a dual labour market it is almost imposs- ible to implement a productivity-based wage policy.

The conflicts and difficulties just described make it clear that, although it is a relatively simple and easily understood model, a productivity-oriented wage policy will not be a perfect coordination instrument for the eurozone. Its success largely depends on the homogeneity of the eurozone. Furthermore, while such a policy does provide meaningful orientation in the absence of shocks, it is not an adequate tool when differential price shocks with different degrees of respon- siveness exist alongside very different country-specific labour markets.

THE RELEVANCE OF WAGE POLICY AS THE CAUSE AND THE SOLUTION
OF IMBALANCES IN THE EUROZONE

Developments prior to the outbreak of the euro crisis have shown that in a world of absolutely fixed exchange rates or in a common currency area, a lasting diver- gence in prices and unit labour costs between one country and its main trading partners creates unsustainable external deficits, and may risk the coherence of a currency union.[110]

A monetary union in agreement about an inflation target of close to 2 per cent has to coordinate wage developments in its member states. This is the case because the most important determinant of inflation is growth in unit labour costs (Figure 5.16).

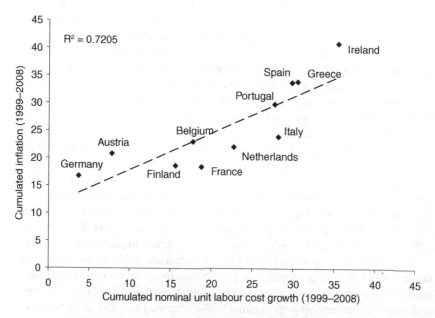

Figure 5.16 Relationship between inflation and unit labour costs (source: European Com- mission, Ameco; taken from Zemanek *et al.*, 2009).

The reasons for divergence in competitiveness and ultimately for current account imbalances can be traced back to the labour market policies pursued in individual countries. In Germany, following the introduction of the euro, labour market stakeholders agreed on a policy of moderate wages and flexible work arrangements, which allow the export-oriented industry to flourish. The new German approach to labour market policy coincided with the beginning of the currency union, and ultimately led to a huge divergence in the growth of unit labour costs between countries. Since the start of the EMU, German unit labour costs, the most important determinant of prices and competitiveness, have risen only slightly (Figure 5.17). In most Southern European countries, on the other hand, nominal wage growth exceeded national productivity growth. The commonly agreed upon inflation target of 2 per cent was also exceeded by a small but stable margin. France was the only country to exactly meet the target path for nominal wage growth, as it was perfectly compatible with the national productivity performance and the inflation goal of 2 per cent.[111]

The illustration shows that a significant gap accumulated over time. At the end of the first decade, the cost and price gap between Germany and Southern Europe amounted to some 25 per cent; between Germany and France to 15 per cent. In other words, Germany's real exchange rate had depreciated significantly, while in the south exchange rates had appreciated, despite the absence of national currencies.[112]

Wage policy can play an important role in closing the competitiveness gap as well as in avoiding deflationary developments in the EMU as a whole. Wages in

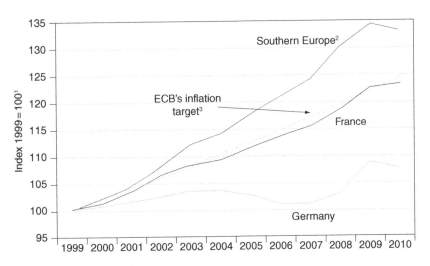

Figure 5.17 Divergence in unit labour cost growth in the monetary union (source: Flassbeck and Spiecker, 2011).

Notes
1 Index of unit labour cost of total economy 1999 = 100.
2 Greece, Portugal, Spain and Italy.
3 Yearly increase of 2 per cent.

Germany need to rise for some time by more than is justified by the traditional wage rule (national productivity growth plus the common inflation target). Meanwhile, Southern European countries must pursue a policy of extreme wage restraint. Figure 5.18 shows an example of such an adjustment, projected over the next ten years. Germany's nominal wages would increase by more than 4 per cent, while Italy's, Greece's, Portugal's and Spain's would increase by much less. It is worth noting that even in this scenario, the surplus–deficit relations within the EMU will not change quickly. Germany's advantages and its market share gains remain until 2022. Accordingly, a turnaround in deficit and surplus positions cannot be expected soon. However, an announcement of willingness on the part of member countries to pursue such an adjustment would help to tackle the problem in the long run, as it would dramatically increase the credibility of short-term adjustment efforts. Certainly, the adjustment process illustrated in Figure 5.18 could be much quicker. The faster labour costs decrease in Southern Europe and increase in Northern Europe, the sooner labour costs will reach a sustainable level. The path of the adjustment process will depend a lot on the political will in each country.[113]

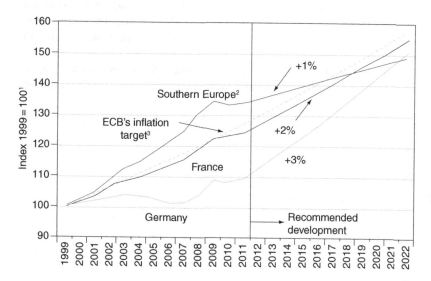

Figure 5.18 Possible paths for labour cost adjustment (source: Flassbeck and Spiecker, 2011).

Notes
1 Index of unit labour cost of total economy 1999 = 100; proposal 2012–2020; Germany +3 per cent, i.e. nominal wage growth c.+4.5 per cent; France +2 per cent, i.e. nominal wage growth c.+3 per cent; Southern Europe +1 per cent, i.e. nominal wage growth between +1 per cent and +3.5 per cent.
2 Greece, Portugal, Spain and Italy.
3 Yearly increase of 2 per cent.

5.3.3 Implementing productivity-oriented wage coordination

Beyond the conceptual difficulty of establishing standards for a productivity-oriented wage policy, it is also debatable whether such a policy could be implemented while preserving collective bargaining autonomy. As part of recent efforts to manage the sovereign-debt crisis in the eurozone, the implementation of a productivity-oriented wage policy now has a prominent place on the political agenda. Moreover, there have already been a few attempts at regional coordination aimed at developing a productivity-oriented wage policy. However, cross-border wage policy coordination is a form of collective action, the stability of which is contingent upon a series of preconditions. In fact, the question arises as to whether national wage negotiating systems are open to cross-border coordination in the first place, or if instead, they are so heterogeneous as to rule out effective coordination. It would appear that wage policy coordination is only possible if an adequate level of homogeneity exists between countries in terms of the organizational structures involved in wage negotiations.

Against this background, in the following section I will examine previous coordination initiatives in the eurozone to determine if such initiatives provide a model for developing a productivity-oriented wage policy. In this connection, I will also investigate the extent to which the existing wage negotiation systems in EU member states would appear to allow for a common wage policy.

5.3.3.1 Previous approaches to wage policy coordination in the eurozone

For years, the BEPGs of the EU have expressed their support for a productivity-oriented wage policy. In addition, the Euro-Plus Pact of 2011 further solidified the aim of implementing a productivity-oriented wage policy. The consensus that has emerged with regard to such a wage policy is founded on the understanding that economic divergence can have adverse effects on other member nations. Since fluctuating exchange rates are now excluded as an avenue for economic adjustment, competitiveness is now largely modulated by price levels. In this regard, stagnant wages serve as the functional equivalent of currency devaluation. The result is permanent wage competition, which has led to major differences in competitiveness between European nations. Since 2000, countries such as Germany have been able to gain a major advantage in competitiveness by ensuring wage increases fall well below growth in productivity. Seen from the perspective of the member states, this can be regarded as a negative externality, since it allows Germany to win additional market share. Conversely, countries such as Spain and Greece have concluded wage agreements for years that substantially exceeded increases in productivity, and this has weakened their competitiveness, leading in turn to significant negative account balances. In the future as well, countries may find that they have an incentive not to pursue the goal of a productivity-oriented wage policy. For example, this would be the case if a nation saw the potential for advantage in concluding wage agreements that undercut a productivity-oriented wage policy, or if political and economic exigencies made wage growth below productivity growth unavoidable.

In any event, the ability for government to impose a productivity-oriented wage policy from on high are extremely limited because of collective bargaining autonomy.[114] Accordingly, past coordination efforts on the part of unions have exceeded government initiatives in their scope. For years, unions have attempted to improve their position through a greater level of cross-border union coordination. From the point of view of the unions, the need for greater coordination stems from the changes brought about by the realization of a European single market. The single market has progressively eroded the unions' power and sphere of action. The single market favours transnational competition between production locations, including the transnational interchangeability of the workforce. The monetary union intensifies competition between production locations by turning over currency and monetary policy to a supranational authority, while also curtailing the scope of action for fiscal policy (as per the SGP). This has narrowed options for the autonomous correction of imbalances, leaving the labour markets and their institutions to bear the heaviest burden of economic adjustment processes. There are no collective institutions in the realm of labour relations whose transnational regulatory strength can match the scope of transnational market integration that has already taken place.[115]

Against this backdrop, European trade unions have made significant efforts to establish a basis for cross-border collective bargaining since the 1990s.[116] The European Metalworkers' Federation (EMF) has been at the forefront in adopting a "European" framework for collective bargaining, laying down common rules and guidelines for the wage bargaining for its member organizations in the early 1990s.[117] The EMF and its member organizations agreed on a "regular annual compensation for price increases in order to protect real wages, so that workers have a share in productivity gains". Finally, the adoption of the European Coordination Rule, which specifies quantitative and normative criteria for wage bargaining, can be perceived as a further step towards the international coordination of collective bargaining.

The EMF's coordination approach includes three basic structures:

1   The coordination rule, which is intended as the standard for national collective bargaining agreements that serve to "compensate for the inflation rate and for the equal participation of worker's incomes in productivity advances".

2   The EUCOB Information Network, which offers regular, standardized reports about current collective bargaining policy. It provides for the rapid reciprocal exchange of information and for the evaluation of coordination efforts.

3   The cross-border (interregional) collective bargaining partnerships have the function of broadening the base for cooperation between the unions beyond the coordination rule. The focus of these collective bargaining partnerships is on multinational corporations with several sites located in the respective regions participating in the collective bargaining partnership.

Yet not only procedural rules and guidelines for the cross-border coordination of collective bargaining have been adopted in the European metalworking sector. In parallel, a set of institutions for the transnational coordination of bargaining policies has been established.[118] One of the most active "clusters" of coordination is the bargaining coordination network for Central Western Europe, that is, Germany, the Netherlands and Belgium.[119] In 1997, the North Rhine–Westphalia branch of IG Metall, the Belgian organizations of CCMB and CMB, as well as the two Dutch unions FNV Bondgenoten and CNV Bedrijvenbond, set up a transnational network for the exchange of collective bargaining information and trade union officials. Several other networks have been founded in other European regions. The most active ones include IG Metall's network in Central and Eastern Europe (Austria and Bavaria, the Czech Republic, Slovakia, Slovenia and Hungary); IG Metall's network for Denmark, Sweden and coastal areas of Germany; as well as the Nordic IN network, which consists of manufacturing sector unions from Sweden, Norway, Finland, Denmark and Iceland. The transnational collective bargaining networks of the EMF were established with the aim of institutionalizing information exchange and cooperation in the field of collective bargaining between unions from neighbouring countries. Although national unions – and in particular the German IG Metall, which can be regarded as the "backbone" of the interregional network structure – have been decisive in establishing these networks, the EMF represents a transnational organization that strongly supports activities within the networks by providing financial, organizational and personnel support.

We thus find that the EMF's collective bargaining networks are the product of both top-down and bottom-up processes. In this way, they could serve as an appropriate institutional framework for the union-side implementation of the EMF's European coordination rule. The viability of such an institution will primarily depend on the readiness of national union officials to join with affiliates in other countries to address common policy issues and implement Europe-wide policy goals that were set in a rather top-down fashion. Yet a readiness to collaborate across borders is on display in existing networks, particularly the transnational bargaining network in the region of North Rhine–Westphalia, Belgium and the Netherlands. Cross-border communication and events occur on a continued and regular basis within this network. Union representatives meet at least twice per year in order to exchange information on collective bargaining efforts. Additionally, ad-hoc topical seminars on other issues such as vocational training have been carried out.[120]

The previously described forms of coordination represent informal exchanges of information and they are based on non-binding goals. They do not result in a specific process for conducting collective bargaining, nor do they directly involve the EMF in the negotiations. Given this backdrop, in the following section I will elucidate (1) the problems arising from the divergence of interests between the parties involved that make an agreement unlikely; and (2) the empirical experience gathered to date from attempts to implement wage policy coordination.

5.3.3.2 The instability of wage policy coordination in terms of collective action theory

In view of the existing forms of transnational union coordination discussed in the preceding section, how likely is the implementation of a coordination rule for wage policy? It would appear that a failure to implement defined targets would be an ever-present possibility, as specific national interests could easily trump and undermine a country's commitment to the coordination project. One cannot rule out the possibility that economic competition between nations, in tandem with other unfavourable conditions, could induce the actors to reorient their behaviour to benefit their own short-term interests. For example, the interests of large and small economies may diverge. Large nations with fewer international trade interdependencies might be less interested in a policy directed at reducing wage costs to favour competitiveness than small nations with more extensive international trade interdependencies.

The risk of strategic non-compliance is clearly evident when one views the international coordination of wage policy as a type of collective good. The basic problem in providing collective goods is that non-cooperating actors (that is, actors who avoid sharing the costs for providing the good) cannot be excluded from the benefits of that collective good. In this particular instance, this means that those national unions concluding wage agreements that do not conform with the transnational coordination targets nevertheless benefit from the coordination process so long as sufficient numbers of other unions are in adherence. This situation is a conundrum right out of game theory, for under these starting conditions, the actors' (long-term) collective interests are diametrically opposed to their (short-term) self-interest. Thus, on the one hand, it is in the actors' collective interests to coordinate bargaining based on wage policy targets, since only the coordination process can promise an optimally Pareto-efficient solution (that is, optimal curtailment of a counterproductive "race-to-the-bottom" in wage and social policy). On the other hand, a purely self-interested strategy would favour non-cooperation. As long as a sufficient number of other unions decide to cooperate, a double advantage emerges for the non-cooperating "freeriders": they profit from the coordination-based containment of a race to the bottom in wage and social policy, while at the same time, they improve their international competitiveness by undercutting the coordination target in their own collective bargaining agreements.

The stability of collective action depends on four factors of particular importance for the strategic choices made by the participating actors. These factors are (1) the availability of selective incentives, (2) the size of the group, (3) the time frame of the cooperation problem and (4) the degree of heterogeneity between interest positions:[121]

1   Availability of selective incentives: selective incentives aim to reward cooperation or sanction non-cooperation. They are directly linked to the self-interests of the participating actors, and they assure cooperation in

providing collective goods in so far as the perceived reward and avoidance of sanction exceeds the benefits of non-cooperation. In the case of the transnational coordination of collective bargaining policy, the trade union committees directing the coordination process would have to establish such selective incentives for their national member organizations. However, they are not actually in a position to do so, since they have far fewer resources at their disposal than their member organizations in all of the relevant dimensions (authority, budget and personnel). As a result, they are only in a position to set up a relatively weak sanction mechanism. Member organizations that behave like notorious freeriders risk harming their reputation. Yet member organizations that step out of line hardly risk damaging their reputation if they merely violate non-binding coordination agreements. The example of the smaller trade unions in Germany shows how ineffective reputational concerns can be as a sanction instrument for unions. In any event, this form of oversight is contingent upon the existence of a functioning evaluatory system that can reliably identify freeriders.

In addition, the implementation of coordination agreements may encounter barriers due to the nature of bargaining autonomy of unions and employers. Generally, there is no identity between those who conclude the agreement with the other party and those who ultimately would have to enforce the coordination agreement. More specifically, while the agreement is negotiated by delegates or representatives of unions, the individual companies will carry out the actual wage agreement. Given the non-identity between negotiating and enforcing parties, implementation issues are likely to occur and give space to strategic behaviour. Individual companies may incline to diverge from the coordination agreement if this may serve their individual interest. At least, there is no enforcement mechanism at hand which ensures the agreement to be actually implemented.[122]

2   Group size: collective action theory proposes that as group size increases (that is, the number of participating actors), the probability of a cooperative solution will fall, since with increasing group size, coordination problems mount and the expected influence of each individual actor on the occurrence of the cooperative solution diminishes. The criterion of group size is a matter of dispute. Some theorists claim that the argument is only valid if the costs of the cooperation increase proportionally or overproportionally with increasing group size.[123] If cooperation costs increase underproportionally, even "large" groups will have a real chance of cooperation. We can assume that this is the case for the transnational coordination of collective bargaining policy. It would appear the costs of cooperation would tend to rise underproportionally, since not all of the relevant actors have to participate in order for the cooperation process to be effective. Rather, what is required is a "critical mass" of cooperating actors, whose collective bargaining agreements taken together are of sufficiently large economic relevance that their coordination has a collective steering impact on wage development in Europe.[124]

3   Time frame of the cooperation problem: with respect to the time frame, the issue is whether the cooperation problem to be dealt with is a one-time or recurrent situation. The likelihood of a cooperative solution will generally tend to increase when a problem is recurrent.[125] This is because the advantages of cooperation become more substantial the more frequently and the longer the actors see themselves confronted with a cooperation problem. Moreover, if a given problem keeps arising, this allows for learning processes that can lead to mutual confidence building and a stabilization of the actors' expectations. Since collective bargaining agreements are not one-time events but must be negotiated repeatedly, the transnational coordination of collective bargaining represents a continuously recurring problem, and this favours cooperation on the part of national unions. However, one stumbling block in this respect is that national collective bargaining agreements are concluded at different points in time, and are also valid for varying periods.

4   Degree of heterogeneity of interests: finally, a core argument in collective action theory is that the chances of arriving at a cooperative solution increase when the interests of the relevant actors are more heterogeneous. At first glance, this hypothesis might seem paradoxical, since the problems of agreeing upon a common goal clearly intensify when the represented interested are highly heterogeneous. However, the crucial factor is the extent of divergence between the intensity of desire to reach an already established goal. A high degree of this kind of heterogeneity between actors makes cooperation more likely, since this configuration implies that one actor or a few actors have enough interest in a collective goal that they are prepared to bear the costs of its realization singlehandedly, or at least to assume a disproportionate share of these costs.[126] If one considers the goal of coordinating collective bargaining transnationally, considerable heterogeneity does exist between national interests along two dimensions. For one thing, there are differences in national interests between countries with greater trade dependencies and those with lower trade dependencies. In the latter case the balance of costs and benefits arising from a competition-oriented collective bargaining policy (that is, one that lowers wage costs in the interest of increased competitiveness) tends to be less favourable than for those nations with greater trade interdependencies. With decreasing trade interdependency the costs arising from a competitive collective bargaining policy (in the form of an associated attenuation of domestic demand) increase relative to their benefits (in the form of increased exports). Consequently, countries with fewer trade interdependencies are less able to externalize the costs arising from a competition-oriented collective bargaining policy – and thus, they manifest less interest in extreme wage restraint. A second basic gap in national interests divides high-wage from low-wage countries. To the extent that the relocation of production facilities is undertaken in response to transnational differences in labour costs, the high-wage countries are the losers and the low-wage countries the winners in this

competition. Accordingly, the coordination of national collective bargaining policy is primarily of interest to the high-wage countries. It is important to note that such divergence in interests does not mean there is no underlying common interest in wage policy cooperation. None of the groups has an interest in setting off a downward wage spiral. Still, cooperation initiatives will tend to originate from countries with a disproportionately high interest in cooperation, and we can expect these countries to make concessions to countries with less to gain. From a formal perspective, the coordination rule will meet with approval from low-wage countries to the extent that it tends to envisage retaining the status quo in transnational wage differentials rather than levelling them upward. Similarly, it is conceivable that within a certain margin of tolerance, slow wage growth might be tolerated by the less interested countries.[127]

Another kind of heterogeneity of interests can occur when the aim of wage policy is not the direct improvement of aggregate welfare, but instead short-term maximization of workers' income, without adequate consideration for the interests of the unemployed. This relates to an unequal consideration of the interests of insiders and outsiders of labour markets. Unions focusing primarily on wage increases favour interests of employed (insiders) over unemployed (outsiders). Favouring insiders, it is optimal for wage policy to deviate from a declared policy of permanent wage restraint, and to implement greater wage increases, as soon as the central bank, confident that employers and unions will pursue wage restraint, decides to embark on an expansive monetary policy. In the short term, this scenario will allow workers to obtain wage increases without having to deal with lay-offs, since the economy is in the midst of a monetary policy-induced boom. In the medium term, this strategy will clearly lead to greater inflation and higher rates of unemployment. Even if higher unemployment might not seem relevant to wage policymakers because it would only emerge several years later, the time horizon will actually be shorter if the declaration of wage restraint is time-inconsistent. Irrespective of the true intent of the wage policymakers, the central bank will not give credence to such signals, and will favour a prudent monetary policy that does not rely upon the declared wage policy.

The analysis reveals that the theoretical conditions favouring a cooperative solution are not clear cut. It is impossible to arrive at a confident conclusion about the stability of wage policy coordination based on the preconditions set by collective action theory. Therefore, it makes sense to turn next to an empirical examination of the effectiveness of transnational coordination. This task would appear simple at first glance: one merely has to test how well national collective bargaining agreements have adhered to coordination targets.

In addition, the coordination between wage bargaining partners produces a variety of concerns related to corporatism.[128] In line with Schmitter and Streit,[129] neo-corporatism is understood as the involvement of interest associations in the political steering process leading to a partial loss of autonomy of political decision-makers and a formal cooptation of the associations. In this process, political decision-makers and associations employ the instrument of reciprocity or political bargaining in order to secure cooperation of these associations.[130] In Germany, this corporatist approach has been applied in the context of labour market reforms: in 1999, a concerted actions labelled "Bündnis für Arbeit" was established, bringing the government, employer associations and unions together with the aim of improving labour market conditions in a consensual manner. However, the concerted action failed and was finally terminated in 2003. There are a number for reasons rendering such official cooptation of interest groups ineffective and also incompatible from a viewpoint of democratic theory. In particular, corporatist arrangements are even less compatible with procedural and substantive principles of democracy than the political role which organized interests tend to play in welfare states. Moreover, the interplay of corporate actors does not secure the desired outcome. Often corporatism tends to disfavour groups not participating in the concerted action, as cooperation pays for associational entrepreneurs only if they hope to secure significant net advantages. This leads costs to be diffused widely or pushed on to groups which are not represented in the concerted action.[131]

5.3.3.3 Empirical studies of previous efforts at wage policy coordination

Existing empirical studies differ significantly regarding the validity of their findings. Earlier studies that were conducted by European trade union organizations in the context of a monitoring programme for wage agreements show contradictory findings for a number of countries, depending on the examined data. Moreover, an ETUC study concluded that, excluding the countries for which data were contradictory, four of the nine remaining countries concluded wage agreements in line with coordination targets.[132] Another study of the metalworking industry, which examined the wage policy strategies of unions in Germany, France and Italy from 1999 to 2003, came to the conclusion that the unions basically adhered to coordination targets. However, they did not abide by targets when employers and governments exerted significant pressure on them during negotiations.[133]

A more recent study examined compliance with coordination guidelines based on the German–Dutch–Belgian wage coordination network established in 1997, which included the participation of the North-Rhine–Westphalia region of the German union IG Metall; two Belgian unions, CCMB and CMB; and two Dutch unions, FNV Bondgenoten and CNV Derijvenbond. The aim of this network is to coordinate wages in the light of the EMF's coordination guidelines.[134] The study chose 1999 as the index year to examine the effectiveness of the coordination guidelines.

Figures 5.19–5.21 and Table 5.3 illustrate the successes of coordination efforts. In Belgium it is apparent that, on average, hourly wages were significantly nearer the targets set by the EMF following the introduction of the wage

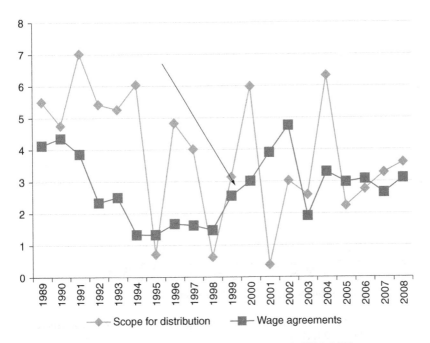

Figure 5.19 Belgium, increases in hourly wages (per cent), 1989–2008

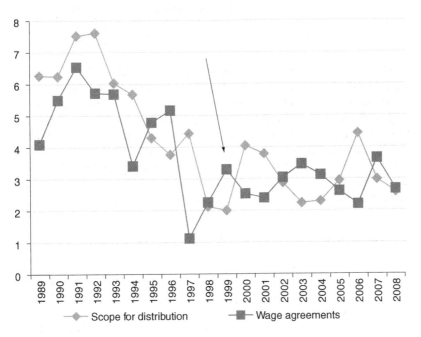

Figure 5.20 Germany, increases in hourly wages (per cent), 1989–2008

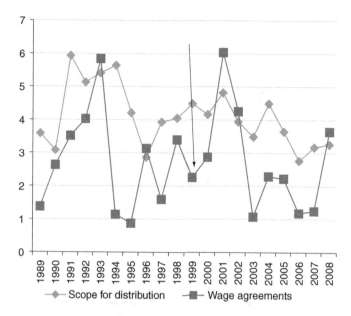

Figure 5.21 Netherlands, increases in hourly wages (per cent), 1989–2008 (source: Pusch, 2011).

negotiation network in 1999 than during the previous ten years. While wage growth was only equivalent to 50 per cent of the target range prior to coordination efforts, wage growth targets were 92 per cent fulfilled during the period of coordination.

In Germany, one can also see closer adherence to the EMF guidelines on the part of IG Metall. In Germany, target fulfilment increased from 78 per cent (1989–1998) to 94 per cent (1999–2008). In the Netherlands as well, adherence to wage growth targets improved following coordination, but at 67 per cent it lagged behind Germany and Belgium. In the Netherlands as well, growth between 2003 and 2007 fell significantly short of the EMF guidelines.

Therefore, the most comprehensive and most recent study of the EMF wage negotiation network shows substantial improvements in adherence to wage growth targets, and at the same time, consistent adherence to the productivity rule.

5.3.3.4 Institutional frameworks for coordinated wage policy in EU member states

Our theoretical exploration showed that collective action theory casts considerable doubt on the viability of coordination. However, the few existing empirical studies demonstrate that coordination can be effective.

Accordingly, in the next section I will examine the extent to which existing wage negotiation systems in EU member states would allow for a common wage

Table 5.3 Wage coordination

	Belgium		Germany		Netherlands	
	Wage increases [EMF scope for distribution], in %	Exploitation of scope for distribution (%)	Wage increases [EMF scope for distribution], in %	Exploitation of scope for distribution (%)	Wage increases [EMF scope for distribution], in %	Exploitation of scope for distribution (%)
1989–1998	27 [54]	50.00	54 [69]	78.26	31 [64]	48.44
1999–2008	36 [39]	92.31	33 [35]	94.29	31 [46]	67.39

Source: Pusch (2011); author's calculations.

policy. The underlying question is whether national wage negotiating systems are at all suitable for cross-border coordination, or if, instead, they are so hetero-geneous as to rule out the possibility of a viable coordination regime. It would appear that wage policy coordination is only possible if a sufficient level of homogeneity exists between wage negotiating structures. To address this issue, I will first outline the existing wage negotiating systems in EU member states with regard to their existing level of coordination and their capacities for coordin-ation. A related question is whether it would be advisable to harmonize existing wage negotiating systems with the aim of creating a coordinated wage policy.

CLASSIFICATION BY WAGE NEGOTIATION LEVEL

The predominant level at which wage negotiations are conducted is an important characteristic that differentiates European collective bargaining systems. In Germany, as in most of the older EU states in Northern, Western and Southern Europe, the most prevalent and structurally important form of national collective bargaining system continues to be industry-wide, multi-employer agreements. The United Kingdom is the only country where wage agreements are concluded almost exclusively at the firm level, while in Belgium and Ireland the prevalent form of wage agreements are industry-wide, national agreements.[135]

Wage negotiations actually take place at multiple levels in all of the EU member states.[136] One can find a sectoral and firm-specific component in every country. In five nations, there are wage negotiations at a central level that either encompass the entire economy (Finland), the private sector (Belgium and Greece) or the industrial sector (Denmark).[137] Countries differ substantially with respect to the importance of each individual level in their national collective bar-gaining processes. In Belgium, the central level is critical, whereas in Finland it is not of key importance in every wage cycle. In Denmark and Greece, it is of only secondary importance. Meanwhile, in Ireland, firm agreements are concluded after a foundation for negotiations has been previously established at the central, national level. In Denmark and Sweden, one can observe a notable shift towards negotiations at the industry level, since bilateral and tripartite agreements have lost importance. In both of these countries, however, subsequent on-site agree-ments are often renegotiated at the company level after the industry-wide agree-ments have been concluded. The same is true of Spain and Italy. Central wage negotiation systems exist in the Netherlands, even though most negotiations are actually conducted at the sectoral level, but considerable influence is exerted through central coordination at the national level (Table 5.4).[138]

While one can find sectoral-level wage negotiations in all countries, their importance within the overall national collective bargaining system differs. In Ireland and in United Kingdom, sectoral wage negotiations are limited to a few industries. In other countries (France, the Netherlands, Portugal and Spain), it is primarily small and mid-sized companies that conclude sectoral collective bar-gaining agreements, whereas large companies typically negotiate firm-wide con-tracts. There are also differences in collective bargaining practices between the

Table 5.4 Levels of wage bargaining at the EU level

	Central level	Sectoral level	Company level	Overall classification
Austria	0	XXX	X	Centralized
Belgium	XXX	X	X	Centralized
Denmark	XX	XX	X	Intermediary
Finland	XX	XX	X	Centralized
France		X	XXX	Decentralized
Germany		XXX	X	Intermediary
Greece	X	XXX	X	Intermediary
Ireland	XXX	X	X	Centralized
Italy		XXX	X	Intermediary
Luxembourg		XX	XX	Intermediary
Netherlands	0	XXX	X	Centralized
Portugal		XXX	X	Intermediary
Spain		XXX	X	Intermediary
Sweden		XXX	X	Intermediary
United Kingdom		X	XXX	Decentralized

Source: Boss *et al.* (2004, 78); EIRO (2000); Dohse *et al.* (1998).

Notes
X = Wage bargaining level exists, but not important.
XX = Wage bargaining level important, but not the prevailing method.
XXX = Prevailing method of wage bargaining.
0 = Important higher-level coordination.

sectors. The public sector typically concludes centralized contracts, while in sectors with many large companies, the company level is of greater significance. Moreover, national collective bargaining systems differ with respect to the geographical scope of the wage agreements. Whereas in most countries, wage agreements are applicable to the entire nation, their scope is limited to specific regions in Germany, France and Spain.[139]

Furthermore, there are differences in the relationships between the various negotiating levels. In a few countries, the sectoral and company levels are complementary. In these cases, the sectoral wage agreements are usually regarded as a lower limit for wage increases, which can then be exceeded by individual firms according to their specific circumstances. By contrast, in Belgium and Ireland there is an upper limit set at the national level, which must be respected by the negotiating parties at the sectoral or firm levels.

CLASSIFICATION BY DEGREE OF CENTRALIZATION

In the literature, the major initial attempts to classify the collective bargaining process have been concentrated virtually exclusively on centralization factors.[140] Sometimes, a difference is also drawn between coordinated and non-coordinated systems.[141] This differentiation has sometimes been further extended to contrast strategic and non-strategic wage negotiation systems. A centralized system is only considered strategic if it is vertically coordinated, that is, if decision changes in wage growth rates made at the top actually produce the intended results through the system; similarly, a decentralized system that is coordinated is only regarded as strategic if horizontal coordination is assured between individual unions and there is one union taking a leadership position in wage bargaining.[142]

The great majority of countries would be rated as intermediate with respect to the centralization of their wage bargaining systems. Central collective bargaining systems exist in five countries (Belgium, Ireland, Finland, Austria and the Netherlands); even through actual wage negotiations take place primarily at the sectoral level, considerable influence is exerted through central coordination at the national level.

Decentralized wage negotiation systems are found in the United Kingdom and in France. A particularity of the British wage negotiation system compared to Europe as a whole continues to be the absence of legal stipulations in many areas. As in Ireland, the principle of voluntarism carries widespread validity. Thus, for example, wage bargaining is generally permitted but not legally mandated. There is no requirement that employers bargain with unions.

Regardless of the degree to which wage negotiations are centralized in a given nation, at the EU level the introduction of the currency union resulted in a de facto process of decentralization in the relationship between the central bank and the wage negotiating parties, and this has made Europe-wide coordination of monetary and wage policy more difficult. The integration of monetary policy across Europe reduced the signalling effect of monetary policy. Prior to the currency union, IG Metall's wage-setting leadership and the German Central Bank's credible threat that it would retaliate against inflationary wage agreements with a more restrictive monetary policy led to an implicit coordination of monetary and wage policy. In the current monetary union, such coordination between the economic actors is not assured.[143] With the decentralization of wage policy, the ECB lacks a clear addressee for signalling its monetary policy and a free-rider problem arises between the unions. When a single union's contribution to overall inflation is small and no targeted response is possible on the part of the ECB, the union's readiness for wage restraint would appear to decrease.[144]

LEVEL OF ORGANIZATION AND THE SCOPE OF WAGE SCALE COVERAGE

Beyond the level at which negotiations occur, another critical factor for wage coordination is the degree to which workers and employers are organized in interest groups, the extent that wage agreements are binding and the number of jobs covered by wage agreements. There are major differences in this regard between individual countries. Workers in the Scandinavian nations are highly organized. However, the level of organization among firms is not especially high in Scandinavia, and the coverage scope of collective bargaining agreements is in the mid-range. Overall, the predominant model in the EU is for relatively low levels of union organization (with a trend towards lower organization over time), and a relatively high level of organization among firms. As a consequence, the scope of wage agreement coverage is generally quite high, ranging from nearly 100 per cent in Austria to 40 per cent in the United Kingdom. In the Baltic nations, the scope of coverage is actually below 20 per cent. In most Western European EU states there is a relatively high rate of coverage between 70 per cent and 99 per cent, whereas in the majority of the newer EU states, the rates of wage agreement coverage are often below 50 per cent (Table 5.5).[145]

COORDINATION MECHANISMS IN NATIONAL COLLECTIVE BARGAINING SYSTEMS

Wage policy is not necessarily uncoordinated in every country at the macroeconomic and national levels.[146] In the United Kingdom and France, coordination is limited to adhering to a government-mandated minimum wage. The government exerts a stronger influence in Belgium and Luxembourg, where there is a wage indexing mechanism. In other EU nations, the coordination of wage policy takes place at the national level between the associations representing the negotiating parties. To some extent, such coordination takes place explicitly, with central wage guidelines set by union and management umbrella organizations (in Belgium, Finland, Ireland, the Netherlands and Spain).[147] In part, the coordination is implicit, with wage leadership undertaken by one sector. Employer and employee organizations use pilot agreements of this kind as a guide when concluding other wage agreements, especially in Austria, Denmark, Germany and Sweden.

A new development in wage policy has been the formation of commissions and roundtables. These bodies agree upon macroeconomic guidelines for wage

Table 5.5 National wage bargaining systems

	Rate of unionization (%)	Rate of companies unionization (%)	Coverage	Degree of legal bindingness
Austria	37	96	97	Significant
Belgium	40	80	82	Significant
Denmark	68	48	52	Non+existent
Finland	65	58	67	Significant
France	<7	71	75	Limited
Germany	25	76	80	Significant
Greece	<15	N.A.	97	Significant
Ireland	37	44	N.A	Not significant
Italy	32	40	90	Non-existent
Luxembourg	N.A.	N.A.	N.A.	N.A.
Netherlands	19	80	79	Limited
Portugal	<20	N.A.	80	Limited
Spain	<15	70	67	Limited
Sweden	77	60	72	Non-existent
United Kingdom	21	57	40	Non-existent

Source: Boss *et al.* (2004, 80); Auer (2000, 58); Dohse *et al.* (1998, 68).

policy; such superordinate institutions have been set up in ten countries to date.[148] Their structure and degree of influence differs greatly from nation to nation, and their decision-making ranges from non-binding declarations of principle about wage policy issues to setting legally binding guidelines for wage development.

In Germany, the current system for collective bargaining relies on negotiated regional wage agreements between management and labour. However, at least in Germany, these regional agreements are embedded within a number of specific legal frameworks (governing collective bargaining, the right to strike, the extension of regional collective bargaining agreements) and are part of a political consensus between the negotiating parties. Sectoral unions negotiate with sector-wide employer organizations, whose membership reflects a significant proportion of the firms. Regional wage agreements largely eliminate wage competition between firms in the same industry, and when a single firm is established as the wage leader in a sector, competition is eliminated throughout the sector. Competition on the labour market is reduced overall, and at the same time, redirected to competition about non-salary benefits and labour productivity.

Germany had a past history of soft corporate coordination through moderating policies and/or through informal agreements on worker obligations and benefits; however, this form of coordination is rightly viewed as a failure. The "Concerted Action" programme that was part of the German Stability and Growth Law, and the "Alliance for Jobs" may be regarded as prototypes of soft coordination. The Concerted Action programme failed when workers were asked to make major sacrifices during times of significant inflation; this led workers to turn away from the unions as their representatives. The "Alliance for Jobs" was burdened by a number of labour policy goals that went well beyond mere wage policy, and demanded, among other things, that workers exercise restraint about their real wages for the sake of "regional economic policy" without offering clear or adequate reciprocation. Such soft forms of coordination are similar in that they require a consensus on the part of the major actors (i.e. the collective bargaining parties, the government and the central bank). They also do not provide for sanctions. The most successful examples of such coordination can be found in smaller countries such as the Netherlands, the Scandinavian nations and Austria.

5.3.4 Interim findings

From a theoretical as well as practical perspective, a productivity-oriented wage policy entails conflicts and difficulties. In light of the foregoing discussion, it would appear that a productivity-oriented wage policy is not the perfect coordination tool for a heterogeneous economic area. It could provide meaningful guidance in the absence of shocks, but its success would be contingent in large part on the homogeneity of the eurozone. In their practical attempts to implement coordination in recent years, trade unions have focused primarily on trying to improve their negotiating position through greater cross-border coordination of union activities. In this process, they have sought to enforce a coordination rule strongly reflective of a productivity-oriented wage policy. The prospects for the success of coordination efforts cannot be definitely determined by merely considering the four requirements set forth in the theory of collective action. What is clear, however, is that unions particularly lack the kinds of selective incentives that would assure reliable cooperation under collective action theory. This means that the coordination process can only succeed on the basis of a narrower scope of voluntary coordination that leaves union negotiation committees functioning as mediators and centres for information exchange. In the context of such a non-hierarchical, decentralized coordination process, the critical actors are the national unions. Furthermore, the chances for success hinge on the unions' readiness to set aside short-term interests in favour of longer-term common goals. Yet the unions' willingness to engage in voluntary cooperation is contingent upon the three other determinant factors for collective action described previously. With respect to each of these three factors, I have demonstrated the existence of relatively favourable starting conditions for voluntary coordination. Such favourable factors include: cooperation problems recur on a regular basis; cooperation costs tend to increase underproportionally compared to group size; cooperation does not require participation of all relevant actors, but only a critical mass; and finally, the coordinating process is marked by significant heterogeneity of interests.

Empirical studies examining the EMF wage-negotiating network have shown that a productivity-oriented wage policy can generate considerable successes. In Germany, Belgium and the Netherlands, the available scope for wage increases was more broadly exhausted after the introduction of the EMF network in 1999. Compliance with the guidelines for productivity-oriented wage increases was notable, especially in Germany. The fulfilment of wage growth targets increased from 78 per cent (1989–1998) to 94 per cent (1999–2008).

However, it must be noted that national systems for determining wages differ substantially in a number of respects. An EU-wide centralized wage policy would require a macroeconomic strategy coordinated with monetary policy, and this does not appear to be possible.[149] To create the necessary conditions for a joint European wage policy, existing national systems would have to be harmonized. Overall harmonization of wage policy institutions along with their employment-policy strategies does not seem like a realistic possibility due to several fundamental considerations. First, there is a lack of sufficient agreement about the underlying causes of European labour market problems and about how appropriate institutions should be structured. Economists have suggested a variety of different causes. Some regard the primary problem as being the rigidity of the labour market, and thus, they fear that establishing a consistent wage policy would reduce the flexibility of national labour markets, thereby compromising the effectiveness of the only policy instrument remaining since the loss of divergent exchange rates as an adjustment mechanism.[150] Other economists place an emphasis on the magnitude and duration of non-salary benefits.[151] Yet others see the primary cause of underemployment as an excessively restrictive monetary and finance policy.[152] Some economists reject harmonization due to fundamental economic policy considerations: they feel that an exchange of information and experience is the essential prerequisite for ensuring labour market competition. This perspective understands competition as a discovery process in a Hayekian sense, a process that allows superior institutions and practices to naturally prevail.[153] In keeping with the multiplicity of explanations proffered by economists, there is a similar variety in palliative recommendations and strategies for reform. In addition, we should not forget that wage policy institutions have developed historically in individual countries and thus embody different national preferences. It is not a self-evident fact that labour market institutions that have generated good results in one country would function in a satisfactory way in another.[154]

For our study, it is important to recall that voluntary transnational coordination efforts do, in fact, exist. At the same time, they are fraught with major uncertainties due to the risk that participating actors will engage in unpredictable and strategically motivated behaviour. As long as such coordination is non-binding, it cannot achieve a significant degree of effective coordination.

5.4 Coordinating monetary and fiscal policy

Another option for cross-policy coordination relates to monetary and fiscal policy. As we have seen, theoretical and empirical research on externalities confirms that there are strong interdependencies between fiscal and monetary policy (see Section 3.3.2.1). What is less clear is whether there is a definitive need for coordination. The majority of theoretical and empirical analyses support the notion of a need for coordination due to the interdependencies between fiscal and monetary policy. Yet those economists who reject the need for coordination do not base their opposition on the contention of no interdependencies between fiscal and monetary policy. Instead, they cite problems related to transparency and incentives as well as political and economic obstacles to achieving this kind of coordination.

A form of cross-policy coordination already exists today through the relationship between the SGP and monetary policy. One could interpret the SGP in part as an instrument to prevent cross-border fiscal policy spillovers. To prevent externalities that extend beyond single policy areas, the SGP also contains an inherent coordinating element, as it prescribes regulations only for national fiscal policies, while monetary policy remains independent. In this way, negative externalities that stimulate increases in inflation or a higher interest rate (in turn "crowding out" private sector investment) can be reduced. Thus, the monetary and fiscal policy coordination in the SGP consists of restricting each nation's freedom of action in fiscal policy in favour of preserving the ECB's monetary policy freedom. It is only the fiscal policy side (that is, the debt policy of national governments) that is subject to fixed rules. This is intended to benefit the monetary policy side because of the ECB's expanded scope of action with respect to price level stability. This effectively subordinates fiscal policy to monetary policy. Monetarists can also lend their support to this form of coordination, since it gives the central bank maximum freedom to preserve price level stability within the scope of an assignment approach.

Based on these considerations, in the next section I will examine more far-reaching coordination options. I will show that classical and Keynesian approaches come to different conclusions about the desirability of assigning a self-limiting role to the ECB within the scope of an effort to coordinate monetary and fiscal policy.

5.4.1 The classical argument against coordinating monetary policy

With the exception of the monetary and fiscal coordination contained in the SGP, the consultation procedure known as the Macroeconomic Dialogue represents the only form of "soft" coordination established to date. No hard coordination takes place at present between monetary policy and other policy fields, because according to the prevailing view, an independent central bank with a primary responsibility of assuring price stability cannot plausibly engage in the sort of bargaining with other policy actors that would be required to implement coordination. If it did, it would mean potentially entertaining a trade-off between higher inflation and other goals, such as faster growth or lower unemployment.[155] The issue is not whether such an outcome is desirable (the contrast with the Fed's dual mandate is obvious), but whether it is constitutionally allowed, and it would appear that existing law offers little room for manoeuvre.

The main argument against coordination is that an arrangement under which monetary authorities depend on fiscal authorities (and vice versa) would directly compromise Article 130 of the AEUV, confuse the roles of fiscal and monetary policy and jeopardize the credibility of the ECB.[156] Even if the relationship between fiscal and monetary authorities remains unchanged under coordination, the mere fact that centralization reduces the number of independent fiscal players in the eurozone will likely increase the pressure on the ECB to monetize excessive public debt. If the bank shows signs that it would capitulate to this pressure and permit member states to externalize the costs of excessive deficits, then the prior constraints on fiscal profligacy would be effectively removed. Under these circumstances, a common policy approach to coordination generates greater inconsistency in the macroeconomic policy mix. Other commentators criticize proposals for enhanced fiscal and monetary policy coordination on the grounds that they would create a forum in which member states could bring pressure on monetary policy.[157] Policy coordination might help to solve the problems of social choice and collective action, but in so doing it jeopardizes the credibility of monetary policy. Since monetary credibility is a fundamental principle in the design of EMU, politicians and economists alike have largely discounted common policy as a realistic cure for the eurozone's ills.[158] The ECB has struggled with pursuing a coordinated monetary policy directed at achieving economic growth.[159] Many traditional central bankers believe that although monetary policy may have short-term growth effects related to higher inflation, over the longer term, the monetary supply and monetary policy are actually growth neutral. Instead, the conditions for growth must be improved through "structural reforms" in member states. In addition, they point out that the short-term nominal interest rates that the ECB generally controls have been low since the inception of the EMU, both in nominal and real terms, and that seen in this light, the orientation of the ECB has tended to be slightly expansive.

5.4.2 The role of the ECB in a Keynesian-based coordinated economic policy

From the Keynesian perspective, there are a number of reasons to believe that monetary policy can have positive as well as negative effects on growth in the short and medium term. According to this view, the ECB might become worried about accelerated inflation even during a weak economic upturn, unlike the Fed or the Bank of England. Since nominal interest rates have little room for downward movement during periods with a low inflation target, the options for an expansive monetary policy are quite limited. In addition, Keynesians point out that in the past, interest rates have decreased far too slowly during times of weak growth. The Keynesian recommendations for reform thus take the following trajectory:[160]

1   The ECB should keep a closer eye on growth and employment targets and from time to time test the growth potential of the eurozone by means of a controlled monetary expansion, along the lines of what the US Federal Reserve did in the second half of the 1990s. Such a policy takes into account that potential growth and the NAIRU are not exogenously determined variables, but are in fact jointly determined by actual real GDP and employment trends, both of which are also influenced by monetary policy.[161]

2   In the longer view, long-term real interest rates, which the central bank influences through its base rate, should remain below the growth rate in real GDP. This has an expansive effect and prevents ongoing redistribution in favour of investment income.

3   The legal mandate of the ECB should be changed so that price stability, economic growth and employment are equally important goals for the ECB, similar to the situation in the United States. In the context of a coordinated macropolicy, monetary policy should assume responsibility for growth and employment, especially when there is no inflationary pressure from wages policy or fiscal policy. Setting a dual goal that consists of a nominal interest rate target (inflation) and a real growth target (GDP expansion) is somewhat analogous to the Taylor Rule, according to which both of these aims are weighted equally. The Taylor Rule is a de facto guiding principle for the US Fed.

4   The ECB should not independently set the target inflation rate. Instead – as in the United Kingdom – the target rate should be set by European-level policymakers, such as the European Parliament. Under such an arrangement,

the ECB would then be required to adopt the targets set by the European Parliament.[162] Furthermore, the promotion of growth and employment should be viewed as monetary policy objectives alongside maintaining price stability.

5   It has been argued that the ECB must not only combat inflation that exceeds its targets, but must also combat excessively low inflation with equal vigor.[163] The ECB should formulate its inflation target as a single figure or corridor. Moreover, the target should be treated as a medium-term goal, with the prime lending rate adjusted dynamically to ensure target fulfilment.

6   The coordination of monetary, fiscal and wage policy at various levels is of key importance for a reorientation of monetary policy. Provided the ECB is to be more committed to the goals of promoting growth and employment, then the ECB should take over responsibility for both wage and fiscal stability. However, even if a growth- and employment-oriented realignment of monetary policy in the EMU were achieved, considerable risks to macro-economic instability could still be expected if wage restraint continued to be pursued and unemployment remained high. One issue is the asymmetrical and sometimes significantly delayed effects of monetary policy during the course of an economic cycle. Should there be a failure to react in time to an emerging downturn or a negative shock, leading the economy to plunge into a deep recession, then monetary policy will be powerless to do anything about it. In addition, a more expansive monetary policy for the eurozone as a whole still cannot take into account regional and structural asymmetries. For both of these reasons, it is essential to coordinate monetary policy with fiscal policy, as well as to elevate growth and employment to monetary policy objectives with equal importance as price stability. Procedurally, the Macroeconomic Dialogue should be used to increase cooperation with other policy areas, e.g. in the Macroeconomic Dialogue, but without encroaching on its independent choice of policy tools.[164]

5.4.3 The ECB's quasi-fiscal monetary policy in the sovereign-debt crisis

To achieve the coordination of fiscal and monetary policy, it is not necessary to involve all of the fiscal and monetary policy actors that exist. The ECB's interventions during the financial crisis have shown that the ECB has recognized a need to engage in monetary policy that has fiscal implications. To this extent, the ECB has already exceeded the remit of a central bank under classical monetary policy.

The financial crisis that began in August 2007 when the subprime mortgage market collapsed in the United States and that dramatically intensified in September 2008 with the insolvency of Lehman Brothers posed a double challenge for the ECB. For one, the ECB needed to stabilize European financial markets. As banks began questioning each other's solvency, they drastically curtailed interbank lending, leading European money markets to come to a rapid standstill.

The only way banks could overcome the ensuing liquidity bottleneck was by refinancing themselves through the central bank. Moreover, the ECB needed to prevent the financial market crisis from spreading to the real economy, which could have led to a drastic decline in growth and a major decrease in employment. To deal with this double challenge, the ECB was compelled to directly provide the private sector with adequate liquidity, while at the same time stimulating the economy through low interest rates.

The ECB relied first on standard monetary policy measures to manage liquidity. This quickly led the ECB to give up control of the monetary supply in order to provide banks with unlimited liquidity.[165] Yet even more serious from a fiscal policy view was that the ECB had to weaken its usual safety mechanisms in order to expand the liquidity available to banks. Among other moves, it lowered the credit quality threshold for its main refinancing operations from A– to BBB–. This was especially important for stabilizing the banking sector in eurozone nations such as Greece, Italy, Spain, Portugal and Ireland. All of these countries had suffered bond rating downgrades, and largely financed their sovereign debt through the domestic banking sector.

As the crisis in Greece worsened in 2010, the ECB found itself compelled to further intensify its interventions. In May 2010 the ECB decided to begin purchasing government securities from banks in order to indirectly finance the sovereign debt of governments in the eurozone.[166] In order to assist over-indebted peripheral countries and support their banks with liquidity, the ECB bought government securities on the secondary market and took them over from banks in the PIIGS nations (Portugal, Ireland, Italy, Greece and Spain) as a guarantee for liquidity assistance. These functions were part of the ECB's open market operations.[167] Yet the ECB did not merely pursue a relaxed monetary policy by decreasing the prime lending and main refinancing rates. It also pursued a policy of quantitative easing (QE) analogous to the policy of the US Federal Reserve. The official line was that the ECB intended in this way to assure a process of "orderly monetary policy transmission". However, these interventions violated the intention of the Maastricht Treaty. Article 123 of the AEUV explicitly forbids the direct sale of government bonds in order to finance states in the eurozone.[168]

The bond purchases by the ECB were not meant to have a fiscal policy effect. In fact, the deliberate purchase of securities from severely indebted euro nations included an element of subsidizing them, one that weakens fiscal discipline. This policy causes the interest rates for the bonds of weaker countries to fall, while rates rise for countries on more solid financial footing. In effect, the ECB is passing along the credit risk from the bonds of weaker euro nations to the bonds of stronger ones.[169]

This quasi-fiscal policy ends up affecting the ECB's financial and political independence. The ECB assumes liability. This endangers the financial independence of the ECB that is necessary so that the ECB can meet its mandate to maintain price level stability without relying on the financial support of the government, and, by extension, being subjected to political compromises (i.e. "lower interest rates in exchange for safeguarding solvency").[170] Yet the political independence of the ECB is also endangered. For one thing, the ECB invites reproach for bowing to political pressure to save Greece in making its decision to purchase government bonds. This intervention casts doubt on its credibility as an autonomous institution for preserving monetary stability. However, until today the ECB maintained its independence as it formally adopts decisions on bond purchases at its own discretion as is required under EU law. In the event of member state insolvency or a haircut on public debt, however, the assets contained in the ECB's portfolio could lead to losses in the triple-digit billions, sapping its reserves. At this point, ECB losses would be passed along to taxpayers in eurozone nations.

5.4.4 Monetary and fiscal policy coordination between the ECB and the European Stability Mechanism

The purchase of government debt by the ECB was not only condemned as an instance of the central bank improperly engaging in public sector financing. It also led to the problem of moral hazard. Leaving aside the contentious question of whether the ECB decided to purchase bonds to assure monetary policy transmission or to relieve the burden on government finances, such purchases of sovereign debt clearly harbour the potential to create disincentives. If a government can count on the ECB to intervene in the event it is overwhelmed by high interest rates, it will be relieved of the regulating pressures of the market, and will not have sufficient incentive to avoid future indebtedness.

The moral hazard problem highlights that the purchase of government securities as an instrument of monetary policy has broader consequences for the fiscal policy behaviour of the euro nations whose bonds are purchased by the ECB. In the wake of ECB initial interventions, there have been attempts to mitigate the "moral hazard" problem by making the rescue packages conditional. Access to credit granted under the rescue packages (the EFSF and the ESM) is contingent on the recipient's undertaking austerity measures and structural reforms. However, in a world without cross-policy coordination, the ECB cannot negotiate conditions for purchasing government debt. This problem became apparent over the course of the sovereign-debt crisis, as pressure mounted on the ECB to purchase government debt.

As a consequence of the moral hazard risk created by the purchase of sovereign debt, it was necessary to find a mechanism that would maintain the incentive for reforms. Therefore, the ECB announced in the summer of 2012 that it would only agree to purchase government debt on the secondary market after the affected nation had submitted an application for assistance to the ESM and agreed to a set of stipulations. This was intended to guarantee that the country would meet certain conditions in exchange for the purchase of bonds by the ECB, and that these countries would not neglect reform efforts.

In the context of this study, the ECB's decision to link its purchase of government securities to the requirement that the nation in question apply for help through the ESM represents an impressive shift in ECB policy. Previously, the ECB was a stalwart advocate of the monetarist assignment doctrine, according to which every actor should be independent and accomplish its assigned task without the benefit of coordination. National governments had independent responsibility for the sustainability of their fiscal policy, while the ECB was tasked with maintaining stable price levels in the absence of coordination with fiscal or wage policy. The ECB's decision in the summer of 2012 represented a marked easing of its strict assignment policy.

In the future, coordination will continue between the activities of the ESM and the ECB. Such coordination has already been anchored in law, since it was explicitly provided for in the law that established the ESM. According to Article 18, para. 2 of the ESM Treaty, the ESM may only undertake purchases of bonds on the secondary market after the ECB has determined "the existence of extraordinary circumstances on the financial markets and a risk to financial stability". Therefore, the ESM and the ECB will have to interact when undertaking the purchase of government securities, not only for bond purchases by the ESM but also for bond purchases by the ECB.

In short, the crisis has led to a two-fold expansion of monetary and fiscal policy coordination, and thus, to a break with the classical assignment policy, as illustrated by Table 5.6. The first dimension of expansion was assured by the institutional inclusion of the ECB in the troika for establishing conditional fiscal policy assistance programmes. As a consequence, conditional assistance programmes and their monitoring by the ESM in the context of rescue packages cannot take place without the ECB. In effect, virtually all conditional fiscal policy assistance programmes will be coordinated with the ECB. In the second

Table 5.6 Classification of coordination

		Horizontal coordination	
		Cross-border coordination	*Cross-policy coordination (fiscal, monetary, wages)*
Vertical coordination	Soft coordination	Macroeconomic dialogue; BEPG; Luxembourg process; EU2020-Strategy; EU semester	
	Hard coordination	*Macroeconomic imbalance procedure*	
		SGP	
		Conditionality on rescue programs	
	Centralized coordination	Monetary policy	Until 2012; ECB bond purchases without conditions
		Since mid-2012: Bonds purchases contingent on ESM conditionality	

Source: author's own description.

dimension of expanded coordination, the ECB now couples its purchase of sovereign debt (based on monetary policy considerations) with the condition that the affected member state has submitted an application to the ESM for assistance, and has agreed to let the ESM develop a conditional aid programme. With this step, for the first time, the ECB relinquishes decision-making authority for a fiscal policy measure in that it couples its own decision-making to an independent decision by a member state.

Notes

1 See for a comprehensive analysis Kullas and Koch (2010, 3).
2 See for the following Herrmann (2011).
3 Regulation (EU) No. 1175/2011 of the European Parliament and of the Council of 16 November 2011 amending Council Regulation (EC) No. 1466/97 on the strengthening of the surveillance of budgetary positions and the surveillance and coordination of economic policies; Regulation (EU) No 1173/2011 of the European Parliament and of the Council of 16 November 2011 on the effective enforcement of budgetary surveillance in the euro area.
4 See for the following Kullas and Koch (2010, 15).
5 See Sachverständigenrat (2009, 88); Blanchard and Illing (2006, 769).
6 Sachverständigenrat (2009, 88).
7 Article 121, para. 4 of AEUV.
8 Kullas and Koch (2010, 15).
9 See for the following Herrmann (2011).
10 Kullas (2011, 31ff.).
11 Manasse (2010).
12 Article 126, para. 6 of AEUV.
13 Article 126, para. 8 of AEUV.
14 Blankart and Fasten (2009, 40).
15 A third type of state is the unitary state. In unitary states the central government is liable for all debts throughout the state. As a result, only the central government can take on debt. The regional governments are just departments of the central government and cannot take on any debt.
16 Blankart and Fasten (2009, 41).
17 Diekmann *et al.* (2012).
18 Deubner (2010, 802).
19 See for the following Diekmann *et al.* (2012).
20 Blankart and Fasten (2009, 40).
21 Blankart and Fasten (2009, 45).
22 For the following see Konrad and Zschäpitz (2010, 186ff.).
23 Konrad and Zschäpitz (2010, 187), Schulz and Wolff (2008).
24 Deubner (2010, 802); for a different view see Blankart and Fasten (2009, 51f.).
25 Deubner (2010, 802).
26 Joumard and Kongsrud (2003).
27 Landmann (2012).
28 11 March 2011 decision of the heads of state and government of the eurozone member states.
29 For the following, see Gerken *et al.* (2011, 9); Folkers (1999, 29f.).
30 German Federal Ministry of Finance (2011).
31 Heinen (2010).
32 Blankart and Fasten (2009, 42).
33 Gerken *et al.* (2011, 10).

34 See for the following the contribution of the German Federal Ministry of Finance (2011); Gerken *et al.* (2011).
35 Voigt and Blume (2011).
36 Hagen (1992).
37 Kiewiet and Szakaly (1996).
38 Bohn and Inman (1996).
39 German Federal Ministry of Finance (2011).
40 Hetschko *et al.* (2012, 15).
41 See Reinhart and Rogoff (2010, 29; 169).
42 See Karl-Bräuer-Institut (2011, 51) and Rogoff and Zettelmeyer (2002).
43 See Zenker (2003, 2); Wissenschaftlicher Beirat and Bundesministerium für Wirtschaft und Technologie (2011, 22).
44 See Krueger (2002, 10).
45 See Wissenschaftlicher Beirat and Bundesministerium für Wirtschaft und Technologie (2011, 20) and Zenker (2003, 1).
46 Eurogroup (2011, 2).
47 See Europäischer Rat (2010).
48 See Wissenschaftlicher Beirat and Bundesministerium für Wirtschaft und Technologie (2011, 18).
49 Delpla and von Weizsäcker (2011), German Council of Economic Experts (2012).
50 Nauschnigg (2009).
51 De Grauwe and Moesen (2009).
52 Delpla and von Weizsäcker (2011).
53 See Delpla and von Weizsäcker (2011).
54 See Horn (2009, 28).
55 See the German Council of Economic Experts (2012).
56 See Delpla and von Weizsäcker (2011).
57 See Horn (2009, 12).
58 See Delpla and von Weizsäcker (2011, 2).
59 See Issing (2009, 77).
60 See Bernoth and Engler (2012).
61 See Diekmann (2012, 31).
62 See Bordo *et al.* (2011).
63 See Bernoth and Engler (2012), Hagen and Wyplozs (2008) and Enderlein *et al.* (2012).
64 Bernoth and Engler (2013).
65 See Hagen and Wyplosz (2008) and Enderlein *et al.* (2012).
66 See Koske and Pain (2008).
67 See Dullien (2008).
68 See Brenke (2012).
69 See Dietrich *et al.* (2010, 371).
70 See Article 2, subsection A of the Regulation on the Correction and Prevention of Macroeconomic Imbalances.
71 See Article 3, para. 1 of the Regulation on the Correction and Prevention of Macroeconomic Imbalances.
72 See Article 121, para. 3 of the TFEU.
73 See Article 5, para. 1 of the Regulation on the Correction and Prevention of Macroeconomic Imbalances.
74 See Article 2, subsection B of the Regulation on the Correction and Prevention of Macroeconomic Imbalances.
75 See Article 121, paragraph 2 of the TFEU; and Article 6, para. 1 of the Regulation on the Correction and Prevention of Macroeconomic Imbalances.
76 See Dullien (2010, 15).
77 See European Commission (2009, 28).

78 See Gerken and Kullas (2011).
79 See Deutsche Bundesbank (2010, 21).
80 See the EC communication dated 11–12 January 2011; the EC communication dated 7 June 2011 (400); and the Council recommendations 11391/11 on Germany's national reform programmes for 2011.
81 See Dullien and Schwarzer (2009).
82 See European Commission (2010).
83 See Deutsche Bank Research (2011, 11).
84 See Agnello and Schuknecht (2010).
85 See Eurostat (2010).
86 See Reitschuler and Cuaresma (2004).
87 See Deutsche Bank Research (2011, 11).
88 See consideration 14 of the Regulation on the Correction and Prevention of Macro-economic Imbalances.
89 See communication from the EC dated 11–12 January 2011.
90 For the first report of Council recommendations, see 11391/11.
91 Greece: Memorandum of Understanding on Specific Economic Policy Conditionality, 2 May 2010.
92 By contrast, the ECB's monetary analysis (the so-called second pillar) also takes systematic note of the mid-term and long-term consequences of monetary policy on the financial markets.
93 Ribhegge (2011, 209).
94 Calmfors (1998).
95 Article 127 of the Treaty of the European Union.
96 ECB (2000, 54).
97 Boss *et al.* (2004, 38f.).
98 See for the following Hein and Truger (2004, 17ff.).
99 Allsopp and Vines (1996).
100 Hein and Truger (2004, 17).
101 Hein and Truger (2004, 19ff.).
102 Boss *et al.* (2004, 76).
103 ECB (2008).
104 Sinn (2008, 21); Council of Economic Experts (2003/2004).
105 Franzese (2001), Soskice and Iversen (2001), Hein (2002c).
106 Hein and Truger (2004, 18).
107 Angelo and Mesch (2003, 117).
108 Boss *et al.* (2004, 46ff.).
109 Ribhegge (2011, 222f.).
110 See for the following Flassbeck and Spiecker (2011).
111 Flassbeck and Spiecker (2011).
112 Flassbeck and Spiecker (2011).
113 Flassbeck and Spiecker (2011).
114 Priewe (2009).
115 Angelo and Mesch (2003, 99), Sisson and Marginson (2002), Marginson and Traxler (2005).
116 Glassner and Pusch (2010, 5), Angelo and Mesch (2003, 114ff.).
117 Schulten (1998).
118 Glassner and Watt (2010).
119 See for the following Glassner and Pusch (2010, 13ff).
120 Glassner and Pusch (2010, 13ff).
121 See for the following Traxler (1999, 115ff.).
122 This issue typically arises on the implementation of outcomes of corporatist arrangements involving associational parties and political stakeholders (Streit, 1988, 615).
123 Pamela and Gerald (1988).

124   Traxler (1999, 115ff.).
125   Axelrod (1984).
126   Olson (1965,35).
127   Carlin and Soskice (2006).
128   Streit (1988).
129   Schmitter (1979), Streit (1988).
130   Streit (1988, 608).
131   Streit (1988, 620, 613).
132   Dufresme and Mermet (2002).
133   Erne (2004).
134   Pusch and Glassner (2010, 565).
135   Schulten (2010).
136   For the following see Boss *et al.* (2004, 77ff.).
137   EIRO (2000).
138   Enderlein (2004, 115).
139   Baum-Ceisig (2002).
140   Cameron (1984), Calmfors and Drifill (1988), Iversen (1999).
141   Crouch (1985), Soskice (1990), Hall and Franzese (1998).
142   Traxler and Kittel (2000).
143   Hall and Franzese (1998), Iversen (1998).
144   Hancké and Soskice (2003).
145   Schulten (2010).
146   EIRO (2000).
147   Baum-Ceisig (2002).
148   EIRO (2000); Fajertag and Pochet (1997).
149   Boss *et al.* (2004, 82); Ribhegge (2011, 214).
150   See for the following Boss *et al.* (2004, 81f.), Siebert (1997), Dohse *et al.* (1998, 6ff.).
151   Nickell (1997).
152   Martin (2000).
153   Padoa-Schioppa (1987).
154   Freeman (1988).
155   See for the following Begg *et al.* (2003, 72).
156   Begg *et al.* (2003, 68); Issing (2002).
157   Alesina *et al.* (2001).
158   Begg *et al.* (2003, 72).
159   Bibow (2007).
160   See for the following Priewe (2007a, 142f.), Hein and Truger (2004, 5ff.).
161   Hein and Truger (2004, 26).
162   Hein and Truger (2004, 26).
163   Hein and Truger (2004, 26).
164   Hein and Truger (2004, 27).
165   Ribhegge (2011, 127ff.), Hess (2010, 473ff.).
166   ECB (2010).
167   Statutes of the ESCB and the ECB, Article 18.1.
168   Statutes of the ESCB and the ECB, Article 21.1.
169   Belke and Schnabl (2010, 10).
170   Belke and Schnabl (2010, 10).

6 Summary

The objective of this study was to investigate the necessity for economic policy coordination within the eurozone, as well as to elaborate possible options for configuring such coordination. Unlike previous research in the area of economic policy coordination, this study has attempted to find a way past the typical criticism of coordination attempts that invokes uncertainties regarding the underlying economic model. Past research typically displays a series of underlying assumptions concerning the functional relationships between monetary, fiscal and wage policy. As a result, the relevance of their findings is contingent upon whether the assumed interrelationships are valid. This study approached the subject instead from the perspective of institutional economics, and attempted to analyse instances of economic policy coordination and the incentives resulting from existing and potential forms of coordination. In this context, I compared the different approaches to coordination on the part of monetarist and Keynesian theorists, and evaluated them with respect to the effects of their institutional configurations.

The point of departure for the study was an empirical survey of macroeconomic heterogeneity within the eurozone. This survey formed the basis for examining whether there is a need for coordination in the first place. I have shown that macroeconomic asymmetries have persisted since the creation of the eurozone, and their persistence justifies an analysis of the stabilizing potential of a coordinated economic policy. To date, the EMU has not been able to induce greater convergence in macroeconomic heterogeneity. To some extent, heterogeneity has even increased. Moreover, it is also clear that individual countries have come under pressure to reform as a result of the ECB's common interest rate policy, which is oriented to average values. Indeed, even given identical macroeconomic conditions in member states, it is plausible that the ECB's interest rate policy could generate asymmetric shocks. To the extent this is true, uneven economic growth would be the result, leading to a growing need for alternative mechanisms for absorbing shocks. The empirical findings outlined in the study demonstrate the need to analyse the stabilizing potential of a coordinated economic policy.

The first reason that economic adjustment instruments are needed within the EMU is the fact that the EMU is not a unitary currency area. The eurozone is a monetary union, but at the same time it is not an OCA. The euro area does not fulfil some important OCA criteria, especially those related to labour mobility as well as price and wage flexibility. As a monetary union, the euro area is potentially exposed to asymmetric shocks. Second, for the foreseeable future, the only available instruments for functional adjustment are wage and fiscal policy, both of which are constrained in their operational scope. Adjustments in the area of wage policy have limited flexibility on account of labour market regulation and centralized wage negotiations. Similarly, fiscal policy is subject to strict constraints because of European legal requirements. Against this backdrop, there is a clear need for a detailed examination of the stabilizing potential of a coordinated economic policy.

Based upon the empirical survey conducted at the outset, I proposed a coordination classification schema that differentiated between vertical and horizontal forms of coordination. The horizontal axis defines coordination in a way not previously proposed in the literature: on this axis, a difference is drawn between cross-border coordination between euro nations (for example, as part of fiscal policy through the SGP) and cross-policy coordination (for example, between monetary and wage policy). This differentiation is necessary in order to clearly understand the history of coordination in the eurozone up to the present time, and to adequately explain the different economic implications of each form of cooperation. The vertical axis, by contrast, serves to differentiate between various forms of coordination depending on the degree to which they are binding. On this axis, a difference is drawn between three basic types of coordination – namely, soft, hard and centralized coordination.

After elaborating this classification schema, I explored the existence of externalities as a potential justification for economic coordination, as economic heterogeneity alone does not make coordination essential. A justification for coordination only arises on the basis of externalities (or spillovers), the existence of public goods (or club goods), and the existence of interdependencies between policy areas. For the area of cross-border coordination, this study came to the following conclusions: externalities may affect macroeconomic indicators in other national economies, joint club goods, the exchange rate for the common currency, European price levels or the interest rate. Both theoretical as well as empirical research suggests that spillovers result from national fiscal and wage policy. However, no definitive answer can be given as to whether the externalities here are negative or positive.

In contrast to cross-border coordination, economic theory does not provide a clear answer about the preconditions required for successful cross-policy coordination. This is attributable to theoretical disagreement, which extends to the question of whether there is a need for cross-policy coordination. Only the Keynesian model offers support for such coordination, if we agree that there are interdependencies between the different policy areas. From the perspective of neo-Keynesian theory, only a short-term need exists for coordinating monetary, wage and fiscal policy. If instead one follows a classical monetarist perspective, each policy area should be considered separate from the others. Therefore, for the purposes of this study, it was important to also take an empirical look at the question of whether interdependencies may exist. Past research demonstrates the existence of spillover effects between individual policy areas. According to the studies, interdependencies exist between monetary and fiscal policy and also between monetary and wage policy.

Based on these findings, I went on to examine coordination regimes in the EU before the eruption of the sovereign-debt crisis. I was able to show the following: first, the coordination efforts undertaken prior to the sovereign-debt crisis were not able to sufficiently internalize externalities. With its fixation on public sector indebtedness, the SGP fails to consider other causes of negative cross-border externalities and the risks of a bailout. In addition, lacking an effective sanction mechanism, the SGP is not able to resolve the time inconsistency problem. Briefly stated, in its pre-debt crisis mode, the SGP was incapable of contributing to the internalization of cross-border fiscal externalities. A similar pattern can be seen in the other forms of coordination, which either took the form of cross-border coordination (BEPG, the Luxembourg Process) or cross-policy coordination (Macroeconomic Dialogue), but as a whole, can all be considered examples of "soft" coordination. Second, the institutions and actors in the EU prior to the eruption of the crisis in 2009 were characterized by major asymmetries with regard to the coordination of national economic policies. On the one hand, there was an independently acting central bank with sole responsibility for monetary policy; on the other hand, there were more or less strict coordination processes for all other policy areas, each of them generally restricted to a single policy area (SGP, monetary policy, the Luxembourg Process) or if they did enable cross-policy coordination (Macroeconomic Dialogue), this was limited in practice to information exchange, the softest possible form of coordination. In addition, a neoclassical argument clearly underlies the EU's toolbox for economic policy interventions. Each of the aims of economic policy cited in the BEPGs (i.e. budgetary consolidation, productivity-oriented wages, monetary policy to assure price level stability, structural policy to increase flexibility) are meant to be pursued independently of one another. The assumption is that there are no negative side-effects for the other objectives – in any event, possible negative effects are left unaddressed. Thus, the course of fiscal policy was not made contingent upon how monetary policy and wage policy were managed nor on the pace of structural reform.

This study examined broader options for fiscal coordination. It focused on the reforms to the SGP undertaken in recent years as well as broader attempts to coordinate fiscal policy (national debt brakes, Eurobonds, insolvency proceedings). At the very least, the reform of the SGP addressed the time inconsistency problem by strengthening sanctions and the obligations for assistance. However, the SGP still has the disadvantage of exclusively focusing on indebtedness (but this will be partially offset by the new Macroeconomic Imbalance Procedure).

This study's examination of the options for fiscal policy coordination also made it clear that the specific method of coordination must be considered in light of the organizing principles underlying the monetary union. Mutual liability for debts is possible in a union state system – in fact, creditors anticipate it. In a federal system, by contrast, mutual liability is excluded. The various forms of fiscal policy coordination that are possible differ in their suitability depending on whether liability is mutual. The Fiscal Compact imposes national debt brakes on all eurozone members, and these brakes are being introduced or reformed in a number of countries. Debt limits perform a similar function to that of the SGP: the debt limit is an instrument that does not employ market incentives to achieve budgetary discipline, but instead introduces deficit limits set and administered from above to limit indebtedness. The SGP and debt brakes are better adapted to a union state system with joint liability than to a "market-based" federal system without joint liability. The same is true for Eurobonds. They result to some degree in joint liability, even if there is an attempt to retain the disciplining force of the market. For this reason, Eurobonds are better suited to a union state system.

A credible no-bailout system and the option of state insolvency are two forms of coordination that aim to create market incentives to encourage debt reduction. An insolvency procedure creates legal protection for creditors and debtors. In addition, it establishes incentives for creditors to carefully examine the credit-worthiness of their debtors. This harnesses market-based incentives to reduce the tendency for indebtedness. Insolvency procedures are well adapted to a federal system with no joint liability.

Beyond purely fiscal coordination, I have also shown in this study that the once strict separation of functions in accordance with the monetarist "assignment approach" has undergone significant changes in the course of the debt crisis: first, in setting up new macroeconomic monitoring procedures, a hard cross-policy coordination approach was selected. This hard approach is accompanied by soft cross-policy coordination (for example, under the Europe 2020 strategy and the European Semester). The Macroeconomic Imbalance Procedure is the very first instance of mandatory cross-policy coordination. As such, it is complementary to the SGP, which is limited to purely fiscal matters. However, the Macroeconomic Imbalance Procedure scorecard still needs to be improved. The warning thresholds and manner with which the scoreboard is to be integrated into economic coordination processes in the eurozone still need more specific definition. In an ideal case, the scoreboard could function as a complement to implicit coordination, which is based on pressure from capital markets. The scorecard could prove useful in terms of promoting information transparency and generating political pressure to act. Furthermore, its existence might be a persuasive signal that the nations of the eurozone intend to take their coordination tasks more seriously in the future than they have in the past. However, significant shortcomings of the macroeconomic surveillance remain due to uncertainties. There is uncertainty about a country's responsibility for a specific economic development. For example, reasons for current account imbalances can be attributed to both surplus or deficit countries. Also, resolving certain problems may not be properly dealt with by governments, as they are rooted in conduct of economic actors (e.g. trade surpluses, private debt). These uncertainties about the causes and elimination of imbalances render the macro-economic surveillance hard to implement.

Finally, another form of cross-policy coordination can be seen in the shift in the direction of monetary policy, which has been expanded to include a fiscal policy dimension through the purchase of government bonds. The conditionality of rescue programmes for distressed states also makes it clear that the EU has shifted to a form of economic coordination that is broader and more comprehensive. The avowed aim is to resolve the fiscal policy problems in the crisis-shaken countries of the eurozone through reform programmes that extend to every area of economic policy.

The most underdeveloped forms of coordination can be seen at present in the realm of wage policy. In this area, the principle of a productivity-oriented wage policy has run into conflicts and difficulties both in theory and in practice. The model of a productivity-oriented wage policy is not the perfect coordination tool for a heterogeneous economic area. It can provide meaningful guidance in the absence of shocks, but its success is contingent in large part on the homogeneity of the eurozone. In the coordination undertaken to date, the unions in particular have attempted in recent years to improve their position through the cross-border coordination of their activities. In these attempts, they have largely tried to follow a coordination rule based on a productivity-oriented wage policy. The prospects for the success of their coordination efforts cannot be definitely determined by considering the four requirements set forth in collective action theory. What is clear, however, is that unions particularly lack the kinds of selective incentives that would assure reliable cooperation under collective action theory.

The few empirical studies undertaken to date show that the implementation of a productivity-oriented wage policy can be successful in national collective bargaining agreements. However, it must be noted that national wage determination systems differ substantially in a number of respects. An EU-wide centralized wage policy would require a macroeconomic strategy coordinated with monetary policy, and this does not appear to be possible, nor desirable. To create the preconditions for a joint European wage policy, harmonization with monetary policy would be essential. In any event, the overall harmonization of wage policy institutions in addition to employment policy strategies does not seem feasible for several reasons. First, there is a lack of sufficient agreement among politicians and academics regarding the underlying causes of European labour market problems and how appropriate institutions should be structured. Economists have suggested a variety of different causes. Some regard the primary problem as being the rigidity of the labour market, and thus they fear that establishing a consistent wage policy would reduce the flexibility of national labour markets, thereby compromising the effectiveness of the only policy instrument available since the loss of differential currency exchange rates. Other economists place the emphasis on the magnitude and duration of wage replacement benefits. Yet others see the primary cause of the unemployment problem as an excessively restrictive monetary and fiscal policy. In keeping with the multiplicity of different explanatory approaches, there is great variety in the recommendations for reform. Furthermore, we should not forget that wage policy institutions have developed historically in individual countries and thus embody different national preferences. It is not self-evident that labour market institutions that have generated good results in one country would function well when transplanted to another.

This study additionally highlighted that the sovereign-debt crises has led to a two-fold expansion of monetary and fiscal policy coordination, and thus to a break with the classical assignment policy. The first dimension of expansion lies in the institutional inclusion of the ECB in the troika for establishing conditional fiscal-policy assistance. As a consequence, conditional assistance programmes and their monitoring by the ESM cannot take place without the ECB. In effect, virtually all conditional fiscal-policy assistance is to be coordinated with the ECB. In the second dimension of expanded coordination, the ECB has coupled its purchase of sovereign debt with the condition that the affected member state submits an assistance application to the ESM and lets the ESM develop a conditional aid programme. Fiscal policy interventions by the ECB are thus linked with a bailout programme that aims to fundamentally alter the economic policy structure in the recipient state. This leads to the close coordination of monetary policy with other economic policy areas. We thus find that the traditional assignment approach is increasingly falling by the wayside.

Bibliography

Acocella, N., Bartolomeo, G., Tirelli, P. (2007a) Fiscal Leadership and Coordination in the EMU, *Open Economies Review*, 18(3): 281–289.

Acocella, N., Di Bartolomeo, G., Tirelly P. (2007b) Monetary conservatism and fiscal coordination in a monetary union, *Economics Letters*, 94: 56.

Agnello, L., Schuknecht, L. (2010) Booms and busts in housing markets. Determinants and implications. ECB Working Paper No. 1071.

Agresti, Anna-Maria, Mojon, Benoit (2001) Some Stylized Facts on the Euro Area Business Cycle. ECB Working Paper No. 95.

Ahmed, S., Ickes, B., Wang, P., Sam Yoo, B. (1993) International Business Cycles, *American Economic Review*, 83(3): 335–359.

Aizenman, J. (1994) On the need for fiscal discipline in a union, National Bureau of Economic Research Working Paper No. W4656.

Alesina, Alberto (2003) The Coordination of Monetary and Fiscal Policies in Europe, in: Deutsche Bundesbank (ed.), *Auszüge aus Presseartikeln*, Deutsche Bundesbank, pp. 24–27.

Alesina, Alberto, Perotti, R. (1995) The Political Economy of Budget Deficits, IMF Staff Papers No. 42, pp. 1–31.

Alesina, A., Perotti, R. (1997) The Welfare State and Competitiveness, *The American Economic Review*, 87(5): 921–939.

Alesina, Alberto, Tabellini, Guido (1987) Rules and Discretion with Non-Coordinated Monetary and Fiscal Policies, *Economic Inquiry*, 25: 619–630.

Alesina, Alberto, Galí, Jordi, Uhlig, Harald, Blanchard, Olivier, Giavazzi, Franceso (2001) *Monitoring the European Central Bank, Nr.3: Defining a Macroeconomic Framework for the Euro Area*, CEPR.

Alesina, Alberto, Angeloni, Ignazio, Schuknecht, Ludger (2005) What does the European Union do?, *Public Choice*, 123: 275–319.

Allsopp, C., Vines, D. (1996) Fiscal policy and EMU, *National Institute Economic Review*, 158: 91–107.

Altissimo, Filippo, Ehrmann, Michael, Smets, Frank (2006) Inflation Persistence and Price-Setting Behaviour in the Euro Area: A Summary of IPN Evidence. ECB Occasional Paper No. 46.

Angelo, S., Mesch, M. (eds) (2003) *Wirtschaftspolitische Koordination in der Europäischen Währungsunion, Wirtschaftswissenschaftliche Tagungen der AK Wien, Vol. 7*, LexisNexis.

Angeloni, Ignazio, Ehrmann, Michael (2007) Euro Area Inflation Differentials, *The B.E. Journal of Macroeconomics*, 7: art. 24.

Arnold, I., Verhoef, B. (2004) External Causes of Euro Zone Inflation Differentials: A Re-examination of the Evidence, *Intereconomics*, 39: 254–263.

Auer, P. (2000) *Employment Revival in Europe. Labour Market Success in Austria, Denmark, Ireland and the Netherlands*, ILO.

Axelrod, Robert (1984) *The Evolution of Cooperation*, Basic Books.

Barro, Robert J. and Gordon, David (1983) A Positive Theory of Monetary Policy in a Natural Rate Model, *Journal of Political Economy*, 91: 589–610.

Bartolomeo, Giovanni di, Engwerda, Jacob, Plasmans, Joseph, Van Aarle, Bas, Michalak, Tomasz (2005) Macroeconomic Stabilization Policies in the EMU: Spillover, Asymmetries, and Institutions, Cesifo Working Paper No. 1376.

Bartsch, Klaus, Hein, Eckhard, Truger, Achim (2001) Zur Interdependenz von Geld- und Lohnpolitik. Makroökonometrische Ex-post und Ex-ante Simulationen verschiedener Szenarien für die Bundesrepublik Deutschland, WSI – Discussion Paper No. 100.

Baum-Ceisig, Alexandra (2002) *Lohnpolitik unter den Bedingungen der Europäischen Wirtschafts- und Währungsunion.* e-Book, available at: https://repositorium.uni-osnabrueck.de/handle/urn:nbn:de:gbv:700-2003120631.

Bayer, Kurt (1999) Perspectives for Future Economic Policy Coordination within EMU, *Empirica*, 26: 271–279.

Bayoumi, Tamim, Eichengreen, Barry (1993) Shocking Aspects of European Monetary Integration, in: Torres, Francesco, Francesco, Giavazzi (eds), *Adjustment and Growth in the European Monetary Union*, 1993, Cambridge University Press, pp. 193–229.

Bayoumi, Tamim, Masson, Paul (1995) Fiscal Flows in the US and Canada: Lessons for Monetary Union in Europe, *European Economic Review*, 39(2): 253–274.

Beck, Guenter, Hubrich, Kirstin, Marcellino, Massimiliano (2009) Regional Inflation Dynamics Within and Across Euro Area Countries and a Comparison with the United States, *Economic Policy*, 24: 141–184.

Beetsma, R., Bovenberg, A.L. (1998) Monetary Union Without Fiscal Coordination may Discipline Policymakers. *Journal of International Economics*, 45: 239–258.

Beetsma, R., Bovenberg, A. (1999) The Interaction of Fiscal Policy and Monetary Policy in a Monetary Union: Balancing Credibility and Flexibility, in: Razin, A., Sadka, E. (eds), The Economics of Globalization: Policy Perspectives from Public Economics, Cambridge University Press, pp. 373–405.

Beetsma, R., Giuliodori, M. (2004) What are the Spillovers from Fiscal Shocks in Europe? An Empirical Analysis. ECB Working Paper No. 325.

Beetsma, R., Jensen, H. (2004) Mark-up Fluctuations and Fiscal Policy Stabilization in a Monetary Union, *Journal of Macroeconomics*, 66: 357–376.

Beetsma, R., Debrun, X., Bovenberg, A.L. (2001) Is Fiscal Policy Coordination in the EMU Desirable? CESifo Working Paper, No. 599.

Begg, I. (2003) Hard and Soft Economic Policy Coordination under EMU: Problems, Paradoxes, and Prospects, Center for European Studies, Working Paper No. 103.

Begg, I., Hodson, D., Maher, I. (2003) Economic Policy Coordination in the European Union, *National Institute Economic Review*, 183: 66–77.

Belke, Ansgar, Baumgärtner, Frank (2002) Fiskalische Transfermechanismen und asymmetrische Schocks in Euroland, Vierteljahreshefte zur Wirtschaftsforschung, 71: 384–399.

Belke, Ansgar, Gros, Daniel (1998) Asymmetric Shocks and EMU: Is a Stability Fund Needed?, Intereconomics, 33: 274–288.

Belke, Ansgar, Heine, Jens (2001) On the Endogenity of an Exogenous OCA-Criterion: The Impact of Agglomeration on the Synchronisation of Regional Business Cycles in Europa, HWWA Discussion Paper No. 119.

Belke, Ansgar, Kösters, Wim (2000) Asymmetrische Schocks, Arbeitsmärkte und finanzpolitische Anpassung in der EWU, in: Belke, A., Berg, H. (ed.), *Arbeitsmarkt und Beschäftigung : Deutschland im internationalen Vergleich*, Duncker & Humblot, pp. 39–75.

Belke, Ansgar, Schnabl, Gunther (2010) Finanzkrise, globale Liquidität und makroökonomischer Exit, IBES Discussion Paper, No. 184.

Bernoth, Kerstin, Engler, Philipp (2012) Konjunkturelle Ausgleichszahlungen als Stabilisierungsinstrument in der Europäischen Währungsunion, DIW Wochenbericht No. 44.

Bernoth, Kerstin, Engler, Philipp (2013) A Transfer Mechanism as a Stabilization Tool in the EMU, DIW Economic Bulletin 1/2013.

Bibow, Jörg (2013) The ECB: How Much of a Success Story, Really? In: Hein, E., Priewe, J., Truger, A. (eds), European Integration in Crisis, 2007, Metropolis-Verlag.

Bizer, Kilian, Sesselmeier (2004) Werner, Koordinierte Makropolitik in der Europäischen Union, Darmstadt Discussion Papers No. 137.

Blanchard, O. (1991) *Wage Bargaining and Unemployment Persistence*, National Bureau of Economic Research.

Blanchard, O. (2000) *Macroeconomics*, 2nd edn, Pearson.

Blanchard, O., Illing, G. (2006) *Makroökonomie*, Pearson.

Blanchard O., Kiyotaki, N. (1987) Monopolistic competition and the effects of aggregate demand. *American Economic Review*, 77: 647–676.

Blanchard, Olivier, Wolfers, Justin (1999) *The Role of Shocks and Institutions in the Rise of European Unemployment: The Aggregate Evidence*, National Bureau of Economic Research.

Blanchard, Olivier, Amighini, Alessia, Giavazzim Francesco (2010) *Macroeconomics: A European Perspective*, Prentice Hall.

Blankart, Charles B., Fasten, Erik R. (2009) Wer soll für die Schulden im Bundesstaat haften? Eine vernachlässigte Frage der Föderalismusreform II, *Perspektiven der Wirtschaftspolitik*, 10(1): 39–59.

Bofinger, Peter (2003) The Stability and Growth Pact Neglects the Policy Mix Between Fiscal and Monetary Policy, *Intereconomics*, 38(1): 4.

Bofinger, Peter, Mayer, Eric (2003) Monetary and Fiscal Policy Interaction in the Euro Area with Different Assumptions on the Philipps Curve, Würzburg Economic Papers No. 40.

Bofinger, Peter, Mayer, Eric (2005) Staying Together or Drifting Apart: Inflation Targeting and Fiscal Policy in an Estimated Euro Area Model with Sticky Prices and Sticky Wages, CEPR and University of Wuerzburg.

Bohn, H., Inman, R. (1996) Balanced-Budget Rules and Public Deficits: Evidence from the U.S. States, *Carnegie-Rochester Conference Series on Public Policy*, 45: 13–76.

Bonnevay, F. (2010) Pour un Eurobond: Une stratégie coordonnée pour sortir de la crise, Institut Montaigne.

Booth, A. (1995) *The Economics of the Trade Union*, Cambridge University Press.

Booth, A. (ed.) (2002) *The Economics of Labour Unions, vols I and II*, Edward Edgar.

Bordo, M.D., Markiewicz, A., Jonung, L. (2011) A Fiscal Union for the Euro: Some Lessons from History. NBER Working Paper No. 17380.

Boss, Alfred, Gern, Klaus-Jürgen, Meier, Carsten-Patrick, Scheide, Joachim (2004) *Mehr Wachstum in Europa durch eine Koordination makroökonomischer Politik?*, Springer.

Braun, Sebastian, Spielmann, Christian (2010) Wage Subsidies and International Trade: When Does Policy Coordination Pay?, Kiel Working Paper No. 1599.

Brenke, Karl (2012) Mechanismen zur Harmonisierung der Konjunkturverläufe in der eurozone – eine skeptische Sicht, DIW Wochenbericht No. 44.

Breuss, Fritz, Weber, Andrea (2001) Economic Policy Coordination in the EMU: Implications for the Stability and Growth Pact, in: Hughes-Hallett, Andrew, Mooslechner, Peter, Schürz, Martin (eds), *Challenges for Economic Policy Coordination within Monetary Union*, Springer, pp. 143–168.

Bruneau, C., De Bandt, O. (2003) Monetary and Fiscal Policy in the Transition to Monetary Union: What do SVAR Models Tell Us?, *Economic Modelling*, 20: 959–985.

Bruno, Michael, Sachs, Jeffrey (1985) *Economics of Worldwide Stagflation*, Harvard University Press.

Buiter, W.H. (1985) Macroeconomic Policy Design in an Interdependent World Economy: An Analysis of Three Contingencies. National Bureau of Economic Research Working Paper No. 1746.

Bundesministerium der Finanzen (2011) Nationale Fiskalregeln – ein Instrument zur Vorbeugung vor Vertrauenskrisen?, Monatsbereicht.

Burda, Michael (2001) European Labour Markets and the Euro: How Much Flexibility Do We Really Need?. ENEPRI Working Paper No. 3.

Busch, Andreas (1995) *Preisstabilitätspolitik und Inflationsraten im internationalen Vergleich*, VS Verlag.

Busch, Klaus (1994) *Europäische Integration und Tarifpolitik, Lohnpolitische Konsequenzen der Wirtschafts- und Währungsunion*, Bund-Verlag.

Buscher, H., Gabrisch, H. (2009) Is the European Monetary Union an Endogenous Currency Area? The Example of the Labour Markets. IWH Discussion Paper No. 7.

Buti, Marco, Giudice, Gabriele (2002) Maastricht's Fiscal Rules at Ten: An Assessment, *Journal of Common Market Studies*, 40: 823–848.

Buti, M., Roeger, W., In't Veld, J. (2001) Stabilizing Output and Inflation: Policy Conflicts and Co-operation under a Stability Pact, *Journal of Common Market Studies*, 39: 801–828.

Buti, M., Eijffinger, S., Franco, D. (2002) Revisiting the Stability and Growth Pact: Grand Design or Internal Adjustment?. CEPR Discussion Paper No. 3692.

Calliess, C., Schoennfleisch, C. (2012) Auf dem Weg in die europäische "Fiskalunion"? – Europa- und verfassungsrechtliche Fragen einer Reform der Wirtschafts- und Währungsunion im Kontext des Fiskalvertrages. *Juristen Zeitung*, 2012: 477–487.

Calmfors, L. (1993) Centralization of Wage Bargaining and Labour Market Performance: A Survey. OECD Economic Studies No. 21.

Calmfors, L. (1998) Macroeconomic Policy, Wage Setting, and Employment – What Difference Does the EMU Make? *Oxford Review of Economic Policy*, 14: 125–151.

Calmfors, L. (2006) The Revised Stability and Growth Pact: A Critical Assessment, *The Journal for Money and Banking of the Bank Association of Slovenia*, 55: 23–27.

Calmfors, L., Driffill, J. (1988) Bargaining Structure and Macroeconomic Performance, *Economic Policy*, 4: 14–61.

Cameron, David. (1984) Social Democracy, Corporatism, Labour Quiescence, and Representation of Economic Interest in Advanced Capitalist Society, in: Goldthorpe, J. (ed.), *Order and Conflict in Contemporary Capitalism: Studies in the Political Economy of Western European Nations*, Clarendon, pp. 143–178.

Canova, F., Dellas, H. (1993) Trade Interdependence and the International Business Cycle, *Journal of International Economics*, 34: 23–47.

Caporale, Guglielmo, Girardi, Alessandro (2011) Fiscal Spillovers in the Euro Area. DIW Discussion Paper No. 1164.

Carlin, W., Soskice, D. (2005) The 3-Equation New Keynesian Model: A Graphical Exposition, *Contribution to Macroeconomics*, 5: 1–36.

Carlin, W., Soskice, D. (2006) *Macroeconomics: Imperfections, Institutions and Policies*, Oxford University Press.

Cassela, A. (2002) Tradable Deficit Permits, in: Brunila, A., Buti, M., Franco, D., *The Stability and Growth Pact: The Architecture of Fiscal Policy in EMU*, Palgrave Macmillan, p. 394.

Cavallari, L. (2009) Fiscal and Monetary Interactions when Wage-Setters are Large: Is There a Role for Corporatist Policies?, *Empirica*, 37: 291–309.

Ciccarone, Giuseppe, Di Bartolomeo, Giovanni, Marchetti, Enrico (2007) Unions, Fiscal Policy and Central Bank Transparency, *The Manchester School*, 75: 617–633.

Claeys, P. (2004) Monetary and Budgetary Policy Interaction: An SVAR Analysis of Stabilization Policies in Monetary Union. EUI Working Paper, No. 22.

Clar, M., Dreger, C. and Ramos, R. (2007) Wage Flexibility and Labour Market Institutions: A Meta-Analysis. IZA Discussion Paper No. 2581.

Clements, Bendict, Kontolemis, Zenon, Levy, Joaquim (2001) Monetary Policy Under EMU: Differences in the Transmission Mechanism?. IMF Working Paper No. 01/102.

Coleman, James (1995) *Grundlagen der Sozialtheorie. Band 1*, Oldenbourg.

Collignon, Stefan (2003) *The European Public: Reflections on the Political Economy of a Future Constitution*, Federal Trust for Education & Research.

Communication from the Commission to the European Parliament, the Council, the European Economic and Social Committee of the Regions: Enhancing Economic Policy Coordination for Growth and Jobs – Tools for Stronger EU Economic Governance. COM(2010)367, 30 June 2010.

Cooper, R.N. (1985) Economic Interdependence and Coordination of Economic Policies, in: Jones, R.W., Kenen, P.B., *Handbook of International Economics*, vol. 2, Elsevier Science B.V, pp. 1195–1234.

Council of Economic Experts (2003/2004), Staatsfinanzen Konsolidieren – Steuersystem Reformieren, Annual Opinion 2003/2004.

Crouch, C. (1985) Conditions for Trade Union Wage Restraint, in Lindberg, L., Maier, C. (eds), *The Politics of Inflation and Economic Stagnation: Theoretical Approaches and International Case Studies*, Brookings Institute.

Cukierman, A. (2004) Monetary Institutions, Monetary Union and Unionized Labor Markets: Some Recent Developments, in: Beetsma, R., Favero, C., Missale, A., Muscatelli, V.A., Natale, P., Tirelli, P. (eds), *Monetary Policy, Fiscal Policies and Labour Markets: Key Aspects of Macroeconomic Policymaking in EMU*, Cambridge University Press, pp. 299–326.

Cukierman, A., Dalmazzo, A. (2006) Fiscal–Monetary Interactions in the Presence of Unionized Labor Markets, *International Tax and Public Finance*, 13: 411–435.

Cukierman, A., Lippi, F. (1999) Central Bank Independence, Centralization of Wage Bargaining, Inflation and Unemployment: Theory and Some Evidence, *European Economic Review*, 43: 1395–1434.

Cukierman, A., Lippi, F. (2001) Labor Markets and Monetary Union: A Preliminary Strategic Analysis, *Economic Journal*, 111: 541–565.

Currie, David, Holtham, Gerald, Hughes-Hallet, Andrew (1989) The Theory and Practice of International Policy Coordination: Does Coordination Pay?, in: Bryant, R.C., Currie, D., Frenkel, J., Masson, P, Portes, R. (eds), *Macroeconomic Policies in an Interdependent World*, IMF, pp. 14–66.

Czada, Roland (1997) Vertretung und Verhandlung. Aspekte politischer Konfliktregulierung in Mehrebenensystemen, in: Benz, Arthur, Seibel, Wolfgang (eds), *Theorieentwicklung in der Politikwissenschaft: Eine Zwischenbilanz*, Nomos, pp. 237–259.

Dalsgaard, T., de Serres, A. (2000) Estimating Prudent Budgetary Margins for EU Countries: A Simulated SVAR Model Approach, *OECD Economic Studies*, 30(1): 115–147.

Dao, Mai (2008) International Spillover of Labor Market Reforms. IMF Working Paper No. 08/113.

De Grauwe, Paul (2006) What Have We Learnt About Monetary Integration Since the Maastricht Treaty?, *JCMS*, 44(4): 711–730.

De Grauwe, Paul, Moesen, W. (2009) Gains for All: A Proposal for a Common Eurobond, *Intereconomics*, 33: 132–141.

Decressin, J., Fatas, A. (1995) Regional Labour Market Dynamics in Europe, *European Economic Review*, 39(9): 1627–1655.

Delors Report (1989) Bericht zur Wirtschafts- und Währungsunion in der EG, presented by Committee for the Study of Economic and Monetary Union on April 17, 1989. EU Commission Working Document No. 10.

Delpla, Jacques, von Weizsäcker, Jakob (2011) Eurobonds : The Blue Bond Concept and its Implications. Bruegel Policy Brief, March 2011.

De Masi, Paula (1997) IMF Estimates of Potential Output: Theory and Practice. IMF Working Paper No. 97/177.

Deroose, Servaas, Langedijk, Sven, Roeger, Werner (2004) Reviewing Adjustment Dynamics in EMU: From Overheating to Overcooling. European Economy Economic Papers No. 198.

Deubner (2010) Wege aus der europäischen Staatsschuldenkrise, *Wirtschaftsdienst*, pp. 783–804.

Deutsche Bank Research (2010) Schuldenbremsen für Euroland.

Deutsche Bank Research (2011) Makroökonomische Koordinierung.

Deutsche Bank Research (2012) Schuldenbremsen für Euroland.

Deutsche Bundesbank (2010) *Zur Problematik makroökonomischer Ungleichgewicht im Euro-Raum*, Monatsbericht.

Diekmann, Berend, Menzel, Christoph, Thomae, Tobias (2012) Konvergenzen und Divergenzen im "Währungsraum USA" im Vergleich zur eurozone, *Wirtschaftsdienst*, 92(1): 27–32.

Dietrich, D., Holtemöller, O., Lindner, A. (2010) Wege aus der Schulden- und Vertrauenskrise in der Europäischen Wirtschafts- und Währungsunion, *Wirtschaft im Wandel*, 8: 370–375.

Directorate-General for Economic and Financial Affairs of the European Commission (2003) Broad Economic Policy Guidelines (BEPG) (2003) 2003–2005 Period, *European Economy*, 74: 4.

Dixit, Avinash, Lambertini, Luca (2001) Monetary–Fiscal Policy Interactions and Commitment versus Discretion in a Monetary Union, *European Economic Review*, 45: 977–987.

Dohse, D, Krieger-Boden, C., Soltwedel, R. (1998) Die EWU: Beschäftigungsmotor oder Beschäftigungsrisiko?, *Zeitschrift für Wirtschaftspolitik*, 1: 109–120.

Du Caju, P.D., Gautier, E., Momferatou, D., Warmedinger, M.W. (2008) Institutional Features of Wage Bargaining in 22 EU Countries, the US and Japan. ECB Working Paper No. 974.

Dufresne, Anne, Mermet, Emmanuel (2002) *Trends in the Coordination of Collective Bargaining in Europe*, European Trade Union Institute.

Dullien, Sebastian (2004) *The Interaction of Monetary Policy and Wage Bargaining in the European Monetary Union*, Palgrave Macmillan.

Dullien, Sebastian (2008) Eine Arbeitslosenversicherung für die eurozone, *Stiftung Wissenschaft und Politik*, Studie, S1.

Dullien, Sebastian (2010) *Ungleichgewichte im Euro-Raum*, WiSO-Diskurs.

Dullien, Sebastian, Fritsche, Ulrich (2008) Does the Dispersion of Unit Labor Cost in the EMU Imply Long-run Convergence, *International Economics and Economic Policy*, 5(3): 269–295.

Dullien, Sebastian, Schwarzer, Daniela (2009) The Euro Zone Needs an External Stability Pact. SWP Comments, C09.

Eichengreen, Barry (1993) European Monetary Unification, *Journal of Economic Literature*, 31(3): 1321–1357.

Eichengreen, Barry, Wyplosz, C. (1998) The Stability and Growth Pact: More Than a Minor Nuisance?, in: Begg, D., von Hagen, J., Wyplosz, C., Zimmerman, K.F. (eds), Special issue of *EMU: Prospects and Challenges for the Euro, Economic Policy: A European Forum*.

EIRO (2000) *Wage Policy and EMU*, EIRO.

Enderlein, H. (2004) *Nationale Wirtschaftspolitik in der europäischen Währungsunion*, Campus.

Enderlein, H., Delors, J., Schmidt, H., *et al.* (2012) Completing the Euro: A Road Map Towards Fiscal Union in Europe. Report of the Tommaso Padoa-Schioppa Group.

Engel, C., Rogers, J. (1996) How Wide is the Border?, *The American Economic Review*, 86: 1112–1125.

Engel, C., Rogers, J.H. (2004) European Product Market Integration After the Euro, *Economic Policy*, 39: 347–384.

Erne, R. (2004) Organized Labour: An Actor of Euro-democratization, Euro-technocracy or Re-nationalization?, PhD thesis, European University Institute, Florence.

Eurogroup (2011) Statement by the Eurogroup, www.consilium.europa.eu/uedocs/cms_data/docs/pressdata/en/ecofin/118050.pdf (accessed 12 July 2013).

Europäischer Rat (1999) Schlussfolgerungen des Vorsitzes.

Europäischer Rat (2010) Schlussfolgerungen des Vorsitzes des Europäischen Rates vom 16, www.consilium.europa.eu/uedocs/cms_data/docs/pressdata/de/ec/118604.pdf (accessed 12 July 2013).

European Central Bank (2000) Die Beziehung der EZB zu den Organen und Institutionen der Europäischen Union, *Monatsbericht der Europäischen Zentralbank*, October.

European Central Bank (2003) Der Zusammenhang zwischen Geld- und Finanzpolitik im Euro-Währungsgebiet, *Monatsbericht der Europäischen Zentralbank* February: 41–55.

European Central Bank (2008) *Monatsbericht 10 Jahre EZB*, EZB.

European Central Bank (2010) Decision of the European Central Bank of 14 May 2010, establishing a securities markets programme (ECB/2010/5) (2010/281/EU).

European Commission (1990) Ein Markt, eine Währung, Potentielle Nutzen und Kosten der Errichtung einer Wirtschafts- und Währungsunion, Eine Bewertung. Europäische Wirtschaft No. 44.

European Commission (2004) EMU after 5 years. European Economy, Special Report, No. 1, July.

European Commission (2006) The EU Economy: Review 2006 – Adjustment Dynamics in the Euro Area – Experiences and Challenges, *European Economy*, 6.

European Commission (2009) *Quarterly Report on the Euro Area I, 2009*, Europäische Kommission.

European Commission (2010) Wirtschaftspolitische Steuerung in der EU.

Eurostat (2010) Experimental House Price Indices for the Euro Area and the European Union. Research Paper.

Fabeck, Rudolf (1995) *Fiskalpolitische Koordination in der EG: Möglichkeiten udn Grenzen der internationalen Koordination der Fiskalpolitik*, Peter Lang.

Faber, R.P., Stokman, A.C. (2005) Price Convergence in Europe from a Macroperspective: Product Categories and Reliability. DNB Working Paper No. 34.

Fajertag, G. and Pochet, P. (eds) (1997) *Social Pacts in Europe*, ETUI.

Fatas, Antonio (1998) Does EMU Need a Fiscal Federation?, *Economic Policy*, 26: 163–192.

Fatas, Antonio, von Hagen, J., Hughes-Hallet, A., Strauch, R.R., Sibert, A. (2003) Stability and Growth in Europe: Towards a Better Pact, *Monitoring European Integration*, 13: 1–108.

Feldstein, Martin (1988) Distinguished Lecture on Economics in Government: Thinking about International Economic Coordination, *Journal of Economic Perspectives*, 2(2): 3–13.

Feuerstein, Switgard (1992) Studien zur Wechselkursunion, Makroökonomische Konsequenzen der Wechselwirkungen zwischen festen und flexiblen Wechselkursen, Heidelberg, Dissertation.

Fischer, Christoph (2009) Price Convergence in the EMU? Evidence from Micro Data. Deutsche Bundesbank Discussion Paper No. 6.

Flanagan, R.J. (1999) Macroeconomic Performance and Collective Bargaining: An International Perspective, *Journal of Economic Literature*, 37(3): 1150–1175.

Flassbeck, Heiner, Spiecker, Friederike (2011) The Euro: A Story of Misunderstanding, *Intereconomics*, 46(4): 180–187.

Fleming, Marcus (1962) Domestic Financial Policies Under Fixed and Under Floating Exchange Rates, *International Monetary Fund Staff Papers*, 9: 369.

Folkers, C. (1999) Neue Maßstäbe in der Europäischen Union: Grenzen für Staatsverschuldung und Staatsquote durch den Maastrichter Vertrag und seine Ergänzungen. Diskussionsbeiträge des Instituts für Europäische Wirtschaft 25.

Frankel, Jeffrey A. (1987) The International Monetary System: Should it Be Reformed?, *American Economic Review*, 77(2): 205–210.

Frankel, Jeffrey A. (1989) Obstacles to International Macroeconomic Coordination, *Journal of Public Policy*, 3(3): n.p.

Frankel, Jeffrey A. and Rockett, Katharine (1988) International Macroeconomic Policy Coordination When Policymakers Do Not Agree on the True Model, *The American Economic Review*, 78(3): 318–340.

Frankel, Jeffrey, Rose, Andrew (1998) The Endogeneity of the Optimum Currency Area Criteria, *Economic Journal*, 108(449): 1009–1025.

Frankel, Jeffrey A., Goldstein, M., Masson, P.R. (1988) Simulating the Effects of Some Simple Coordinated versus Uncoordinated Policy Rules. NBER Working Paper No. 2929.

Franzese, Robert (2001) Institutional and Sectoral Interactions in Monetary Policy and Wage, Price-Bargaining, in: Hall, P., Soskice, D. (eds), *Varieties of Capitalism: The Institutional Foundations of Comparative Advantage*. Cambridge University Press, pp. 104–144.

Freeman, R. (1988) Labour Market Institutions and Economic Performance, *Economic Policy*, 6: 64–80.

Frenkel, Michael, Nickel, Christiane (2002) How Symmetric Are the Shocks and the Shock Adjustment Dynamics Between the Euro Area and Central and Eastern European Countries?. IMF Working Paper No. 02/222.

Frenz, Walter, Ehlenz, Christian (2010) Der Euro ist gefährdet: Hilfsmöglichkeiten bei drohendem Staatsbankrott?, *EWS*, 21(3): 65–70.

Fröhlich, H.-P., Klös, H.-P., Kroker, R., Link, F.J., Schnabel, C. (1994) Lohnpolitik in der Europäischen Währungsunion, Gutachten, Beiträge zur Wirtschafts- und Sozialpolitik. Institut der deutschen Wirtschaft No. 215.

Gakova, Zuzana, Dijkstra, Lewis (2010) Labour Mobility Between the Regions of the EU-27 and a Comparison with the USA. Princeton Working Paper No. 100976.

Gerken, Lüder, Kullas, Matthias (2011) CEP Default Index. CEP-Studie.

Gerken, Lüder, Van Roosebeke, Bert, Voßwinkel, Jan (2011) Anforderungen an die Sanierung der Euro-Staaten Schuldenbremse plus Nebenbedingungen. CEP-Studie.

German Council of Economic Experts (2012) The European Redemption Pact (ERP): Questions and Answers, Working Paper No. 1/2012.

German Federal Ministry of Finance (2011) Monthly Report, August.

Giordani, P. (2004) Evaluating New-Keynesian Models of a Small Open Economy, *Oxford Bulletin of Economics and Statistics*, 66: S713–733.

Gischer, H., Weiss, M. (2006) Inflationsdifferenzen im Euroraum: Zur Rolle des Balassa-Samuelson-Effekts, in *List Forum für Wirtschafts- und Finanzpolitik*, vol. 32, List Gesellschaft e.V., pp. 16–37.

Glassner, Vera, Pusch, Toralf (2010) The Emergence of Wage Coordination in the Central Western European Metal Sector and its Relationship to European Economic Policy. IWH Discussion Papers No. 13.

Glassner, Vera, Watt, Andrew (2010) The Current Crisis Reveals Both: The Importance and the Limitations of the Transnational Coordination of Collective Bargaining Policies, *Social Europe Journal*, 5(1): 21

Gnan, in: von der Groeben, Schwarze (eds), Vertrag zur Europäischen Union und zur Gründung der Europäischen Gemeinschaft, 6th edition, 2003, Article 103 ECT.

Gottschalk, Jan (2002) Keynesian and Monetarists Views on the German Unemployment Problem: Theory and Evidence. Kiel Institute of World Economics Working Paper No. 1096.

Gräf, B. (2007) *US-Leistungsbilanzdefizit: Keine Panik! Aktuelle Themen 389.* DB Research.

Grober, Günther (1988) Empirical Evidence of Effects of Policy Coordination Among Major Industrial Countries Since Rambouillet Summit of 1975, in: *Economic Policy Coordination, Proceedings of an International Seminar Held in Hamburg, International Monetary Fund and HWWA-Institut für Wirtschaftsforschung*, p. 110.

Grubb, Dennis, Jackman, Richard, Layard, Richard (1983) Wage Rigidity and Unemployment in OECD Countries, *European Economic Review*, 21(1–2): 11–39.

Grüner, H.P. and Hefeker, C. (1999) How Will EMU Affect Inflation and Unemployment in Europe?, *Scandinavian Journal of Economics*, 101(1): 33–47.

Grüner, Hans Peter, Hayo, Bernd, Hefeker, Carsten (2005) Unions, Wage Setting and Monetary Policy Uncertainty. ECB Working Paper Series No. 490.

Guzzo, V., Velasco, A. (1999) The Case for a Populist Central Banker, *European Economic Review*, 43: 1317–1344.

Häde, U. (2007), Europarechtliche Einwirkungen auf die nationale Finanzverfassung, in: Konrad, Jochimsen, *Finanzkrise im Bundesstaat*, 2. Aufl, pp. 197.

Hagen, J. von (1992) Budgeting Procedures and Fiscal Performance in the European Communities. Economic Papers No. 96.

Hagen, J. von, Mundschenk, S. (2002) Koordinierung der Geld- und Fiskalpolitik in der EWU, *DIW-Vierteljahreshefte zur Wirtschaftsforschung*, 71: 325–338.

Hagen, J. von, Wyplosz, C. (2008) EMU's Decentralized System of Fiscal Policy. Economic Papers No. 306.

Hall, Peter A., Franzese, Robert (1998) Mixed Signals: Central Bank Independence, Coordinated Wage Bargaining, and European Monetary Union, *International Organization*, 52: 505–535.

Hallet, Andrew, Mooslechner, Peter, Schuerz, Martin (eds) (2001) *Challenges for Economic Policy Coordination Within European Monetary Union*, Springer.

Hamada, Koichi, Kawai, Masahiro (1997) International Economic Policy Coordination: Theory and Policy Implications, in: Fratiani, Michele, Salvatore, Dominick, von Hagen, Jürgen (eds), *Macroeconomic Policy in Open Economies, Handbook of Comparative Economic Policy, Vol. 5*, Greenwood.

Hancké, Bob, Soskice, David (2003) Wage-Setting and Inflation Targets in EMU, *Oxford Review of Economic Policy*, 19: 149–160.

Hattenberger, in: Schwarze (ed.), EU-Kommentar, 2009, 2nd ed., Art. 103 EGV.

Hein, Eckhard (2002) Koordinierte Makropolitik in der EWU – Zur Notwendigkeit und den Problemen der Umsetzung, in: Hein, Eckhard, Truger, Achim (eds), *Moderne Wirtschaftspolitik = Koordinierte Makropolitik*, Metropolis.

Hein, Eckhard (2002a) Koordinierte Makropolitik in der EWU – Zur Notwendigkeit und zu den Problemen der Umsetzung, *WSI-Mitteilungen*, 5: 251–259.

Hein, Eckhard (2002b) Monetary Policy and Wage Bargaining in the EMU: Restrictive ECB Policies, High Unemployment, Nominal Wage Restraint and Inflation Above the Target, *Banca Nazionale del Lavoro Quarterly Review*, 55: 299–337.

Hein, Eckhard, Niechoj, Torsten (2005) Leitlinien für ein dauerhaftes Wachstum in der EU? Konzept und Wirkungen der Grundzüge der Wirtschaftspolitik, *Wirtschaft und Gesellschaft*, 31(1): 11–40.

Hein, Eckhard, Truger, Achim (2004) Macroeconomic Co-ordination as an Economic Policy Concept: Opportunities and Obstacles in the EMU. WSI Discussion Paper No. 125.

Heinen, N. (2010) Schuldenbremsen für Euroland, Deutsche Bank Research.

Heinz, Frigyes Ferdinand, Rusinova, Desislava (2011) How Flexible are Real Wages in EU Countries?. ECB Working Paper No. 1360.

Heise, A. (2001) *New Politics: Integrative Wirtschaftspolitik für das 21.* Westfälisches Dampfboot.

Heise, A. (2002) Theorie optimaler Lohnräume – Zur Tarifpolitik in der Europäischen Währungsunion, *Vierteljahrshefte zur Wirtschaftsforschung*, 71(3): 368–383.

Heise, A., Küchle, H., Lecher, W. (1994) Anpassungsanforderungen an die Lohnpolitik in der Gemeinschaft auf dem Weg zur und nach Vollendung der EWU unter Berücksichtigung des Beschäftigungsaspektes: Die Sicht der Gewerkschaften, Studie des WSI im Auftrag der Kommission der Europäischen Gemeinschaften.

Herrmann, Karolin (2011) *Bewertung aktueller Korrekturversuche am Stabilitäts- und Wachstumspakt, KBI kompakt*, Karl-Bräuer-Institut des Bundes der Steuerzahler e.V.

Hess, Julian (2010) Finanzielle Unterstützung von EU-Mitgliedsstaaten in einer Finanz- und Wirtschaftskrise und die Vereinbarkeit mit EU-Recht, *Zeitschrift für das juristische Studium*, 4: 473ff.

Hetschko, Clemens, Quint, Dominic, Thye, Marius (2012) Nationale Schuldenbremsen für die Länder der Europäischen Union: Taugt das deutsche Modell als Vorbild?, School of Business & Economics Discussion Paper No. 12.

Hey, J. (2008) Finanzautonomie und Finanzverflechtung in gestuften Rechtsordnungen, *Veröffentlichungen der Vereinigung der Deutschen Staatsrechtslehrer*, 66: 277.

Hill, R.J. (2004) Constructing Price Indexes Across Space and Time: The Case of the European Union, *The American Economic Review*, 94: 1379–1410.

Hodson, Dermot (2011) *Governing the Euro Area in Good Times and Bad*, Oxford University Press.

Hodson, Dermot, Imelda Maher (2001) The Open Method as a New Mode of Governance: The Case of Soft Economic Policy Co-ordination, *Journal of Common Market Studies*, 39(4): 719–746.

Honohan, Daiv, Lane, Philip (2003) Divergent Inflation Rates in EMU, *Economic Policy*, 37: 359–394.

Horn, N. (2009) Die Stellung der Anleihegläubiger nach neuem Schulverschreibungsgesetz und allgemeinem Privatrecht, *Zeitschrift für das gesamte Handelsrecht*, S.12ff.

Horne, Jocelyn, Masson, Paul (1987) Internationale Kooperation und Koordination der Wirtschaftspolitik, *Finanzierung und Entwicklung, Vierteljahrsheft des INternationalen Währungsfonds in Zusammenarbeit mit dem HWWA-Institut für Weltwirtschaft*, 28.

Huemer, Gerhard (2009) 10 Jahre Makroökonomischer Dialog in der Europäischen Union, *Wirtschaftspolitische Blätter*, Sonderausgabe "EU-Integration".

Hughes-Hallett, Andrew, Mooslechner, Peter, Schürz, Martin (eds) (2001) *Challenges for Economic Policy Coordination within Monetary Union*, Springer.

Issing, Ottmar (2005) The Enlargement of the EU and the Euro Zone, Speech at the Spring 2005 World Economic Outlook Conference, Frankfurt am Main, 27 April.

Issing, Ottmar (2001a) How to Promote Growth in the Euro Area, *International Finance*, 3(2): 309–327.

Issing, Ottmar (2001b) Why Price Stability?, in: Herrero, Alicia García, Gaspar, Vitor, Hoogduin, Lex, Morgan, Julian, Winkler, Bernhard (eds), *Why Price Stability?*, European Central Bank, pp. 179–202.

Issing, Ottmar (2002) Anmerkungen zur Koordinierung der makroökonomischen Politik in der WWU, *DIW-Vierteljahreshefte zur Wirtschaftsforschung*, 71: 312–324.

Issing, Ottmar (2004) The Role of Fiscal and Monetary Policies in the Stabilisation of the Economic Cycle, speech at the international conference *Stability and Economic Growth: The Role of the Central Bank*, Mexico City, 14 November.

Issing, Ottmar (2009) Why a Common Euro-zone Bond isn't Such a Good Idea, *Europe's World*, Summer: 77–79.

Italianer, Alexander (2001) The Euro and Internal Economic Policy Coordination, in: Hallet, Andrew, Mooslechner, Peter, Schuerz, Martin (eds), *Challenges for Economic Policy Coordination Within European Monetary Union*, Springer.

Iversen, Torben (1998) Wage Bargaining, Central Bank Independence, and the Real Effects of Money, *International Organization*, 52: 469–504.

Iversen, Torben (1999) *Contested Economic Institutions: The Politics of Macroeconomics and Wage Bargaining in Advanced Economies*, Cambridge University Press

Jacobs, Jan P.A.M., Kuper, Gerard, Verlinden, Johan (2007) Monetary Policy in the Euro Area: The Impact of Fiscal Closure Rules. IEE Working Paper No. 2007/01.

Jacquet, P., Pisani-Ferry, J. (2001) Economic policy co-ordination in the Eurozone: What has been achieved? What should be done?. SEI Working Paper No. 40.

Jerger, J. (2002) How Strong is the Case for a Populist Central Banker? A Note, *European Economic Review*, 46: 623–632.

Jerger, J., Landmann, O. (2006) Dissecting the Two-handed Approach: Who's the Expert Hand For What?, *Applied Economics Quarterly*, 52: 265–288.

Joumard, I., Kongsrud, P.M. (2003) Fiscal Relations across Government Level. Economics Department Working Paper No. 375.

Karl-Bräuer Institut (2011) *Von der Wirtschafts- in die Haftungsunion*, Karl-Bräuer Institut.

Kenen, Peter (1969), The Theory of Optimum Currency Areas: An Eclectic View, in: Mundell, Robert, Swoboda, A. (eds), *Problems of the International Economy*, University of Chicago Press, pp. 41–60.

Kiewiet, D., Szakaly, K. (1996) Constitutional Limitations on Borrowing: An Analysis of State Bonded Indebtedness, *Journal of Law, Economics & Organization*, 12(1): 62–97.

Kim, S. (1999) Do Monetary Policy Shocks Matter in the G-7 Countries? Using Common Identifying Assumptions about Monetary Policy across Countries, *Journal of International Economics*, 48: 387–412.

Kim, S. (2001) Effects of Monetary Policy Shocks on the Trade Balance in Small Open European Countries, *Economic Letters*, 71: 197–203.

Kim, S., Roubini, N. (2000) Exchange Rate Anomalies in the Industrial Countries: A Solution with a Structural VAR Approach, *Journal of Monetary Economics*, 45: 561–586.

Kittel, Bernhard (2001) How Bargaining Mediates Wage Determination: An Exploration of the Parameters of Wage Functions in a Pooled Time Series Cross Section Framework. Max Planck Institut fur Gesellschaftsforschung Discussion Paper No. 01.

Knopp, Lothar (2010) Griechenland-Nothilfe auf dem verfassungsrechtlichen Prüfstand, *Neue Juristische Wochenschrift*, 1777.

Koll, Willi (2011) Governance in der Krise. IMK Policy Brief.

Konrad, Kai A., Zschäpitz, Holger (2010) *Schulden ohne Sühne?*, C.H. Beck.

Koppitz, Matthias (2010), *Für und Wider makroökonomischer Koordinierung in der Europäischen Wirtschafts- und Währungsunion: eine ontogenetische Parabel*, Siegen.

Koske, I., Pain, N. (2008) The Usefulness of Output Gaps for Policy Analysis. OECD Economics Department Working Papers No. 621.

Krämer, Hagen (2010), Der Konstruktionsfehler des Euro-Stabilitätspaktes, *Wirtschaftdienst*, 6: 379–384.

Kreiner, Claus (2002) Do the New Keynesian Microfoundations Rationalise Stabilisation Policy? *Economic Journal*, 112: 384–401.

Krueger, Anne O. (2002) *A New Approach to Sovereign Debt Restructuring*, IMF.

Krugman, Paul (1993) Lessons of Massachusetts for EMU, in: Torres, F., Giavazzi, F. (eds), *Adjustment and Growth in the European Monetary Union*, Cambridge University Press, pp. 241–259.

Kullas, Matthias (2011) Kann der reformierte Stabilitäts- und Wachstumspakt den Euro retten?, CEP (Center for European Policy), October 2011.

Kullas, Matthias, Koch, Jessica (2010), Reform des Stabilitäts- und Wachstumspakts – Schneller, Schärfer, Konsequenter?, Studie des Centrum für Europäische Politik.

Landmann, Oliver (2012) Die Krise der Europäischen Währungsunion, in: Held, Martin et al. (eds), *Lehren aus der Krise für die Makroökonomik: Jahrbuch Normative und Institutionelle Grundfragen der Ökonomik, Vol. 11*, Metropolis-Verlag.

Le Cacheux, Jacques (2007) To-Coordinate or Not to Co-ordinate: an Economist's Perspective on the Rationale for Fiscal Policy Co-ordination in the Euro Zone, in: Linsenmann, Ingo, Meyer, Christoph, Wessels, Wolfgang (eds), *Economic Government of the EU*, Palgrave, pp. 37–52.

Leith, Campbell, Wren-Lewis, Simon (2000) Interactions between Monetary and Fiscal Policy Rules, *Economic Journal, Royal Economic Society*, 110(462): 93–108.

Leterme, Yves (2010) Pour une Agence européenne de la Dette, *Le Monde* 25 February.

Levin, Jay (1983) A Model of Stabilization Policy in a Jointly Floating Currency Area, in: Bhandari, J.S., Putnam, B.H. (eds), *Economic Interdependence and Flexible Exchange Rates*, MIT Press, p. 329.

Lindbeck, A. (1998) New Keynesian and Aggregate Economic Activity, *The Economic Journal*, 108, pp. 167–180.

Linsenmann, Ingo, Meyer, Christoph (2002) Dritter Weg, Übergang oder Teststrecke? Theoretische Konzeption und Praxis der offenen Politikkoordinierung, *Integration*, 4: S285–296.

Lippi, F. (2002) Revisiting the Case for a Populist Central Banker. *European Economic Review*, 46: 601–612.

Lippi, F. (2003) Strategic Monetary Policy with Non-atomistic Wage Setters, *Review of Economic Studies*, 70: 909–919.

Lommatzsch, K., Tober, S. (2006) Euro-Area Inflation: Does the Balassa–Samuelson Effect Matter? *International Economics and Economic Policy*, 3(2): 105–136.

Lutz, M. (2004) Price Convergence Under EMU? First Estimates, in: Deardorff, A (ed.), *The Past, Present and Future of the European Union*, Palgrave MacMillan, pp. 48–73.

MacDougall Report (1977) *The Report of the Study Group on the Role of Public Finance in European Integration, 2 Bände*, European Commission.

McKinnon, Ronald (1963), Optimum Currency Areas, *American Economic Review*, 53(9): 717–725.

Maclennan, D., Muellbauer, J.N.J., Stephens, M. (1998) *Asymmetries in Housing and Financial Market Institutions and EMU*, Nuffield College.

Maennig, Wolfgang (1992) *Internationale Transmission und Koordinierung der Wirtschaftspolitik*, Duncker and Humblot.

Maltritz, Dominik (2012) Determinants of Sovereigns Yield Spreads in the eurozone: A Bayesian Approach, *Journal of International Money and Finance*, 31(3): 657.

Manasse, P. (2010) Stability and Growth Pact: Counterproductive Proposals, available at voxeu.org (accessed 12 July 2013).

Mankiw, N.G. (1992) The Reincarnation of Keynesian Economics, *European Economic Review*, 36: 167–180.

Marginson, P., Sisson, K. (2002) European Integration and Industrial Relations: A Case of Convergence and Divergence? *Journal of Common Market Studies*, 40: 671–692.

Marginson, P., Traxler, F. (2005) After Enlargement: Preconditions and Prospects for Bargaining Coordination, *Transfer*, 11(3): 423–438.

Marin, Bernd (1990) Generalized Political Exchange: Preliminary Considerations, in: Marin, Bernd (ed.), *Generalized Political Exchange: Antagonistic Cooperation and Integrated Policy Circuits*, Campus and Westview Press, pp. 37–65.

Martin, A. (2000) Social Pacts, Unemployment and EMU Macroeconomic Policy. EUI Working Paper RSC No. 32.

Mélitz, J. (2000) Some Cross-country Evidence about Fiscal Policy Behaviour and Consequences for EMU, European Commission, European Economy, Reports and Studies, Public Debt and Fiscal Policy in EMU.

Michaelis, Jochen, Pflüger, Michael (2002) Euroland: Besser als Befürchtet, aber Schlechter als Erhofft?, *Vierteljahrshefte zur Wirtschaftsforschung*, 71: 296–311.

Midelfart-Knarvik, Karen, Overman, Henry, Redding, Steven, Venables, Anthony (2002) The Location of European Industry, *European Economy*, 2: 216–273.

Mishkin, Frederic (1995) Symposium on the Monetary Transmission Mechanism, *Journal of Economic Perspectives*, 9: 3–10.

Mooslechner, Peter, Schürz, Martin (1999) International Macroeconomic Policy Coordination: Any Lessons for EMU? A Selective Survey of the Literature, *Empirica*, 26: 171–199.

190   *Bibliography*

Mundell, Robert (1961) A Theory of Optimum Currency Areas, *American Economic Review*, 51: 657–665.

Mundell, Robert (1963) Capital Mobility and Stabilization Policy Under Fixed and Flexible Exchange Rates, *Canadian Journal of Economics and Political Science*, 29: 475.

Mundell, Robert (1964) Capital Mobility and Size, *Canadian Journal of Economics and Political Science*, 30: 421.

Mundell, Robert (1973) Uncommon Arguments for Common Currencies, in Johnson, H.G., Swoboda, A.K. (eds), *The Economics of Common Currencies*, Allen and Unwin.

Muscatelli, A., Tirelli, P., Trecroci, C. (2002) Monetary and Fiscal Policy Interactions over the Cycle: Some Empirical Evidence. CESifo Working Paper No. 817.

Neck, Reinhard, Haber, Gottfried (1999) Zur Gestaltung der makroökonomischen Politik in der Europäischen Wirtschafts- und Währungsunion: Ein numerischer spieltheoretischer Ansatz, in: Neck, Reinhard, Holzmann, Robert (eds), *Was wird aus Euroland: Makroökonomische Herausforderungen und wirtschaftspolitische Antworten*, Manzsche Verlags- und Universitätsbuchandlung.

Nickell, S. (1997) Unemployment and Labor Market Rigidities: Europe versus North America, *Journal of Economic Perspectives*, 11(3): 55–74.

Niechoj, Torsten (2004), Gewerkschaften und keynesianische Koordinierung in Europa: Chancen, Risiken und Umsetzungshürden. WSI Discussion Paper No. 121.

Nunziata, L. (2005) Institutions and Wage Determination: A Multi-Country Approach, *Oxford Bulletin of Economics and Statistics*, 67(4): 435–466.

Obstfeld, M., Peri, G. (1998) Regional Non-adjustment and Fiscal Policy: Lessons for EMU. NBER Working Paper No. 6431.

OECD (1999) Adaptability to Shocks: The Role of Labour Markets, in: OECD, *EMU: Facts, Challenges and Policies*, OECD.

Olson, Mancur (1965) *The Logic of Collective Action*, Harvard University Press.

Olson, Mancur (1982) *The Rise and Decline of Nations*, Yale University Press.

Oswald, A.J. (1985) The Economic Theory of Trade Unions: An Introductory Survey, *Scandinavian Journal of Economics*, 87: 160–193.

Padoa-Schioppa, T. (1987) *Efficiency, Stability and Equity: A Strategy for the Evolution of the Economic Systems of the EC*, European Commission.

Palm, U. (2000) *Preisstabilität in der Europäischen Wirtschafts- und Währungsunion*, Auflage.

Pamela, Olivier, Gerald, Marwell (1988) The Paradox of Group Size in Collective Action: A Theory of the Critical Mass II, *American Sociological Review*, 53: 1–8.

Papadoupolou, Daphni-Marina (1992) Makroökonomik der Wechselkursunion, Interaktion fester und flexibler Wechselkurse, Hamburg, Dissertation.

Pindyck, Robert, Rubinfeld, Daniel (2009) *Mikroökonomie*, 7th edn, Pearson.

Priewe, Jan (2002) Fiskalpolitik in einem makroökonomischen Wachstums- und Beschäftigungskonzept, in: Truger, A., Welzmüller, R. (eds), *Chancen für die Währungsunion nutzen. Koordinierte Politik für Beschäftigung und moderne Infrastruktur*, Der Setzkasten GmbH.

Priewe, Jan (2007a) Makroökonomische Politik in Europa: Schwächen und Reformoptionen in: Chaloupek, G., Hein, Truger, A. (eds), *Ende der Stagnation? Wirtschaftspolitische Perspektiven für mehr Wachstum und Beschäftigung in Europa*. LexisNexis-Verlag, pp. 133–153.

Priewe, Jan (2007b) Economic Divergence in the Euro Area: Why We Should be Concerned, in: Hein, Eckhard, Priewe, Jan, Truger, Achim (eds), *European Integration in Crisis*, Schriftenreihe des Forschungsnetzwerk Makroökonomie und Makropolitik.

Priewe, Jan (2009) Rückkehr zur Einkommenspolitik: warum die Europäische Währungsunion Lohnkoordination braucht, in: Hagemann, Harald, Horn, Gustav, Krupp, Hans-Jürgen (eds), *Aus gesamtwirtschaftlicher Sicht: Festschrift für Jürgen Kromphardt*, Metropolis-Verlag.

Pusch, Toralf (2009) *Policy Games*, Lit Verlag.

Pusch, Toralf (2011) Wage Policy Coordination in the eurozone: A Robust Concept for Greater Macroeconomic Stability?, *FES, International Policy Analysis*, May: 4–9.

Pusch, Toralf, Glassner, Vera (2010) Lohnpolitische Koordinierung in der EU: Wie Gewerkschaften agieren, *Wirtschaft im Wandel*, 12: 565–571.

Reinhart, Carmen, Rogoff, Kenneth (2010) *Dieses Mal ist alles anders*, Finanzbuch Verlag Gmbh.

Reitschuler, G., Cuaresma, C. (2004) Ricardian Equivalence Revisited: Evidence from OECD countries, *Economics Bulletin*, 5(16): 1–10.

Ribhegge, Hermann (2011) *Europäische Wirtschafts- und Sozialpolitik*, Springer.

Rogers, J.H. (2001) Price level convergence, relative prices, and inflation in Europe. International Finance Discussion Papers No. 699.

Rogoff, K. (1985) The Optimal Degree of Commitment to an Intermediate Monetary Target, *Quarterly Journal of Economics*, 100: 1169–1190.

Rogoff, K., Zettelmeyer, J. (2002) Bankruptcy Procedures for Sovereigns: A History of Ideas, 1976–2001, *IMF Staff Papers*, 49(3): 470–507.

Rothschild, Kurt (2003) A Note on European Integration and Fluctuations, *Applied Economics Quarterly*, 49: 139–147.

Sachverständigenrat (2003, 2004) Staatsfinanzen konsolidieren – Steuersystem reformieren, Jahresgutachten 2003, 2004.

Sachverständigenrat (2009) Die Zukunft nicht aufs Spiel setzen, Wiesbaden.

Sachverständigenrat (2011) Verantwortung für Europa wahrnehmen, Jahresgutachten 2011, 12.

Sala-i-Martin, Xavier, Sachs, Jeffrey (1992) Fiscal Federalism and Optimum Currency Areas: Evidence for Europe from the United States, in: Canzoneri, Matthew, Grilli, Vittorio, Masson, Paul (eds), *Establishing a Central Bank: Issues in Europe and Lessons from the US*, Cambridge University Press, pp. 195–219.

Schäfer, Armin (2005) *Die neue Unverbindlichkeit: Wirtschaftspolitische Koordinierung in Europa*, Campus.

Scharpf, F.W. (2000) Institutions in Comparative Policy Research. MPIfG Working Paper 00/3.

Schatz, Klaus-Werner (2001) Europäische Beschäftigungspolitik: Existiert Handlungsbedarf?, in: Ohr, Renate, Theurl, Theresia (eds), *Kompendium Europäische Wirtschaftspolitik*, Vahlen, pp. 537–576.

Scheide, Joachim (2004) Macroeconomic Policy Coordination in Europe: An Agnostic View, in: Siebert, Horst (ed.), *Macroeconomic Policies in the World Economy, 2003 Kiel Week Conference*, Springer.

Scheide, Joachim, Sinn, Stefan (1987) *Internationale Koordination der Wirtschaftspolitik: Pro und Contra, Kieler Diskussionsbeiträge 135*, Institut für Weltwirtschaft.

Schmidt, André (2011) Fiskalische Stabilität in einer Währungsunion, in: Theurl, Theresia (ed.), *Gute Regeln oder Wirtschaftslenkung?*, Duncker and Humblot.

Schmitter, P.C. (1979) Still the Century of Corporatism?, in: Schmitter, P.C. and Lehmbruch, G. (eds), *Trends Toward Corporatist Intermediation*, Sage, pp. 259–279.

Schulten, Thorsten (1998) Tarifpolitik unter den Bedingungen der Europäischen

Währungsunion, Überlegungen zum Aufbau eines tarifpolitischen Mehr-Ebenen-Systems am Beispiel der westeuropäischen Metallindustrie, *WSI Mitteilungen,* 7: 482–493.

Schulten, Thorsten (2010) Perspektiven des gewerkschaftlichen Kerngeschäfts: Zur Reichweite der Tarifpolitik in Europa, *Aus Politik und Zeitgeschichte,* 13–14: 36

Schulz, Alexander, Wolff, Guntram B. (2008) The German Sub-national Government Bond Market: Structure, Determinants of Yield Spreads and Berlin's Forgone Bailout, Deutsche Bundesbank Research Centre.

Schwarzer, Daniela (2007) *Fiscal Policy Co-ordination in the European Monetary Union,* Nomos.

Sesselmeier, Werner (2002) European Employment Policy?, in: Funk, Lothar, Green, Simon (eds), *New Aspects of Labour Market Policy,* Verlag fuer Wissenschaft und Forschung, pp. 95–114.

Sidiropoulos, M., Zimmer, B. (2009) Monetary Union Enlargement, Fiscal Policy, and Strategic Wage Setting, *Review of International Economics,* 17(3): 631–649.

Siebert, H. (1997) Labor Market Rigidities: At the Root of Unemployment in Europe, *Journal of Economic Perspectives,* 11(3): 37–54.

Sinn, Hans-Werner (2008) Replik zu Kromphardt, *ifo-Schnelldienst,* 61(2): 21–22.

Sisson, K., Marginson, P. (2002) Co-ordinated Bargaining: A Process for Our Times?, *British Journal of Industrial Relations,* 40(2): 197–220.

Skott, P. (1997) Stagflationary Consequences of Prudent Monetary Policy in a Unionized Economy, *Oxford Economic Papers,* 49: 609–622.

Snowdon, Brian, Vane, Howard, Wynarczyk, Peter (1994) *A Modern Guide to Macroeconomics: An Introduction to Competing Schools of Thought,* Edward Elgar.

Sorensen, J.R. (1991) Political Uncertainty and Macroeconomic Performance, *Economics Letters,* 37(4): 377–381.

Soskice, D. (1990) Wage Determination: The Changing Role of Institutions in Advanced Industrialized Countries, *Oxford Review of Economic Policy,* 6: 36–61.

Soskice, D., Iversen, T. (1998) Multiple Wage-Bargaining Systems in a Single European Currency Area. *Oxford Review of Economic Policy,* 14: 110–124.

Soskice, D., Iversen, T. (2000) The Non Neutrality of Monetary Policy with Large Price or Wage Setters. *Quarterly Journal of Economics,* 115: 265–284.

Soskice, D., Iversen, T. (2001) Multiple Wage Bargaining Systems in the Single European Currency Area, *Empirica,* 28: 435–456.

Spahn, Heinz-Peter, Die neukeynesianische Makroökonomie im Spiegel konkurrierender Weltbilder, in: Hagemann, H., Krämer, H. (eds), *Ökonomie und Gesellschaft, Jahrbuch 23: Keynes 2.0, Perspektiven einer modernen keynesianischen Wirtschaftstheorie und Wirtschaftspolitik,* Metropolis-Verlag, 53–83.

Spange, Morten (2003) International Spill-over Effects of Labour Market Rigidities, University of Aarhus Economics Working Papers No. 2003/12.

Steinbach, Armin (2011), Gefährliche, *Inflationsunterschiede in der eurozone,* 6: 398–400.

Steinherr, Alfred (1985) Policy Coordination in the European Economic Community, *Recherches Economiques de Louvain,* 51(3): 285.

Stiftung Marktwirtschaft (2011) *Honorable States? An Examination of True Public Debt in Europe,* available at: www.stiftung-marktwirtschaft.de/fileadmin/user_upload/Generationenbilanz/Kurzpapier_internationaler_Nachhaltigkeitsvergleich_BJ2010_englisch.pdf (accessed 22 January 2014)

Streit, Manfred (1988) The mirage of neo-coroporatism, *Kyklos,* 41: 603–624.

Szelag, Konrad (2007) Actual and Potential Impact of EMU on Economic and Budgetary Policies of the EU. National Bank of Poland Working Paper No. 39.

Szelag, Konrad (2008) A Single Fiscal Policy in the Euro Area: Vision or Utopia?, Working Paper No. 46.

Tatierská, Sandra (2010) Do Unit Labor Costs Drive Inflation in the Euro Area?, NBS Working Paper No. 2/2010.

Taylor, John (2000) Reassessing Discretionary Fiscal Policy, *Journal of Economic Perspectives*, 14: 21–36.

Taylor, John (ed.) (1999), *Monetary Policy Rules*, Chicago University Pres.

Traxler, F. (1999) Wage-Setting Institutions and European Monetary Union, in: Huemer, G., Mesch, M., Traxler, F. (ed.), *The Role of Employer Associations and Labour Unions in the EMU*, Ashgate Publishing, pp. 115–135.

Traxler, F., Kittel, B. (2000) The Bargaining System and Performance: A Comparison of 18 OECD Countries, *Comparative Political Studies*, 33(9): 1154–1190.

Traxler, F., Blaschke, S., Kittel, B. (2001) *National Labour Relations in Internationalised Markets*, Oxford University Press.

Uhlig, Harald (2002) One Money, but Many Fiscal Policies in Europe. CEPR Discussion Paper No. 3296.

Van Aarle, Bas, Garretsen, Harry (2000) Fiscal Stabilization in the EMU, *Review of Economic Studies*, 8: 741–759.

Van Aarle, Bas, Garretsen, Harry (2003) Keynesian, Non-Keynesian or No Effects of Fiscal Policy Changes? The EMU Case, *Journal of Macroeconomics*, 25: 213–240.

Van Aarle, Bas, Garretsen, Harry, Gobbin, Niko (2003) Monetary and Fiscal Policy Transmission in the Euro-area: Evidence from a Structural VAR Analysis, *Journal of Economics and Business*, 55: 609–638.

Van Aarle, Bas, Garretsen, Harry, Huart, Florence (2004) Monetary and Fiscal Policy Rules in the EMU, *German Economic Review*, 5: 407–434.

Vaubel, R. (1983) Coordination or Competition Among National Macroeconomic Policies?, in: Machlup, F., Fels, G. and Mueller-Groeling, H. (eds), *Reflections for a Troubled World Economy: Essays in Honour of Herbert Giersch*, St. Martins, pp. 3–28.

Vogel, Lukas (2007), *Fiskalpolitik in der Währungsunion*, Metropolis-Verlag.

Voigt, Stefan and Blume, Lorenz (2011) *The Economic Effects of Constitutional Budget Institutions*. Available at: http://ssrn.com/abstract=1839428 (accessed 12 July 2013).

Von Lewinski, Kai (2011) *Öffentlichrechtliche Insolvenz und Staatsbankrott*, Mohr Siebeck.

Wagener, H.-J., Eger, T., Fritz, H. (2006) *Europäische Integration. Recht und Ökonomie, Geschichte und Politik*, Vahlen.

Wegner, Gerhard (2004) *Nationalstaatliche Institutionen im Wettbewerb: Wie funktionsfähig ist der Systemwettbewerb?*, Walter de Gruyter.

Wegner, Gerhard (2009) Die Wettbewerbsfähigkeit der EU als Ziel europäischer Wirtschaftspolitik: eine kritische Analyse, in: Scherzberg, A., Wegner, G., Wobbe, Th. (eds), *Dimensionen des Wettbewerbs: Europäische Integration zwischen Eigendynamik und politischer Gestaltung*, Mohr Siebeck GmbH & Company K.

Weidenfeld, W., Wessels, W. (eds) (2006) *Europa von A bis Z*, Bundeszentrale für politische Bildung.

Welfens, Paul J. (1990) *Internationalisierung von Wirtschaft und Wirtschaftspolitik*, Mohr Siebeck.

Werner Report (1970 [1993]) Bericht an Rat und Kommission über die stufenweise Verwirklichung der Wirtschafts- und Währungsunion in der Gemeinschaft vom 8. Oktober

1970, abgedruckt in: Krägenau, Henry, Wetter, Wolfgang, *Europäische Wirtschafts- und Währungsunion, Dokument 2*, Nomos, pp. 98ff.

Weyerstrass, Klaus, Jaenicke, Johannes, Neck, Reinhard, Haber, Gottfried, van Aarle, Bas, Schoors, Koen, Gobbin, Niko, Claeys, Peter (2006) Economic Spillover and Policy Coordination in the Euro Area. European Commission, European Economy Economic Paper No. 246.

Wissenschaftlicher Beirat, Bundesministerium für Wirtschaft und Technologie (2011) *Überschuldung und Staatsinsolvenz in der Europäischen Union*, Wissenschaftlicher Beirat

Zemanek, Holger, Belke, Ansgar, Schnabl, Gunter (2009) Current Account Imbalances and Structural Adjustment in the Euro Area: How to Rebalance Competitiveness. CESIFO Working Paper No. 2639.

Zenker, W. (2003) *Insolvenzverfahren für Staaten: ein Überblick*, Brandenburg Working Group on Insolvency Law.

Index

9781032927848